C•NNECT
THE
D•TS

EKLAVYA
EDUCATION
FOUNDATION

The inspiring stories of
20 entrepreneurs without an MBA
who dared to find their own path

C•NNECT
THE
D•TS

Rashmi Bansal

Copyright © 2010 Rashmi Bansal

First Edition 2010

ISBN - 978-81-904530-2-8

CONTENT, PAGE DESIGN AND TYPESETTING BY

JAM Venture Publishing Pvt Ltd,
51 Gr Floor, Kailandas Udyog Bhawan, Century Bazar, Prabhadevi,
Mumbai - 400025. Email: rashmi@jammag.com

COVER DESIGN

Amrit Vatsa

First published by Eklavya Education Foundation

Core House, near Parimal Garden,
Off CG Road, Ellisbridge,
Ahmedabad 380 086, India.

Printed at Print Vision Pvt Ltd,
Ahmedabad

Disclaimer:

Due care and diligence has been taken while editing and printing the book, neither the Author, Publisher nor the Printer of the book hold any responsibility for any mistake that may have crept in inadvertently. Eklavya Education Foundation - the Publisher, JAM Venture Publishing Pvt. Ltd, the content, typesetting and design vendors, as well as the printers Print Vision Pvt Ltd, will be free from any liability for damages and losses of any nature arising from or related to the content. All disputes are subject to the jurisdiction of competent courts in Mumbai.

<u>DEDICATED TO</u>

My parents, Manorama and Prahlad Chandra Agrawal
For all my dots.

ACKNOWLEDGEMENTS

My deepest gratitude to Sunil Handa - teacher, friend, philosopher and guide. For his unwavering support and encouragement in the writing and publication of this book.

My friends Piyul Mukherjee, and Deepak Gandhi, for patiently reading every chapter as it was written and providing instant and valuable feedback.

Swastik Nigam, A Srinivasa Rao, Saurabh Datar and the students of LEM at IIM Ahmedabad who proofread this book until their eyes popped out.

Madan Mohan, for laying out page after page, correction after minor correction, always with a smile.

Nikhil Sahasrabudhe, Avinash Agarwal, and Surya Ragunaathan for their beautifully accurate transcripts.

Amrit Vatsa for producing yet another inspired cover design.

My daughter Nivedita for lending me her room to work in, and providing some valuable tips on 'how other authors do it'.

My husband Yatin, for keeping the flag flying high at JAM.

My mother, and my house help - Lata and Sonu - for giving me the 'backend support' every woman needs.

And, finally, I thank each and every entrepreneur in this book for opening their hearts and sharing their stories.

Because it is these stories which will move and inspire the next generation to stay hungry and foolish.

And create an exciting new world.

"You can't connect the dots looking forward; you can only connect them looking backwards. So you have to trust... in something – your gut, destiny, life, karma, whatever. This approach has never let me down, and it has made all the difference in my life."

- Steve Jobs, Commencement address
Stanford University (2005)

AUTHOR'S NOTE

Until I was 17 years old I got everything I ever wanted as a student - effortlessly.

I topped my school board examinations.

Won the National Talent Search scholarship.

Numerous prizes and shields in quizzing.

But when I was 17, I applied to four US universities. Two rejected me outright, one put me on 'waitlist' and the last one accepted me, but without financial aid.

I felt crushed.

I came back to India with my parents and applied to St Xavier's College for a Bachelor's degree. No luck.

Finally, I enrolled in Sophia College for a BA in Economics and funnily enough, these three years turned out to be some of the best of my life.

I grew, I excelled, I became independent and confident. Editor of the college magazine, student council member, inter-collegiate festival circuit.

From nerd I became a *pataka* of sorts.

Meanwhile I also started writing for newspapers like *The Indian Post*, *The Sunday Observer*, *Mid-day* and even worked at *The Independent* (owned by *The Times of India* group) while still in my third year of college.

What's the point of all this? That things did *not* happen the way I had wanted. The plan God had for me was something different.

And in the end it all worked out, it was perfect.

I went on to study at IIM Ahmedabad, start my own magazine, and do what I always loved best - write. One fine day I got the opportunity to write a book on IIM Ahmedabad entrepreneurs and I grabbed it.

AUTHOR'S NOTE

That book you know as *'Stay Hungry Stay Foolish'*.

I was on campus for my 15th year reunion in January 2009, when sales of *'Stay Hungry'* crossed 50,000 copies. To celebrate this, the Dean of IIM Ahmedabad presented me with a silver plaque.

This happened in the same classroom where I had often wondered, "What the *hell* am I doing here?"

That day I got the answer.

I connected the dots.

The truth is, there is a plan. A bigger plan. Every experience in your life - whether 'good' or 'bad' - has made you what you are.

A chance encounter.

A stray conversation.

An article you read which somehow stays with you.

These are the unexpected turns on the journey of life. Which lead to a 'destination'.

So go out there and do more, learn more, experience more. Create lots and lots of dots on the canvas of your life.

Paint boldly and brightly - the colours of your choice. Create a life which is like a work of art.

A thing of beauty, a source of joy, an expression of your heart.

Each of the stories in this book is about people who have done that. People who took a leap of faith, dot by simple dot.

Rashmi Bansal

Mumbai, February 2010

CONTENTS

JUGAAD

These entrepreneurs have no formal training in business. They learnt by observation, experimentation and application of mind. Because ultimately, business is not 'rocket science'.

CONTENTS

JUGAAD

These entrepreneurs have no formal training in business. They learnt by observation, experimentation and application of mind. Because ultimately, business is not 'rocket science'.

CONTENTS

JUNOON

Some entrepreneurs are driven by a particular idea, or passion. Something which is different, ahead of its time. These ventures are about making that dream, a living reality.

CONTENTS

JUNOON

Some entrepreneurs are driven by a particular idea, or passion. Something which is different, ahead of its time. These ventures are about making that dream, a living reality.

CONTENTS

ZUBAAN

Creative people need a platform to express themselves. When that talent is unique, the platform must be created. And in doing so, the artist too becomes an 'entrepreneur'.

CONTENTS

PROTOTYPE LTR

Akhil Bansod – born 1972

Studio ABD

As a young NID graduate, Akhil Bansod wondered why deaf designers were always inspired by the West. He went on to pioneer the uniquely Indian Hieline and Radia collection, and now runs his own production/design company.

TELEVISION LIFESTYLE

Paresh Mokashi – born 198?

Harishchandrachi Factory

Paresh Mokashi wanted to be an actor, but found himself on stage playwright and directions on the Marathi stage. A dramas profiler of Dadasaheb Phalke's biography led him to on a new adventure – a widely acclaimed feature film which was his debut... entry at the Oscars in 2009.

AVATAR

Krishna Reddy – born 196?

Ranga Dance Group

In a small town in Orissa, Krishna Reddy assembled a group of daily wage labourers to form his Ranga Dance Group. They soon won the hotly contested India's Got Talent show, an amalgam of dance which combined and rhythm/ology inspired choreography.

CALL OF THE WILD

Kalyan Verma – born 1980

Wildlife Photographer

At 22, Kalyan Verma had a regular job with Yahoo. But one fine day he quit and to pursue his passion - wildlife photography. Today, he is a living example of an artist who is living his dream and making a living out of something he truly loves.

JUGAAD

These entrepreneurs have no formal training in business. They learnt by observation, experimentation and application of mind. Because ultimately, business is not 'rocket science'.

STREET
SMART

Prem Ganapathy,
Dosa Plaza

He came to Mumbai like millions of others, in search of a better future. Inspired by McDonald's, Prem Ganapathy has risen from humble dishwasher to owner of the fast food chain 'Dosa Plaza', with 26 outlets across India.

"Mera English bohoth accha nahin hai," says Prem Ganapathy, the very first time we speak to fix up the interview.

Kehne ko to Hindi bhi perfect nahin hai - the thick Tamil accent makes it hard to follow, at times.

But there is one language where Prem Ganapathy is completely at ease, and that is the language of business.

Branding? You bet, I need it!

Costing? Always keep an eye on it.

Customer satisfaction? *Usse badkar to kuch hai hi nahin.*

Prem Ganapathy (PG) did not have to go to a B-school to learn all this. He found knowledge, outside of college, on the hot and dusty streets of Mumbai.

Starting his career in the 'restorent line' as a dishwasher, PG worked his way up doggedly. From tea stall to roadside dosawallah, to running a small food joint near Vashi railway station - that would have been achievement enough for most people.

Not this man.

Prem Ganapathy went on to open a counter at New Bombay's first mall - Center One - and has not looked back since.

Today there are 26 'Dosa Plaza' outlets all over India and a franchise even in New Zealand.

It has not been easy but it *is* possible. Prem Ganapathy's story gives you hope, that yes, anyone can achieve anything in this country. We can have a hundred Dhirubhai Ambanis. And we must have a million Prem Ganapathys.

STREET SMART

Prem Ganapathy,
Dosa Plaza

Prem Ganapathy was born in Nagalapuram, in Tuticorin district, Tamil Nadu. There were six brothers and one sister - PG was the fourth child in the family.

"My father had a farming business... before that he was trading coal... but he incurred a huge loss, around the time I was born and closed that down." Even farming was not particularly profitable, but somehow they eked out a living.

The senior Ganapathy was also a yoga and gymnastics teacher. Prem recalls that his father was 'different'. "*Unka jo vyavahar tha, normal person se thoda alag tha.*" Honesty for example, was a way of life with him. "My father did not teach me about business - there he was never successful. But he deeply influenced my thinking, my values. I owe him whatever success I have made of myself in life."

Prem belonged to the Nadar community and thus attended the local community school upto class 10. "Kamaraj Nadar - who was the Chief Minister of Tamil Nadu - made education possible for people like me."

The Nadar community in the village had a temple trust which also ran the local school. The SCN high school where Prem studied actually catered to children from 18-20 surrounding villages.

"Now they have classes till class 12," beams Prem. "This year the school came first in the entire district."

SCN high school students may be aspiring for 'bigger things' today. But when Prem completed class 10 there was only one clear career path: Get out of school and get to work! "In our community, you study till class 8, or maximum class 10. *Phir provision store mein, kapde ka dukaan mein, bartanon ke dukaan mein job pe jaata tha.*" Finances were tight in any case. Prem went to Chennai - where his father and brothers were already working - and got employed at the coffee shop owned by a cousin.

"I learnt how to grind coffee beans... *woh sab seekha maine.*" After a break to attend the annual pooja in his village, Prem took another job - again in the coffee and rice trading business. And so he might have continued, learning the tricks of trading, had it not been for a twist of fate.

"*Mera maalik ka ek bhai Bombay se aaya tha 1990 mein. Uske saath main Bombay chala gaya.*"

Why? Why not? Prem was 17 years old, curious to see the world. Without telling a soul, he set off for the City of Dreams. Sounds like the opening sequence of a Hindi potboiler. And well, what happened when he arrived there was even more *filmi*. The only person he knew in Mumbai - the chap he came from Chennai with - took him upto Bandra station and then disappeared.

"*Mujhe kuch bhaasa vagairah kuch maalum nahi tha,*" he recalls. A fellow Tamilian was kind enough to take him to the Mariamman temple nearby where well-wishers started collecting money for Prem Ganapathy's ticket - back to Chennai.

Prem said, "No way! *Main yahin pe kuch kaam karega.*"

Mumbai embraces every new migrant in her grubby *sari palloo*. And so it was that Prem quickly got a job at the Das bakery shop in Sion. What was the work? Cleaning the *pathra*, the trays and ovens where pizzas and burgers were made. After six months, he went back to his village. On returning, he found another job - this time with the bakery at Satguru hotel in Chembur.

In 1991, the owner of Satguru started another venture - in Vashi's APMC market. Prem Ganapthy now found himself working at Gurudev hotel in the *mori* (kitchen sink).

"Dishwasher," he clarifies.

"*Main unko kaafi request karta tha... main tenth tak padhaa hoon. Mujhe thoda English knowledge hai. Mujhe waiter banaao ya toh bahar chai leke jaane ka kaam do. Kuch nahin to kam se kam table clean karne ka job de do...*"

The stomach may be empty, but a man can still have fire in his belly. And clearly, Prem Ganapathy did.

*"Mera dukaan sab jagah kholne ka
tha mujhe. Fast jaane ka tha."*

The trouble was that the owner avoided the young man who, like Oliver Twist, asked for more. Apparently there were some regional cartels and 'Madrasis' were not favoured for the 'front side' jobs such as waiting on tables. They were confined to the kitchen while locals and Mangaloreans got preference.

"I felt very hurt, very upset," says Prem. But he could do nothing, except bide his time.

Prem's luck turned when a new restaurant called Prem Sagar opened next door. Here, he was offered the job of a 'tea boy'. Now why is a tea boy better off than a dishwasher? Because, *baahar chai lekar jaana* fetches you a commission of 10%, and a chance to build 'clients'. Human relationships which can take you - who knows where?

Prem Ganapathy was a natural. While the other tea boys did a business of Rs 300 per day at best, he would routinely manage to net a thousand. What was the secret?

"See... I had good relations with everyone. Next door we had the Tamil Nadu Mercantile Bank. People used to phone and ask for me, by name."

"I greeted everyone cheerfully, made small talk. And my service was very good. I knew which person likes his tea in a particular way. What time he wants it. And whether he will want a soft drink with his lunch. I studied all that."

"Kyunki poora market mein, sabko alag alag taste rehta hai. Toh main unke hisaab se achha service dene ki koshish kiya taaki mera naam ho."

Whether you are selling tea or servicing a Fortune 500 client - the principle is the same. Always!

Soon Prem was earning Rs 100 per day - boarding and lodging was free. But there was more to come. One of his customers at the bank, a Tamilian gentleman, made an offer. He wanted to set up a tea shop in Vashi's Sector 3-4 market. He would invest the money and Prem would run the business - as a 50: 50 partner.

Prem Ganapathy agreed - happily. The *chai ki dukaan* was set up in the back portion of a *kirana* shop. From day one, the shop started doing brisk business. After a couple of months, the investor got greedy. Profits were touching Rs 8000-10000 per month. Why give away 50% of that?

"Mujhe nikal diya aur salary par kisi ko rakh liya."

Prem Ganapathy - clean bowled. Back to the pavilion!

The year was 1992. Prem went to his village for a vacation, and came back to Mumbai with a small loan from an uncle, and a younger brother in tow. With a capital of some twenty thousand, Prem Ganapathy set up a roadside stall of his own.

Business was good, but the neighbouring housing society was making life difficult. Tired of the daily 'kit-kit', Prem bought a *haathgaadi* and set up shop near the bus depot. That venture too was short lived.

But call it 'never say die', or no option but to get up and keep walking. Soon enough Prem found another spot, this time in Vashi's Sector 17, and set up a 'south Indian' stall. He did not know a thing about making either idlis or dosas. The batter he procured from the homes of south Indians living next door; the cooking he learnt by observation, trial and error.

"Soon I realised the quality of the *atta* was not good enough. So I bought a grinder and started making it myself."

Prem Ganapathy's dosa stall flourished from 1992 to 1997, outside the Bombay Mercantile Co-operative Bank.

"Kaafi achha mera naam hua."

And the money was good too. Prem Ganapathy was making Rs 20,000 per month - as profit.

Not that any business is trouble free.

"Us samay starting mein CIDCO aata tha, bhaagna padhta tha. Baad mein municipality aaya. Municipality ke logon ne bhi kaafi takleef diya hai."

You learn to have a 'setting', of course.

By this time Prem Ganapathy was living in a rented house in Vashi's Sector 11. The house served as the 'kitchen' from where all the chutneys, potato bhaji and dosa batter was prepared every morning. The stall needed round the clock attention - two more brothers joined in to manage the operations.

But why was the tiny stall so successful? Idli and dosa is available at Udupis across Mumbai. Why then did people flock to this vendor on the street? Because it was 'different'.

"I put a lot of emphasis on hygiene. Unlike other roadside dosawallahs we always wore shirt and pant, not *lungi*. We wore hairbands, and we kept the cart *ekdum clean*. *Ekdum achha aur fresh cheez banta tha. Achha dhak ke rakhta tha.*"

"Prem Ganpathy South-Indian fast food" declared a board, in bold blue and white lettering. The 'branding' was clear and concise - right from the start.

Not only was the stall popular with the *aam junta*, plenty of car owners stopped by. Including the *'bade log'* in Mercedes. And yet, the food was economically priced. Two idlis at Rs 4, masala dosa for Rs 10. Far cheaper than the popular Navratna restaurant in the vicinity.

By 1997, Prem had managed to save a couple of lakhs. With that capital, he put one of his younger brothers into a *kirana* shop business in Chennai. Prem could have worked another year or two and headed back home as well. But in January 1998, he took a big gamble.

Prem put down Rs 50,000 as deposit and Rs 5000 per month as rental for a shop next to Vashi station. Thus was born 'Prem Ganpathy's Prem Sagar Dosa Plaza.' And here begins the journey of a brand.

How Prem Ganapathy came up with the name 'Dosa Plaza' makes for an interesting story. At the time Prem had a roommate who was an NIIT student. This chap created an email id for Prem and taught him how to surf the internet. Between 3-6 pm, when he enjoyed a breather, Prem would go to a cybercafe, log on and 'search'.

"*Kaafi main food ka bare mein sochta tha ki kaisa kya hota hai. McDonald's, Pizza Hut sabka baare mein idea aaya mujhe.*"

Prem realised that he was 'famous' for dosas. Hence his name should reflect that. Like Pizza Hut, known for its pizzas. He considered several names - Dosa Palace, Dosa Park, Dosa Inn.

Around the same time he also came across the story of the Coca Cola brand name. Apparently, they had added the term 'coca' before cola because it sounded good. Rolled off the tongue easily. Surely he could find a word to add some zing to his 'dosa'?

Now 'Vashi Plaza' is one of the oldest and most famous buildings in New Bombay. Prem often went there on work. And one day it struck him - 'Dosa Plaza' - it had a ring to it. Yes, this could be it!

"*Phir maine ek din 'plaza' ka meaning dictionary mein dekha. Toh open building ko; open space building ko 'plaza' bolte hain.*"

Since he too was operating from an open space, the name was perfect: 'Prem Ganapathy's Prem Sagar Dosa Plaza'.

Prem even built a website for his open air eatery - the first dosa shop in the country to do so, I think! But, there was more to come. Customers were demanding more 'variety'. So after 3-4 months, Prem opened a Chinese stall next door called 'Chinese Plaza'. It was a disaster! "We had no idea how to run a Chinese place. We didn't know how to cook it... the proper ingredients. Also, the location was no good. There was already an 'Alibaba Chinese' next door."

The venture was loss-making and so it was shut down after just 3 months. But it was not money wasted, because '*kuch seekhne ko to mila*.'

Prem Ganapathy started experimenting. He created all-new concoctions with 'Chinese' fillings inside the good old dosa.

"Szchewan dosa."

"Manchurian dosa."

"Paneer chilli dosa."

The NIIT students who hung around at the stall became his test market.

"Try this American Chopsey dosa, *ismein khatta, meetha bhi hai* !"

The students readily agreed, and gave their stamp of approval. And that is how the 'Chinese dosa' became part of the menu at Dosa Plaza. Customers liked it, and came back for more. Prem kept experimenting and inventing new varieties. He searched for recipes. And he went and tried different kinds of cuisines to figure out what could be mixed and matched.

But his role model remained McDonald's. Whenever stuck for an answer he would ask himself, "How would they do it?"

"I noticed McDonald's write 'TM' next to their product. That's how I too got the idea of trademarking my brand and my recipes. Because many people were copying me. 'Sai Sagar Dosa Plaza', 'Udipi Dosa plaza'. And so on and so forth." Prem got the 'Dosa Plaza' trademark registered through an advocate. Today, he has copyrights and trademarks for 27 of his recipes as well.

Apart from a strong focus on his product, Prem was quick to understand the value of 'branding' and publicity.

"*Public ko mere stall pe leke aane ke liye maine kaafi mehnat kiya.*

"Main hamesha personally nahin khada ho paoonga.. is liye ek brand banana zaroori tha!"

New Bombay mein kitna bhi college hai, sab college mein maine stall lagaya. Bada bada banner ke saath."

And slowly but surely, the efforts paid off. By 2002, Dosa Plaza was a certified success story. With two outlets, a staff of 15 odd and a tunover of over Rs 10 lakhs per month, Prem Ganapathy should have been a satisfied young man. But, there was a burning desire - to do more.

"Actually, *mera profit jo tha maine kabhi nikaala nahin. Bas mera ghar chalta tha."*

Prem Ganapathy wanted to grow. Today's bank balance, he was willing to sacrifice. The idea was to invest and create a chain of shops.

"Mujhe aur dukaan kholna hai, aur mujhe achha banana hai; achha service karna hai. Mera vision yehi rehta tha."

Vision and mission is necessary, but chance encounters often play an important role in life.

It happened like this. The team setting up New Bombay's first mall - Center One - often came to Dosa Plaza for lunch. The project manager - a young man named Aman - got friendly with Prem.

"Take a space in our food court!" he advised.

Prem was sold on the idea. Despite stiff opposition from his brothers, he decided to go ahead. It was a big investment (Rs 3 lakhs for the deposit alone, plus equipment cost and interior decoration).

A bank loan may have been possible but Prem did not believe his file was that 'strong'. After all he had no property to offer as collateral - why would he be eligible for funds?

Like most entrepreneurs, Prem fell back on family and friends. *"Kaafi log se main fund liya, loan pe. Friends circle se. Thoda thoda paisa aata tha aur main kaam karta gaya."*

By the time the mall was completed, Prem's counter was ready to roll. In August 2003, Center One mall threw open its doors. Dosa Plaza was a hit from day one.

On the very first day, sales touched Rs 44,000. The first month's turnover was Rs 6 lakhs. The profit margins - a healthy 15-20%.

At this point, Aman advised, "You need to do more branding." He referred Prem to an advertising agency called 'Think Why Not'.

And the dosa dude had no trouble at all stepping into the role of a 'client'.

"Unka saath maine ek hafta to main daily unko lekar aata tha. Food khilata tha. Product samajhne tak un ko maine time diya."

The agency then swung into action and created a logo, mascot, menu card, POPs, posters - the works.

All of which continues to be used by Dosa Plaza, even today.

Advertising is great, but there's nothing as powerful as free publicity. The '108 dosas on offer' fetched Dosa Plaza plenty of coverage in local papers and on television.

Which brings me to an important question. These 108 items you see on restaurant menus... are they for real or just for effect?

Prem assures me that 'anything I order' will be available.

"See, it is mix and match. We have 5-6 sauces. 5-10 chutneys. Dosas are same. Vegetables are mostly same..."

There - you have the 'secret'.

The trick is to train your staff to combine the stuff together and give it a cool name. Like 'salad roast dosa', or 'Mexi roll dosa'. Creative but not too exotic. People should know what they are getting.

The other important aspect of running a chain is to be consistent. Any outlet you go to, the food should taste the same. At Dosa Plaza the all-important sauces and chutneys are therefore prepared at a centralised kitchen.

The success of the Centre One outlet was a turning point. A world of possibilities lay ahead! But starting one new outlet in a mall - 200 metres from his stall at the station - was one thing. How would he manage far-flung locations?

Two things happened. First, Prem Ganapathy learnt about something called a 'franchise'. The company from whom Dosa Plaza bought its billing machines expressed an interest in opening a counter at Thane's Cine Wonder mall.

"Humko franchise chahiye," the owner said. "I did not know what is

a franchise but I said okay, give me some time to think. And I went and found out *yeh kya hai*.. I did all the R & D."

Prem realised that many of the biggest fast food chains in the world operated on a franchise basis. So, why not Dosa Plaza?

I wonder, though, was he ever 'afraid' that the franchisees might just learn his secrets and then start outlets of their own?

"No.. I was never worried because I am in control of the important things. The recipes, masalas and sauces go from my kitchen. The staff is also supplied by me but he pays their salaries."

Essentially the franchisee needs to handle the cash counter and make the upfront investment, plus bear the running expenses. Dosa Plaza earns 6-8% royalty on sales. Which is a cool way to grow, on someone else's capital!

The second big leap for Dosa Plaza was 'systems'. The company invested in software connected to a central server to keep track of billing, inventory and overall operations. And of course, all this was possible because of 'professionalisation'.

In 2004, Prem took on a partner called Easwaran to look after business development and automation. Easwaran had a background in computers and handled the software side of things. At the same time, Dosa Plaza started setting up different 'departments'.

"Initially we were in a hurry to open more outlets... somehow we would run them, at break even. Then we started planning everything... all the details."

Purchase, marketing and most importantly, costing, became crucial.

"We made calculations for every recipe. How many grams of *atta*, how much vegetable do we need? *Sab ko costing ke hisaab se jaana chahiye*."

A training manager was deputed to visit outlets on a rotation basis and make sure that the costing was strictly controlled. But who were these managers and how were they persuaded to join this unknown company which was in the less-than-glamorous business of dosas?

Prem Ganapathy sums it up in one word: 'Relationships'.

"*Mera hotel industry mein sabse relation tha*." Prem could sense that many employees were working with big brand names, but their aspirations were not being met.

Dosa Plaza's operations manager Mendonsa, is one such example. He was recruited from McDonalds. *Magar kaise*?

> *"Mera dost hai, MBA kiya, ab job hi nahin mil raha. Pehle usko bees hazaar ka salary tha MBA ke baad usey 12,000 mein dawa bechne ka naukri mila hai."*

"Maine ek din meeting bulaya, offer kiya. Usko paanch saal kaam karne ke baad MNC company mein jo jagah milna chahiye tha, woh nahin mila. Mujhse baat karke laga ki Dosa Plaza is a growing company."

And he agreed to come on board.

No, the money was not better - it was actually a little less. But Mendonsa bought into a dream.

"Maine usko apna vision bataya. Mera aur baahar mein farak yeh tha ki yahan unko zyada value milega, zyada naam milega. Zyada freedom milega.. Is liye unhone mera company join kiya."

Did Prem Ganapathy offer his employees ESOPs? So far, only Easwaran has a 'stake' in the company. But in a larger sense, the feeling of ownership is there.

Crucial to the success of Dosa Plaza are not just managers, but employees at all levels. 80% of the original kitchen staff is still with Dosa Plaza. The same guys who once earned Rs 1500-2000 per month are now at 'training level'. They may not have a formal education but they too have learnt and grown. And they now earn as much as Rs 15,000 per month.

Prem Ganapathy has also made sure of one thing: caste and community is of no consideration. There are North Indians, South Indians, people from east of India.

"Hard work and talent is what we value here."

Today, Dosa Plaza is 150 employees strong and has 26 outlets. Five are company-owned, the rest run by franchisees.

To market the franchises in north India, the company tied up with 'Franchise India Holding Ltd' on a 67: 33 basis. Ten new franchise outlets are under construction as I write this and what's more, there are enquiries from as far as the US, Japan and Australia. In fact, Dosa Plaza already has a franchise in New Zealand!

In March 2009, the turnover of Dosa Plaza crossed Rs 5 crores.

Remember, the company only counts the royalty from franchises as its income - not actual sales. And I think this might affect the way investors see it - a profitable but 'small' operation. Does Dosa Plaza have what it takes to enter an even bigger league?

Prem Ganapathy thinks so.

"See, we are only opening franchise outlets in places where we can't open ourselves. We already have one 'express' model on the Mumbai Pune highway. Our plan is to open 20 more such outlets."

I think to myself, "Where are the VCs and PE funds?"

Well, Dosa Plaza has been talking to them for a while now. But nothing has clicked. They cannot see the diamond, inside that lump of coal. It does not deter Prem Ganapathy .

"Abhi bhi mein middle mein hoon... isse aur fast jaana chahiye.. nahin to main problem me aa sakta hoon."

And of course problems keep coming - you just have to face them, head on. With new malls coming up in the area, sales at the Centre One outlet slowed down. In fact, Dosa Plaza decided to shut its counter there last year.

Meanwhile, there are others offering South Indian snacks at food courts - more choice for customers, more competition. More problems to face, frontiers to conquer.

I say to my wife, *"Thoda ruko.. Main abhi first generation hai business mein, is liye mujhe isme zyada time dena hi padega."*

He would like his two young children to enter the hotel management industry - even the daughter. But, he adds, "If their vision is different from mine, I won't oppose them..."

Prem Ganapathy is only 36 but he is wise beyond his years.

"Agar chance milta hai padne ka, to padna chahiye. Lekin aadmi job karke bhi seekh sakta hai. Asli student ko har aadmi se, har experience se kuch na kuch seekhne ko milta hai."

Keep learning, keep walking, keep growing!

ADVICE TO YOUNG ENTREPRENEURS

Kapde ka business karo, food ka business karo,

Jo bhi karo sabse hat ke hona chahiye aur branding karna chahiye.

Barabar costing karke, sahi tareeke se handle karoge to kaafi profit hai.. kisi bhi business mein.

Food business mein dekhna padta hai ki item kya hai. Main kahaan khol raha hoon? Jaise ki bus stand ke saamne hai to wahan kya bikega.

Phir thoda specialise hona chahiye. Clean and hygiene par dhyaan dena chahiye. Branding and visiblity.

Wada bhi becha to public ko dikhna chahiye.

Presentation accha hai to ek rupya zyada milega.

Luck hai lekin ghar pe baitha rahega to luck nahin milega. Koshish karega to hi luck saath dega.

Main Bombay aaya woh accident tha.

Food line mein aaya accident tha.

Usme kya accha karna chahiye woh maine practice kiya.

Accha vyavhaar hona chahiye.

Accha product hona chahiye. Aur accha service.

Mere saath kitna bhi problem ho main sab ko convince karta hoon. Saare team ko motivate karta hoon, takleef door karta hoon.

Yehi mera secret hai.

THE
INVENTOR

Kunwer Sachdev,
Su-kam

Kunwer Sachdev is a Bsc graduate but he can take on the best of engineers. An average student in school, he fell in love with Physics late in life and turned it into a profitable business. Today, he runs Su-kam, a Rs 500 crore company in the field of Power Electronics.

There are people who do well in school and go on to become engineers.

There are people who bumble through and one day become inventors.

Kunwer Sachdev is the guy who hated Physics, hated Maths but today he lives and breathes electronics and inverters. The Su-kam R&D Centre looks like an office designed for cubicle workers but it's actually the *karambhoomi* of inventor-engineers.

Just like Kunwer himself. Although when you first meet the man you can't help wondering, "Is this short, boyish looking fellow really the MD of a Rs 500 crore company?"

I think Kunwer can sense my thoughts because there is mischief in his eyes as he greets me. "Tell me why do you want to write about me... You should look at someone big and famous like Ratan Tata."

I explain the purpose of my book - to inspire, to educate, to guide the next generation of entrepreneurs. *Lagta hai thoda maska lagana padega, ki aap bhi famous hain,* I think to myself.

But he breaks into a grin. "You are so much like me! We are both a little crazy, jo *hamein karna hai wahi karte hain.* See - you have so many points to convince me. You will write your book one way or another."

Just like he built this company.

THE
INVENTOR

Kunwer Sachdev,
Su-kam

Kunwer Sachdev is the son of a railway clerk. But, with a difference.

"My father was in the Railways but somehow he always wanted to be an entrepreneur." Along with his government job Mr Sachdev also ran a business. So he shifted his family out of the Railway Colony into Punjabi Bagh, a place 'full of entrepreneurs'.

Kunwer's father ran many different businesses - a grocery shop, a tailor shop - but none of them ever flourished. "He used to bring in people and make them partners. Once the thing was established, then there would be problems... So my father never did well financially."

The family lived through some hard times. The salary fo a railway clerk is meagre, and from that meagre salary Mr Sachdev would invest some portion into his business. "We were not even middle class, we were below middle class. To get a shoe or a shirt on a birthday was a big thing!"

In fact when he was in class six, the situation became so bad that Kunwer was shifted from the well known Hansraj school to a government school. What was the impact of this shift on the young man. "I was too small, so I don't know...," says Kunwer. Overall, it was not an idyllic childhood - that's for sure.

"As far as my family was concerned... I have gone through a strong turmoil in life. I don't like to talk about my childhood days. My father and mother were always fighting and there was no one to confide in. I became a loner."

There is a tinge of emotion - a raw nerve touched - as he narrates all this. But, no self-pity. In fact, looking back, he can see the silver lining to this dark cloud.

"I knew that there is no one behind me, so I had to rely only on myself. I took my own decisions, I became very independent. This has helped me a lot in life."

Kunwer bumbled through school - never particularly interested in studies. "There was not a single teacher who could motivate me," he recalls. Besides, there was no pressure from the family to achieve.

"My father was too involved in his own life, he did not have the time to worry about me, or guide me."

But in his trademark *phir-bhi-kuch-seekha* style Kunwer adds, "Whatever it is, I have never seen my father sitting idle, he was so hardworking." A trait which did rub off on all three sons in the family.

While in school young Kunwer would often have to wake up early and open up his father's grocery store because the helper had not arrived. Eggs and bread are perishables - you don't have a choice! Meanwhile his elder brother had started a small business and there too, Kunwer lent a helping hand.

"My brother used to go on a cycle to sell pens - I went along. Even if I used to get a rupee or two rupees, it was a great feeling."

After class 12, Kunwer continued to work with his brother, but he also joined Hindu college and this was a 'big leap'. An experience which changed his personality completely.

"I came from a school where we spoke in Hindi, at Hindu college, everyone spoke in English In the first year of college, I was very shy. I never talked with anyone... I did not know whether I will be *able* to do it or not."

Then somebody suggested to Kunwer: "Read novels to improve your English." He recalls, the first book he ever picked up was a 'big book, about an architect'. *The Fountainhead* by Ayn Rand.

"For one week, I just looked at the book and thought that I won't be able to do it. Finally I started reading it and in the first year of my life I read around 30 English novels. I overcame my language problems, started talking to people and made friends in college."

What's more, by final year Kunwer was one of the 'most sought after guys' in the college. He was into student politics and also on the organising committee of the Hindu college cultural festival 'Mecca'.

"Whenever I am challenged internally or externally, I try to prove myself. I have seen people in my business talk, but we try to execute also. If we fail, we try again and again and again. I do not give up."

"Every year students collected funds for the festival. The record was one lakh rupees - we collected five lakhs that year! We spent Rs 3 lakhs and gave Rs 2 lakhs for the 'next generation'," he recalls with a flourish.

As far as 'studies' went, well again, that was really not a priority for Kunwer.

"I enrolled for BA in Mathematical Statistics (Hons) and I passed every year - simply because I did not want to be a failure. But I never studied with my heart because I used to feel - what's the use of these theorems?" The important stuff was what he learnt outside the classroom.

"I learnt how to talk to people, to take people along and how to make groups. I learnt to organise things. My height was a big problem... because I was short people used to think what will this child do? But when I was challenged, I used to think that I will do and show them. So I kept on taking challenges in life and I set one or two big goals for myself."

The main one being to 'make it big in business'.

In 1984, Kunwer graduated from college and joined his brothers. He coined the name 'Su-Kam' for the pens and wanted to make it into a 'brand'.

"I used to talk big and that worried my family... *Ki badi badi baatein karta hai.*" Should one dare to dream, or simply accept the reality and aim within arm's reach? That, is a personal choice. Kunwer's dreams kept him awake while his brother was satisfied with his small shop and slept soundly at night.

"After college, I joined my brother but I had a tough time because his thoughts were different from mine. What he wanted to do in life, I did not want to do that. He wanted to hold on to what he had made - that was it."

By that time he had 'settled' down and owned two shops. "You run this shop and I will run that shop," was the offer but it did not excite Kunwer at all.

"We were making money but I wanted to build a brand. I remember at that time, Luxor was a brand, owned by one Mr D K Jain. I wanted to go and sit in that seat of Mr D K Jain. But my brother was not interested in branding... He was not convinced we would be able to sell."

For a while, Kunwer soldiered on. But after two and half years, he realised: "I can't work with him." This created major tension in the family. The question was, what will this boy do on his own?

"For a few days, I sat at home and then I decided that I am not going to do anything in pens." A lesser man might have stuck to pens - the only business he knew. But Kunwer did not want to compete with his brother. And that was that.

There was another slight complication. Since his college days, Kunwer was going steady with Geeta, a junior at Hindu college. Now, there was pressure from his prospective in-laws, to 'settle down'. So Kunwer took up a job. Side by side, he also spent his evenings studying Law.

"Law was something which I always wanted to study, because I had seen so much litigation in my own home. My father fought cases against many people... my mother was suffering, attending court and all that. So studying law was always at the back of my mind."

For the first time in his life, Kunwer studied 'seriously'.

"For three whole years, I attended evening classes and became the darling of my professors. Even though I never wanted to be a practicing lawyer, my professors felt that I should become one!"

While learning is a joy in itself, the love and support of a teacher is a mind-altering drug. It gives the student a special kind of 'high'.

In the meantime, Kunwer also got married. And under rather dramatic circumstances.

"The girl's side was not willing so we had to run away from our houses to get married. I could not take my wife to my family, because... I have seen so many things there, and I did not want to her to experience all that."

The marriage was solemnised among friends; the young couple was 'on their own'. Kunwer was earning some three to four thousand rupees a month at that time. He got some furniture made with his tiny savings but Geeta realised there was no way they could run the house on one salary. So she took up a job. Meanwhile, for Kunwer, the itch to move beyond the 9 to 5 life was getting stronger.

"I had the pressure, that I have to become something in life. What to become used to keep on changing. Sometimes, I used to think of becoming a lawyer. Sometimes, an entrepreneur."

Marriage brought some stability into Kunwer's life, and the courage to quit his job. But clarity remained elusive. Ultimately he started a cable TV business, despite not knowing the 'ABC' of that industry. "I knew only the spelling of the product and nothing else," he grins. "I took up the project I had no clue how to implement it!"

The year was 1989. In those days, 'cable' TV actually meant 'MA' or Master Antenna TV system. There were two Doordarshan channels and one transmitted through the VCR. The additional channel was known as 'cable'. Kunwer's job was to go to multi-storey buildings, meet the Secretary and the Committee and convince them to install his system.

"See, people take flats in a society and there are some common facilities. Same way, people had to install separate antennas for their TV. Instead of that, the society could go for our system and have a common antenna from where the programs would be relayed to every TV in the building. Plus they got the extra channel."

Hotels and shops selling television also went for this system. Each installation could cost from Rs 1 lakh to Rs 10 lakhs and there were just 2-3 companies in Delhi offering this service. Kunwer says he worked with the best of the lot. But it was a steep learning curve.

He managed to get four or five orders because he was a great salesman. But he had no clue how to install the system. That was the company's responsibility, but they were working on Indian Standard Time.

"Some of the people from whom I had taken the orders were very angry with me because their work was not done. One of them was a hotel. They asked me to return the money and said they did not want to deal with me."

Kunwer said to them, "Take the keys of my motorbike. Keep it or sell it and make good your money because whatever you had given me, with that I have bought the things required to install the system. But, if you give me a chance, I will see to it that your work is done."

This was a turning point in Kunwer's life.

"That day I realised that I have to learn how to do this work. So I started working with the people and learnt how to fix the modulator, the amplifier - everything. I started working with my hands. That was

> **"I was brought up in Punjabi Bagh, with people who were entrepreneurs like small shopkeepers. Had I been brought up in the Railway Colony, I would not have been what I am today."**

the day I started *learning* things."

Kunwer went back and read his ninth and the tenth class Physics books.

"I understood half the principles and went back to the basic studies of my life. It was very necessary for me and I also realised that I am very good at it. All the things from which I used to run away were actually so interesting!"

After clearing all his fundas about the system, Kunwer started searching for someone to assist him on the job. One day, at his grandfather's house, someone told him about a boy who needed a job. He asked that boy to join him.

"I trained that boy. I came in contact with many people of this industry and learnt new things. Like that my business expanded and I started employing ten boys. I had a nice cable TV business."

Then in 1992, there was a boom in Cable TV and competition heated up in the installation business. Kunwer decided to start something new, to once again strike out on his own.

"There were very few people like me who had the knowledge about the cable business. So I decided to manufacture my own system." Again, he had no real expertise in manufacturing but he knew he would somehow 'figure it out'.

"I opened a unit and used to be at it day and night. How life went on, I did not even know."

The business flourished and by 1996-97, Kunwer had a factory with 50 employees and was making good money. "I even had my own vehicle," he grins. And how did he finance the business? Did he approach banks for loans? Yes, but except for one disbursement of Rs 2 lakhs in 1997, he was constantly refused.

It was a tough time.

"Let me tell you, there were times when I did not have a single rupee in my pocket. My wife was very supportive, she was teaching and earning quite well but I never asked her for money." Hmmm, typical male ego? Kunwer says he did not have the 'courage'.

"There were times when I used to get the vehicle pushing for 5 to 6 kms because there was no petrol and I did not have the money. You can call me an egoist, but I've never been able to share my sorrows. If I don't have something, I will manage without it, but I do not know to cry for it. Today I am telling all these things... but at the time I never shared anything with my wife or friends."

Mujhe nahin lagta yeh koi samajhdaari ki baat hai... but to each his own.

Luckily for Kunwer, things started improving. In 1998, he thought of getting into inverters. The cable TV business was still doing well, with an annual turnover of Rs 3-4 crores and handsome profits. But many big players had entered the field and demand for his product was declining.

"See, we were not making standard products. I tried to do a lot of R&D, but I did not have the people. I had even bought a spectrum analyzer for Rs 20 lakhs." This was a big sum and it could have gone towards building a house.

But Kunwer's priority was the business. He would rather gamble his surplus on a machine which could take his venture to the next level .Hard to explain the rationale - it makes sense only to a man possessed.

"Whatever I was earning, I was putting it in my business, because that was my life. I did not tell my wife about the spectrum analyzer... because I knew there would be fights. I kept on investing and finally, I got into my inverter business."

Kunwer realised that there was huge demand for inverters in north India, but everyone was making the same kind of inverter. Could he come up with something superior? Well, it was part accident, part design. Here's what happened.

There was an inverter at Kunwer's home which would constantly get spoilt. One day when the mechanic came to repair it, Kunwer had a peek inside the inverter. "I realized they were using a sub-standard PCB. I knew about PCBs because of my cable TV experience."

Kunwer noticed a high quality branded inverter in the market - he bought it. He asked two people in his factory to work on an inverter using this PCB but they did not have any knowledge of Power electronics.

> **"My father always had partners but I have seen him suffering. Somehow that thing was there in my mind, and so I did not ever have a partner in business."**

"You see there are two kinds of electronics. One is the kind used in cable TV (called RF Electronics). The other is Power Electronics used in inverters. Power Electronics engineers are different from RF Electronics engineers. You generally specialise in one or the other!"

But Kunwer had experience in both areas and using the Spectrum analyzer, he started testing and experimenting. I used to read a lot of books and articles - whatever I could get hold of. Those days internet was not popular, so I used to go for exhibitions, buy thick books and lug them home."

"That was a strong drive. Whether people understood or not, I did not bother."

Knowledge for the sake of knowledge - sounds foolish but it is always a way forward.

Take the spectrum analyzer itself. Kunwer used it to test his Cable TV's amplifier and modulator. It was not a standard requirement, no small manufacturer bothered with it. And yet, he did the tests - because he was fanatic about quality and accuracy.

And because *isme mazaa aa raha hai. Ek na ek din kuch fayda bhi zaroor hoga.*

"Definitely, I learnt how different things performed. I learnt many practical things and also showed it to my boys."

Kunwer finally managed to launch an inverter but it did not rock the market. He did not give up. "We kept trying, improvising, and to do that we bought more equipment." This included a power analyzer and some more meters for testing.

The team spent a whole year in making that first inverter, then taking it apart and making it better! The company manufactured just 100 inverters in its first year of operations.

Bigger manufacturers shook their heads and said, "No need to do all this." Kunwer was a' my way or the highway' kind of man. He was determined to *make* his ideas work.

"In school I used to run away from Physics, hate History. Today I can miss my dinner to read books on these subjects. I just can't get enough! I am constantly learning."

Finally, the team came up with an inverter with a smaller circuit which worked on one battery, as against the standard two batteries. The efficiency was also much higher. This inverter caught the market's fancy, sales started picking up.

"Our inverter consumed less power. Other inverters - when you kept the batteries for charging, the technology was so bad, that it never used to get charged properly. When you started the inverter, it would get spoilt. People were frustrated!"

Perhaps the companies made more money by servicing inverters than selling it?

"I never understood that", he says.

"You only wanted to make a very good product?" I ask.

"I don't know, I wanted to make a good product and some thing which I was convinced with. I only knew that I have to work with this technology." So he brought in more people to work on the inverter. People from digital and power electronics background. And they had fresh ideas.

A great product is a good thing to have, but even great products need marketing. A fact that companies focussed on technology often overlook. Su-kam was no exception.

In the year 2000, someone casually mentioned to Kunwer, "You do not have a brand name."

Kunwer retorted, "What nonsense are you talking!"

He knew no one was making a better inverter than Su-kam, in fact they were copying his product.

The man persisted, "*Doosri company ka brand name hai.* You find out from the market."

This played on Kunwer's mind and he did some research. Soon he realised that it was true: Su-kam was not a product people asked for - by name. Something had to be done about this!

Kunwer contacted an advertising agency which was on the same floor as the Su-kam office and told them the problem.

He asked, "Can you help us build a brand name?"

The agency advised that Su-kam should spend at least Rs 25 to 30 lakhs a year on an ad campaign. It seemed way too much, but he agreed on a budget of Rs 20 lakhs. And once he was committed to the idea, Kunwer decided to learn all he could about the advertising business. The result was some completely out of the box ideas.

"In *Times of India*, they used to have different rates for the classified page and for the other pages. So I told them that I want four lines on the classifieds page and I want my ad in this particular space. The one who came to take the ad was not well versed with it and he said okay. Then I made different lines and joined them all into one, so it became one ad."

Kunwer had found a loophole and cleverly exploited it. He used the classifieds to create *display* advertising. Of course, the *Times of India* people realized they'd been had and quickly changed their policy. But in the meanwhile, Su-kam had managed to get noticed, with a fairly low spend. The company then switched to advertising on TV, which was a first for the inverter category.

In time, Kunwer hit upon the idea of making boards which had just one thing written on them: Su-kam.

"There were two or three employees of mine, who were not good at work, so I put them on this job. I made three teams for all-India and gave them the work of putting up boards everywhere. I did not know what the impact would be but it worked wonders. It made the Su-kam brand very popular."

Kunwer's team persuaded dhaba owners to put their name on Su-kam boards and 'advertise' along with their product.

"Some *dhaba* owners did not agree, so we gave them something small like a T-shirt and got their permission. We used to face problems from some people, but then we used to solve it. And in due course, my brand became very popular."

Today any and every brand from Vodafone to Airtel is using the same strategy.

By 2002, Su-kam was in a 'good position'. The turnover crossed Rs 10 crores, even as refinement of the product continued. The following year Su-kam launched very innovative products including the Sinewave Inverter and an inverter with a plastic body, both for the first time in India. The company brought out a UPS range and also expanded geographically.

Su-kam opened its first branch office in Hyderabad, and got its first export order - from Sri Lanka

"I had an employee in Delhi, whom I sent to Bangladesh to look for buyers. But it was the first time for him and he could not get any orders. The next time I went with him. Doing like that, slowly we started getting orders and we started exporting."

The company participated in an overseas exhibition in Africa. A continent which would soon become a major export market for Su-kam.

For once, things were truly going well for Kunwer but then, life took a painful and unexpected turn.

"I was approached by a large company, to manufacture inverters on contract basis."

He reasoned, "Why should I make my products in your name?"

Kunwer refused the offer but had to face consequences. The company he rebuffed pulled some strings and Su-kam was raided by the excise department. Kunwer found himself embroiled in multiple cases.

"Actually I had not realised that I was doing anything wrong. I had grown up in Punjabi Bagh, where the shopkeepers and businessmen never paid importance to income tax and excise laws. I only knew I was doing business and that was something great."

Well, everybody lives and learns...

"I never realised that once I become a man of status, people would be after me. Even my wife told me I was stupid. But that day, I realised that this was not the way of doing business. I do not know how you will write this, because all this is damaging..."

But it is in the past now. Talking about it will help - educate others.

At this point Kunwer realised he would have to turn over a new leaf. And he did. But, it was a difficult period.

"There were so many cases against me and there were chances that I would be behind bars. I had to pay a lot of money which I owed the government. Then all my stocks were sealed and word spread in the market, that the company would be taken over."

The rival company enticed 50% of Su-kam's employees.

"I think that was the worst time of my life in business. I went into depression for a few days. I used to go to the office, not talk to anybody and come back. I did not have anyone who could handle

"I used to talk big and that worried my family... *Ki badi badi baatein karta hai.* My dreams are so big that even if I work for another 50 years there will be more to do!"

the excise people. I had to handle everything single-handedly. I had to look after the company also."

"My wife was at her wits' end but she still supported me and stood by me. Then I came out of that situation. Some people who had left me and gone also came back. We started production once again. We built an R&D department - from scratch."

By this time Su-kam had developed some innovative technologies, which needed protection. "I realised that we have to patent our products to survive in this industry. In 2004, for the first time, I applied for a patent."

With superior products, a well known brand name and strong dealer network, Su-kam has achieved remarkable growth over the last 5 years. In 2004, Su-kam's turnover stood at Rs 100 crores. Today, it is touching Rs 500 crores, of which Rs 80 crores comes from the export market.

Although there *have* been bumps along this seemingly smooth road...

"In 2006, our business was booming and I noticed that certain employees who had grown with me did not share my vision. So in 2007, I fired some of these people and...my business went down." The effects are being felt even three years down the line. Former employees spread rumours in the market about the company.

"It is my own mistake. But this up and down goes on. I will learn from my mistakes!"

But what was the issue, really?

"I wanted them to go out and talk in the market about the new products, new technologies we created together. But they were more interested in cars... good life... they did not share my passion."

Money was not the issue - Kunwer says he's been a generous employer. But an entrepreneur expecting everyone to feel as *much* for the company as he does is - a bit idealistic. Things might have been different if Su-kam had been a listed company. With tangible

"My height was a big problem... because I was short people used to think what will this fellow do? But when I was challenged, I used to think , 'I will do and show them'!"

value attached to its shares.

Around this time Su-kam was once again approached with a buyout offer. It was from an American multinational, one of the largest manufacturers of inverters in the world.

"The last time I had made a mess of it, so this time, I handled them very diplomatically. They called me to the US, I went and met them. They called me to Singapore, I went there also to meet them. But in my heart, I knew I am not going to sell the company."

Reliance had also approached Su-kam with a PE offer and Kunwer decided to take that instead. Reliance India Power Fund - A JV between Reliance (ADAG) & Temasek Holdings Singapore invested Rs 45 crores in Su-kam. The stage was set for a scorching pace of growth.

In 2006, the company set up its first off-shore office in Dubai. The same year Su-kam became the world's second company to manufacture 100 KVA inverter and inaugurated India's first SMF* battery plant. It also armed itself with a trademark registration in the US, where it was now exporting.

And then, there are the awards and accolades.

'National Award for Quality Products for manufacturing inverters of outstanding quality.'

'Recipient of 'Sectoral Award - In recognition of Highest Export in Consumer Electronics.'

'Recognition of In-House R&D by Government of India, Ministry of Science & Technology.'

The latest on that list is the 'Innovation for India 2008' award instituted by the Marico Innovation Foundation. Ah - innovation! It's something most companies preach but few actually practice. But Su-kam is different.

The company has 32 people working on R&D - all engineers. And innovation is actually a mild way to describe it. What they do is keep 'inventing'.

* sealed, maintenance-free battery

"In 2006 we applied for 50 technology patents. Now every month we are applying for two technology patents, because we have so many new ideas." Although truth be told, most of those ideas appear to emerge from Kunwer himself.

"Sometimes he will call you at 11 pm and say... why don't you try such and such thing?" says an R& D engineer.

The Su-kam 'lab' is full of inventions - some of which are commercially viable. Recent successes include the 'power quality monitor' and the 'battery equaliser'. But why come up with a geyser with a timer facility? Because someday there may be a market for it, and meanwhile there is the sheer fun of having 'created something'.

So how does the future look? Will the demand for inverters continue - in India and across the world? Well, Su-kam now sees itself in broader terms - as a 'power back up' company. For example, Su-kam has connected telecom towers to inverters. It's cheap, it's efficient and also 'green' as the inverter actually runs on solar power.

"There is huge scope in the storage of power . There is no one in that field. You see, when power is created, we have to use it up otherwise it is wasted. The question is how can we store it?" Kunwer thinks he has some of the answers. To sum up in a single phrase: "Large inverters!"

"I have this problem of dreaming. I am very clear, that I have to work on this. I had made a 100 KW inverter around three years ago. No one had even thought it was possible at that time..."

But then who would have thought *any* of this was possible?

"I did not realise it then.... I understand everything late in life. I am like a tube light! My wife also tells me that I do not understand the small things in life. But I understand what others have not thought about..."

How he will do it, he does not know. That he will do it, no doubt!

In his mind's eye Kunwer see a day when countries will have tanks of stored power, and 500 KW inverters.

"Actually people have not worked much in this field of power. Even today they use 100 year old distribution and transformer designs... My dreams are so big that even if I work for another 50 years and the new generation also works on it, it will not be completed!"

The 1600 employee strong Su-Kam with five factories no longer excites Kunwer Sachdev. The company now has a professional CEO, who takes care of day to day operations, so he can concentrate on the things he wants to do.

Inventing, reinventing, dreaming of new possibilities. Always charging and always charged up!

<u>ADVICE TO YOUNG ENTREPRENEURS</u>

People take up jobs and remain satisfied with it because they do not know their capabilities. You do something and then gain the confidence.

Decisions are never 'right' or 'wrong', it's the outcome which may be either positive or negative. But you can't sit on the fence, you have to weigh the pros and cons and make decisions in life . That is an essential quality for every entrepreneur!

Mistakes do happen in life. I have also made mistakes and learnt from it. Some people may be with you and some may not. You should be driven by your passion or your interest.

You should not be driven only by the monetary value. It comes and then goes; if you are successful it keeps increasing. This was my passion and I worked towards it. I have not been driven by any other force.

TO SIR
WITH LOVE

Ganesh Ram,
Veta

As an NSS volunteer, Ganesh Ram discovered he had a knack for teaching. From a single coaching centre in 1981, Vivekananda Study Circle has grown into Veta - India's largest trainer in the field of spoken English.

The first time I saw bus shelters in Mumbai with advertisements for 'Veta English Speaking Classes', I said to myself, "Great - about time!"

If 'computers' was the buzzword of the '90s, English ability is the need of today!

I googled 'Veta', to find out who the bright spark was who'd recognized this huge business opportunity. Probably an MBA type with VC funding (judging by the advertising budget!). Or a *bade baap ka beta/ beti* who wants to enter the sunrise industry of education.

I was wrong, completely wrong. Veta has been in existence since 1981!

Before BPOs. KPOs. LPOs.

Before CNN, CNBC, HBO.

Before English was anointed as the skill for every young Indian looking for a job.

Ganesh Ram trained lakhs of students to speak the language - and make their lives better.

In hindsight, you could call him a visionary, but he will assure you, "I never had a vision, or a business plan."

As I sit in his modest office in T Nagar I think, there is no spreadsheet column to sum up elements such as faith, perseverance and common sense.

And the simple but burning desire of a teacher, who wants his students to 'pass'.

TO SIR
WITH LOVE

Ganesh Ram,
Veta

Ganesh Ram was born into a well to do family. A family that was ahead of its time.

"My grandfather went all the way to Benaras Hindu University to do his diploma in engineering. He came back and started the first rice mill in Thanjavur district and became a very rich man."

"Rice Mill Ram Iyer" had three sons, but they did not have much interest in running the business. And, the inevitable happened.

"My grandfather was lured to give a guarantee to a private bank. The bank collapsed and with his name and reputation at stake, he sold most of his property. Despite that, he had some wealth but that too was mismanaged, by the second generation."

What's more, when Ganesh was just a year old, his father passed away. His mother had some money, and support from her parents. But all of a sudden, they became a "low income" family.

Young Ganesh, his mother and siblings moved to Chennai from Kumbakonam. "My brother was 14 years old when my father expired, so he started working at an early age to support the family. Because of him, my elder sister and I could complete our studies."

It was a corporation school and a government college, but it was an education nevertheless. At Government college, Nandanam, Ganesh participated in an NSS project where he taught slum children in the evenings. It was his first exposure to the joy of teaching.

"I was very good at mathematics, I realised this is something I like. If even a slum student can understand what I am teaching it means I have the capacity to train people!"

Meanwhile Ganesh completed his BSc in Physics and landed a job with the Indian Express. In 1981, a Rs 750 stipend and management trainee position was a very big opportunity. But Ganesh had no interest in taking it up.

"I told my mother I want to be independent."

She said, "You are making a big mistake. What will you do?"

Ganesh said, "I will take up social service - or I will do something on my own."

She said, "No, I will not permit you. You are getting a job, you will become an officer and take the family to greater heights."

But Ganesh was adamant, so finally his mother decided to consult the family astrologer.

The astrologer saw Ganesh's palm, his charts and said, "Even if he joins the company, he will not stay there long. Better you let him do what he wants."

So his mother relented.

Now she asked, "What are you going to do?"

Ganesh said, "I think I am good at teaching. I will take up a teaching post or try on my own. You don't worry about me... just give me food and shelter. I will do something!"

You don't always have a definite plan, but you have some inclination. And if you are wise, that will become your compass and lead you, in the right direction.

It was in this phase of wondering 'where to start' and 'what to do' that Ganesh noticed a bungalow with a thatched roof in Nandanam extension.

Boldly, Ganesh went up to the house owner and asked him to rent the place to him.

"What will you do here?" the owner asked.

"I am planning to take tuition classes for students," Ganesh replied.

He said, "OK. Pay me Rs 500 as advance for 3 months and Rs 175 per month as rent."

Now where would Ganesh find Rs 500? Simple - he begged his mother to lend the money, promising to return it in a few months.

> **"I was very good at mathematics, I realised this is something I like. If even a slum student can understand what I am teaching it means I have the capacity to train people!"**

Reluctantly, she agreed. And that was how the journey began...

Ganesh spruced up the bungalow a bit and then started marketing his services. "That means I found three students who had failed in their plus two examinations," he grins.

The young graduate said to them, "It's January right now and you are going to write your examination in the month of April. Within three months I will train you and make you pass. Are you ready to study at my centre?"

They said. "Ok sir, we will come." And, they agreed to pay a sum of Rs 30 per month.

Ganesh cut a ribbon and 'inaugurated' his coaching center on January 12th, 1981 - Swami Vivekananda's birthday. Classes began and all seemed to be going well. Except that rent of Rs 175 was due at month-end and only Rs 90 was coming in so far!

After one week, Ganesh called his students and said, "I have a problem. Can you help me?"

"Tell us, sir. What, sir?" they asked.

"Are you happy with my teaching in the class?" Ganesh asked them.

They said, "Very much sir. We have the confidence that we will get through the mathematics examination."

Ganesh explained his situation and said he did not want to borrow more from his mother, or ask them to pay more. So what *was* the alternative?

When the tunnel looks dark and endless, the man with a mission somehow sees the 'light'. An 'out of the box' solution is, really, the only way to get out of the box!

"Will you bring one student each, your age, your friend who had failed along with you?" Ganesh asked his three pupils.

They said, "Certainly we will do it sir!"

What's more, instead of one they brought two each. And so, in the first month itself Ganesh had nine students. Each student paid Rs 30, adding up to a sum of Rs 270.

"Electricity was Rs 10, rent was Rs 175 , so in the first month I made my profit," Ganesh recalls.

He took that money and put it in the nearby bank. Slowly, through word of mouth alone, Ganesh Ram's classes started attracting students. Not just those who had failed but those who were bright, and wanted to do better.

"Mathematics - anyone who teaches well - can attract a lot of students," Ganesh says modestly.

The classes were originally targeted at 12th class students, but there was interest from other age groups as well. So Ganesh also started batches for class 8 and class 10 students. Within three months, the little bungalow was buzzing with activity from dawn to dusk.

Ganesh asked the landlord, "Can you expand this thatched roof to some open area also?"

The man readily agreed. The entire open area of 1000 sq ft was covered up and soon Ganesh had 2-3 different classrooms. It was now time to find more teachers!

"I slowly requested my brother and sister. You see, I am good at mathematics, she was good at commerce & economics and he was good at English."

So I asked them, "Can you also help me after office hours in the mornings or evenings?"

Both agreed to pitch in. By now, the family realized that Ganesh was on to something. After all, he was depositing money in the bank!

In less than six months Ganesh was running a tuition centre for 'all subjects'. Since there was no in-house resource to teach Hindi, he employed a teacher. His second employee was a biology teacher. And thus the business grew.

But it did not stop at that - Ganesh's mind was constantly ticking. By the end of the first year, he realised that location was an issue.

"I observed that we were in a residential area with no bus facility, so students from other parts of Chennai found it difficult to come to our centre. So why not move into a commercial area?"

By this time Ganesh had saved up money - some 20-25,000 rupees - and that gave him the courage to 'think big'.

"I thought to myself, "Which is the 'best commercial place' in Chennai?" I decided it was T Nagar because it is accessible by bus as well as by train - the local railway station is nearby."

"I moved around T Nagar... looking for a location. But I didn't have a 'vision' or anything. I didn't prepare any business plan and did not expect - first year I'll be here, second year I'll be there... and no formal, you know, management experience also."

Directly from the college, to the business - raw between the ears. But everything Ganesh did was driven by some intuition, or practical thinking.

In T Nagar, Ganesh finally located the right premises at Madley Road ("We still have a centre there!" he adds). Again, there was an open terrace to work with.

Ganesh asked the houseowner, "Can you put a thatched roof for me?"

He said, "Ok."

Ganesh sealed the deal with Rs 5000 as advance and Rs 550 as monthly rental.. Now came an important decision. What name to put up on the board outside?

"In Nandanam, I thought of my centre as 'Vivekananda Study Circle'. Why Vivekananda? Because even during my college days Vivekananda was my role model."

But many people mistook the centre for a library, not a tuition centre. Hence Ganesh decided to change the name to Vivekananda Kalvi Nilayam.

"*Kalvi* means education, *nilayam* means centre - so Vivekananda Kalvi Nilayam. This became a tuition centre and tutorial centre. I started giving advertisements also."

Initial advertisements were posters, banners, wall stencils. Ganesh employed an agency but in the night he would go and personally inspect their work. The personal touch was at the core - of everything.

"I always believe whatever you do, do it well. My principle is: Whatever I do I'll do it sincerely and to my satisfaction."

For example, Ganesh would ensure that extra classes were provided to weak students.

"My objective is to make him pass. So I will not say, 'Your training hours are over.. I will not teach you'. I told my faculty also, we must ensure every student passes the exam."

"My objective is to make him pass. So I will not say, 'Your training hours are over.. I will not teach you.' I told my faculty also, we must ensure every student passes the exam."

Within two years Vivekananda Kalvi Nilayam became the biggest tutorial centre in Chennai, with a strength of nearly 800 students .

Then one day Ganesh's brother Rajagopalan remarked, "I find the students are very poor in spoken English. Why don't we start training for that also?"

Ganesh said, "Why not? You are good at English. If you are interested, you leave the other subjects and concentrate only on this."

As simple as that. Rajagoplaan admitted one batch and by the time they completed the course, they were fluent in English. But how - was it really that easy?

"See, Rajagopalan made the classes casual and humorous. He told short stories and jokes, so even the dull students took interest and understood the concepts."

Rajagopalan had his own style of getting across to students.

"His training was so practical that he would never call a noun a 'noun'. He would call it a 'naming' word. Verb would be an 'action word' and so on."

Rajagopalan's logic was that when we speak our mother tongue we are not aware of the rules of grammar. We learn by observation only. So why can't English be taught in the same way?

It could - he discovered. And the numbers flocking to the class were testimony to that! Ganesh had to hire a big hall with a collar mike and start taking in 100 students at a time.

"Then the 101st student would come up and say, 'Sir can you arrange an extra chair? If not, I will stand in the corner and attend, no problem'."

Ganesh realised he had a winner in his hands. English training could become THE main offering - and not just one of the many classes at the centre.

So what was the hitch? Well, Rajagopalan was free to take classes only in the evening. In the day, he was busy with a government job. But, the time had come to make a decision...

Vivekananda Kalvi Nilayam was making Rs 4 lakhs a month in revenues. Profit margin - close to 80%. Investment - nothing beyond the original Rs 500 (long returned).

One day Ganesh gathered the courage to ask his brother, "Why don't you quit your job?"

It made sense, yet Rajagopalan hesitated. Once again, the family astrologer convinced them it was the right thing to do.

"It was a bold decision... I was barely 24 then! The moment he joined I felt he is much older to me. I should respect his experience. So immediately, I made Rajagopalan the principal of the institute."

Managing the expectations of partners - and more so family members - is an art. But if the canvas is big enough and each one gets his choice of strokes, a Big Picture is what gets painted.

And Ganesh's job was to keep looking for that bigger canvas. He stopped taking classes now and concentrated only on 'administration'. And more importantly, growing the business, taking it forward.

Now that Rajagopalan had quit his job, one option was to start taking English classes morning, afternoon and evening. But Ganesh had different ideas. And ambitions.

He instructed Rajagopalan, "Whatever however you speak, just give me the script so that I can duplicate it."

The idea was to start a 'distance education program'.

Ganesh bought a Tamil typewriter and an English typewriter.

He hired a Tamil typist and an English typist.

Someone to cut the stencils and duplicate the lessons.

Loose sheets were bound into a book.

"There was one magazine named *Kalkandu* in Tamil, it was

"I always believe whatever you do, do it well. My principle is: Whatever I do I'll do it sincerely and to my satisfaction."

predominantly read by youth. Most of the articles were about self improvement. So in that magazine I released one quarter page advertisement."

The advertisement was in Tamil and it read: "Do you want to speak English? Write to us we will send you the course material."

The ad got an excellent response and from then on, Ganesh booked an ad in every issue. "People wrote in, we would send our prospectus.. they would fill up the application form and send a money order. As soon as we got that we would despatch the material."

The course was priced at Rs 90 and every month 200-300 students were signing up. Ganesh decided to start releasing ads in other popular magazines.

"The response was so huge that in entire Tamil Nadu this programme of Vivekananda Kalvi Nilayam became very famous. By mid '86 we were admitting 300 students per day."

In addition to reading material, there were contact classes at important centres. No examination - the proof of the pudding is in the eating; here the proof was in speaking.

Being 'famous' in Tamil Nadu would have been enough for most. But Rice Mill Ram Iyer's grandson was already thinking ahead.

He told his brother, "Let us find someone who can translate our entire Tamil material into Telugu. Then we can start our operations in Andhra Pradesh also!"

A translator was found and Telugu to English program kickstarted.

By this time the volumes had grown so much that stenciling was becoming difficult.

It was time to start printing the material.

In those days printing was a complicated process. There was a compositor who would compose your script using lead letters. This would have to be proofread, corrected and then sent to press.

"It was a long process - no offset printing. Everytime you printed you had to proofread it!"

Still, it was less laborious than stenciling and worth the effort.

3000 copies were printed at a time. They would last 1-2 months and then the process of composing, proofreading and reprinting would be undertaken - once again.

"A herculean task but somehow we managed it", says Ganesh.

Meanwhile, there was a small dilemma. The course was now available in Telugu but the name 'Vivekananda Kalvi Nilayam' did not make sense in Andhra Pradesh. So in 1988, Ganesh chose a new name: "Vivekananda Institute."

All was going well when one fine morning, Ganesh Ram received a letter from the Income Tax department asking, "Are you filing your returns?"

The answer was "No."

"I didn't know anything about tax - I was only doing business. I got very worried about the letter but it was not a notice, only an initial survey."

A friend advised Ganesh to form a private limited company and that is how Vivekananda Kalvi Nilayam Private Limited came into being. And there were other changes as well.

While the English training was growing in leaps and bounds, the tutorial business was also (literally) going through the roof. From the 4th floor, activities expanded to the 3rd floor and then the 2nd floor, until the entire building was occupied by Vivekanada students.

But by 1988, Ganesh realised that the income from the English program alone was more than the tutorial income. And running the tutorial centre required a lot of staff to handle the many different subjects. So, Ganesh decided to close down that business.

Thus, Vivekananda Institute became, exclusively, an English training company.

But teaching English is just a small fraction of what you need to do, to be successful as an enterprise. And the God of All Things lies in the small things... how can you make everything you do just that little bit better?

Ganesh noticed that sometimes the proofreaders were not perfect in their job. So errors crept in - and that bothered him.

At this time, printing took a giant step forward with the advent of phototypesetting. This involved typesetting on a computer and then printing onto a bromide. The bromide was cut and pasted, negative made and then sent for printing.

Still complicated but there was one advantage - you need not proofread the copy each time.

Meanwhile, he continued expanding. Then, there were more 'translations'. A Malayalam translation, Kannada translation, Hindi translation, more students in more markets.

Each new program meant a new set of contact sessions.

"Once in 2 months we would a hire a local school, intimate all the students and interact with them directly. We would clarify their doubts and give them response sheets. A panel of teachers was appointed to correct them... It was a huge activity. "

To manage it all, Vivekananda Institute now had 40-45 employees.

One of the major tasks which the staff had to handle was matching the applications of students with their money orders. There was just too much volume to handle!

"Some students would say we have sent you the money and you are not sending material! Others would send only the application form - no money order with it. It used to be a big problem!"

A friend who was a Chartered Accountant suggested a simple solution, "Buy a computer."

Thus Vivekananda Institute bought its first PC - an XT, which was at the time the 'latest' machine available. A consultant was brought in and the 'matching' process became easily manageable.

By 1990 the business model had stabilised. Apart from English training through five languages, there was now an 'Effective English" program.

"If you take *Competition Success Reviews* of the '90s, you will find our advertisement. We started teaching a higher version of English i.e. English through English."

By 1995, Vivekananda Institute had managed a turnover of Rs 70-80 lakhs. All managed through the same 45 employees. That, in essence, was the beauty of the program!

"My major cost is only advertisement. I advertised in almost all the popular magazines of south India and in Hindi also."

By this time, Vivekananda Institute had touched the lives of close to ten lakh students.

"Every time we reached a milestone we would get a popular personality like Kamal Hassan or Rajnikanth to distribute our material!"

1995 was another turning point, for two reasons. Firstly, desktop publishing put an end to the many headaches of printing. And secondly, Ganesh observed that the correspondence course business had 'peaked'. Things were changing, and Vivekananda Institute too would have to change!

"See, I always apply my mind because we did not have outside agencies, consultants. All our advertisements were written by us and we had an own inhouse agency for releasing them."

"Slowly around '93-'94, I observed that TV was becoming very popular. Particularly the private channels, like Sun TV."

One question which Ganesh always pondered on was: "Who is our target group?" And how can one reach that target most efficiently?

"We never released our advertisement in dailies, we released our advertisements only in monthlies and weeklies because a person will go for distance education only when he has time to read. But slowly the magazine reading habit was coming down."

For example, at one time the popular Tamil magazine *Kumudam* was selling 6 lakh copies and was the no 1 weekly in vernacular. But over the years, the magazine's circulation came down even as it increased its rates in a big way.

"When we were doing roaring business through *Kumudam*, the advertisement cost Rs 6000 per page. But by 1995 they were charging Rs 35,000 per page. Same was the case with Malayala Manorama."

Ganesh did start advertising on TV but while it increased the awareness of the brand name, it did not draw many students. The medium was not suited to the message.

But the bigger issue was that TV was affecting the reading habit; this in turn impacted the popularity of the correspondence course.

"From around 2000 students per day our enrolment was slowly coming down. I was very worried! Am I making a mistake.. or has the market changed?"

After training 15 lakh students in multiple languages, it was time to introspect once again.

Ganesh had noticed advertisements by NIIT and Aptech seeking franchisees and decided that *this* was the business of the future. He too would shift from pure correspondence to 'direct training centres'.

A separate person - Major Rajan - was appointed to take care of the franchising business. Vivekananda Institute took off in Chennai, Hyderabad and Bangalore with the company supplying the course material, training of teachers and brand name in return for a fixed percentage of royalty. The franchisee invested in the infrastructure.

By 2003, Vivekananda Institute had 60 centres all over south India with a Rs 14 crore turnover and over 100 employees. But, there was a brand new problem.

> **"I always apply my mind because we did not have outside agencies, consultants. All our advertisements were written by us and we had an own in-house agency for releasing them"**

Like fake Lux soap and fake Cadbury chocolate, you now had a slew of fake Vivekananda Institutes!

"We could not register the trademark 'Vivekananda Institute'. You cannot own the Vivekananda name - he is common to everybody."

So you had a Swami Vivekananda Institute, Sri Vivekananda Institute, Vivekananda Academy, Vivekanada Vidyalaya - all riding on the reputation Ganesh Ram's Vivekanada Institute had established.

"Moreover, some of my franchisees, having got the technical knowhow thought, 'Why pay him the royalty?' They started offering their own English course under a name like Sri Vivekananda Institute."

Court cases were filed - there is still a case pending in the high court against Salem Vivekananda Institute.

"People thought it was our institute, Salem branch... and I could not do anything!"

All these battles affected the company. Growth became sluggish.

"Then I thought okay, having started this at an early age with our limited knowledge we have done what we have done. Hereafter let us go after some professional help."

The leading ad agencies of India including O&M, JWT and Lintas were invited to pitch for the account. JWT was appointed in January 2004.

"I told them all the problems."

They said, "Times are changing, people's attitude is changing, so what we will do is, we will change your name to VETA.- Vivekananda English Training Academy."

Ganesh was taken aback.

"From around 2000 students per day our enrolment was slowly coming down. I was very worried! Am I making a mistake.. or has the market changed?"

"I didn't want to compromise on my Vivekananda name."

They persisted - giving logos, options, arguments in favour of change.

Ganesh decided, "I am not going to apply my mind because my mind is saturated, whatever you suggest I will implement. I closed my eyes and started implementing their recommendations and that is how Vivekananda Institute became Veta."

The campaign broke in April 2004.

Ganesh requested that the agency should first try the name change in one state - Karnataka. And see how the franchisees felt about it. The response was positive, and it convinced Ganesh to roll out Veta nationally.

The name change also allowed Ganesh to address a problem he had been facing for a while. As per the original understanding, brand advertising would be done by the franchise owner but local advertisements were to be released by franchisees. Unfortunately, the franchisees were not keeping their part of the bargain,
So Ganesh changed the formula.

He said, "I will do the local promotion also and let us split our growth. Right now you are paying me 20% royalty and also for the study material. Instead, we will become equal partners."

Now the franchisee had to pay only the rent and staff salary, as well as ensure a certain minimum quality. Veta would take care of local advertisements, provide free study material and undertake brand building as well.

The new revenue model was readily accepted in Karnataka. But in Chennai, all 13 franchisees came together and refused to co-operate. What's more they were not prepared to change their name to Veta.

The franchise manager was worried but Ganesh said, "All these years I did not have any vision, now only I will have a vision and I want to move towards it."

"All these years things were just 'happening'. I never set a goal or a proper revenue model. I did not plan how much we must achieve or take stock of how much further we had to go..."

Ganesh decided to stand firm - it was upto the franchisees to come along or he would go it alone.

Out of 13 franchisees only one agreed to become part of Veta. No problem, said Ganesh.

"We changed our board in Madley Road to Veta. And in Mylapore to Veta. We announced that 'Vivekananda Institute' is now Veta and functions only from these places."

The 'name change' campaign went exceptionally well, it was even discussed on CNBC's *Storyboard*.

Before releasing the campaign, JWT gave Ganesh one last chance to change his mind.

They said, "We conducted a small survey and we found that down South, everywhere - it is so popular. Such a powerful name - Vivekananda Institute - are you sure you really want to change it?"

After all 'name change" is a painful exercise!

I said, "Let me change my name once and for all."

A life-and-death decision. He laughs...

"From Vivekananda Study Circle to Vivekananda Kalvi Nilayam to Vivekananda Institute... let this be the last time. I did not have any vision or anything - it was growing on its own. Now let me make a conscious decision. And it has been a very good decision"

And what happened to those 12 branches which broke away?

"They thought, if they rebel and protest, I will give up. But right from the beginning I am an independent guy... I won't budge or buckle down."

The franchisees continued operating under the 'Vivekananda' name and once again Ganesh had to file a case.

"This time I had a very good lawyer, she knew how to approach the case and got an injunction."

The franchisees also split into 2-3 groups. One used the name VLC, the other took the name E Square. But the Veta campaign was so loud and powerful people realized that the original Vivekananda Institute was now Veta.

One day Anita Gupta, chief of JWT Chennai asked, "Ganesh Ram, do you regret changing your name? You have spent Rs 4.5 crores on the campaign alone."

Ganesh said,"No ma'am. In fact, I am happy."

"Why?" she asked.

Ganesh replied, "Thank God I am famous only in South India, so I have to convey the name change only in 4 states. Had I gone national with 'Vivekananda Institute' I would have to spend not Rs 4 crores but Rs 40 crores!"

Well, that's one way to look at it - the positive way!

Ganesh believes the name 'Veta' was trendy and sweet, and therefore more easily accepted. Post name change, the focus was once again on expansion, the emphasis was now on opening physical centres. Distance education was no longer a preferred option.

What's more, one could charge more for classroom sessions. While a distance learning course cost Rs 975, the cheapest option at a Veta training centre was Rs 1600. There were silver, gold and diamond packages, depending on the student's need.

"We conduct an assessment test to decide whether a student should take up 120 hours programme or 80 hours programme or 40 hours programme."

JWT advised Ganesh to put together a 'business plan'.

"By 2005 I will have 70 centres... by 2006 I will have 100 centres... something like that. From now on you must have a plan and work towards it."

Thus, revenue parameters and targets were put in place.

In 2004, Veta also changed its auditor. The new appointee was to advise not just on accounts but also on financial matters.

The first question the auditor asked was,"You have not approached the bank so far?"

Ganesh said, "No, why should I? I was only making deposits in the bank... not taking loan. Because my business model did not require it!"

The CA explained that to grow rapidly, as per plan, this would have to change. Ganesh too realized he would have to change his style of operation.

"I realised I was spending a lot of money, building a brand. But in 2004, there were 69 franchisees and only one company owned centre!"

Ganesh had seen his Chennai franchisees walking out. What if now, after he had built his brand, another set of franchisees got together and did the same thing? He decided the time had come to put up more and more company owned centres.

So for the first time, in 2004 (he laughs throatily as he recalls this!), Veta took a loan from the bank. Initially, Rs 4 crores, then a further 6 crores. The building housing Veta's head office was put up as collateral.

With sufficient capital available, Veta started expanding rapidly - the company set up its centres in Delhi, Kolkata, Mumbai and other metros. Soon, it caught the eye of private equity investors.

In 2007, Ganesh sold a small stake in the company to private equity firm SAIF Partners. Was it to 'cash out' on the hard work of so many years? No, says Ganesh. All the money went back into the company, to fuel its growth further.

As things stand today*, Veta has 250 centres, out of which 70 are company owned. Things are moving 'as per plan'.

"In our business the competition is from small-time players, unorganised sector. There is no other 'national brand' as far as English training is concerned."

What about distance education - is it completely dead?

"We are trying to relaunch that also. We have employed a professional consultant who has suggested some changes. We are going to sell the course through home shopping."

An e-learning module is also on the cards.

Two lakh students are studying at Veta centres all over India today. How does that compare with, say, NIIT?

"NIIT charges higher fees. We are a mass brand... Everyone needs to learn English! Our revenue is linked to numbers.. number of students!"

Ganesh sees 500 Veta centres by 2011. A 100% subsidary has been set up in Singapore while a master franchise has been granted in Sri Lanka, Thailand and Indonesia. After all, if the model which worked in Tamil Nadu could work in Andhra and Karnataka; the model working in all of India should work in the rest of Asia!

Meanwhile, Veta also has new verticals, such as corporate training.

So what keeps Ganesh going after 28 years?

"Satisfaction... Fortunately we are in a business where we are

figures as of January 2010

enhancing the lives of so many young people."

True, but at another level, Ganesh was driven by business potential and not 'social service' when he originally targeted those failed students. Talk about 'bottom of the pyramid' in education!

Ganesh Ram has had a good life, a balanced life, a challenging and fun three decades.

The astrologer might have said "it is destined" but it still takes determination.

And desire.

And daring.

ADVICE TO YOUNG ENTREPRENEURS

I have seen people start a business by just copying. They see someone who is successful and start the same thing. No, you need to be innovative.

In 1980s, I took the decision of closing down all my other classes and focusing only on English. I never knew that India would one day be a BPO and IT hub where English would be so important.

You have to do something different, believe in your idea and stick with it.

I never went after something but as things demanded, I kept changing myself and my business model. And I kept trying new things.

And one last word: "What is business? It is common sense!"

It's in the mind. If a youngster today has 100% commitment, service motivation and the desire to do his best… the enterprise will be a success!

WHAT WOMEN
WANT

Sunita Ramnathkar,
Fem Care Pharma

Four months after the birth of her second daughter, this feisty housewife launched 'Fem' fairness bleach. Over the next 27 years, the home-grown skincare company held its own against large multinationals, only recently selling out to Dabur.

You work hard so you can have a beautiful house, car, servants, every comfort in life. But what if you already have all this - then what?

Well, if you are a housewife who is a little crazy and has that itch to 'do something', you start a business. If you are lucky and have a brother who is equally crazy, you rope him in and 25 years later you have a Rs 100 crore company.

That's the story behind Fem - a 'made in India and for India' cosmetics company which battled multinational brands and held its own. Just how did they do it?

To find out, I meet Sunita Ramnathkar at her very functional and modest office in Nariman Point. The feeling you get when you are with her is - she is so alive. Sunita's eyes twinkle, she laughs with abandon, she relives the excitement of demonstrating Fem bleach for the first time - like it happened yesterday.

Sunita's zest for life is infectious. Her understanding of what women want - and what sells - razor sharp. Couple that with the logical and technical genius of her brother Sunil Pophale - an aeronautical engineer from IIT - and you can see how Fem has given the biggest brands in the marketplace a run for their money.

Fem is also the story of a woman who built a career for herself, at a time when women did not have careers. A woman who gave birth to a little girl - and to a company - in a span of six months. And did a great job of bringing up both babies.

Because she never said: "I am just a housewife."

Because she never said: "I am trapped."

Because she said: "I can dream and make my dreams come true."

As can anyone, anywhere, any time they decide to...

WHAT WOMEN WANT

Sunita Ramnathkar,
Fem Care Pharma

Sunita is a South Bombay girl.

"My father was in a transferable post so when I was very young we lived in different places. But as far as I remember - since class two - it's always been Bombay."

Sunita's father was a doctor - a government doctor - and he ended up as superintendent of St George's hospital. Education was a big deal and Sunita received the 'best'.

"I studied at Cathedral and then did my BSc in Chemistry from Elphinstone college. Elphinstone in those days had very good reputation."

Sunita went on to do a mass communications course and after an internship with Pfizer in the PR department, she did what any girl was expected to, back in the '70s. She got married.

"I got married on December 31st 1976, so my reception was in '77 - kind of," she laughs. "I was only 22 - twenty one and a half actually."

It was a well to do family. Huge, airy flat at Marine Drive. Servants, driver, cook - no need to do anything. A dream come true for almost any young girl - but not Sunita.

"I started feeling quite useless, because there were people to take care of just about everything. I was restless - I wanted to do something."

A beautiful baby girl was born, in 1979. But even that did not cure the 'doing' itch. A job could have been an option but did not excite

Sunita. She had this vague notion about doing something 'for Indian women'. That something was the idea of cream bleach.

"At that time there was no cream bleach available in the market. People used bleaching powder with liquid hydrogen peroxide and liquid ammonia, and this whole concoction burnt the face."

But use they did - because something had to be done about ugly facial hair...

And how did Sunita stumble upon this opportunity?

"I just found what I would have liked to use, which was not available."

Any products she explored, apart from bleach?

"Actually, it was only bleach. Nothing else!" she laughs. "And I went after it with a vengeance."

It could have become a small business, run by a housewife for a bit of fun and some pocket money. But fate had other things in store.

"My brother Sunil was just graduating from IIT Powai. He was an aeronautical engineer and knew nothing about cosmetics, let alone bleach. But I told him, here is an idea - why don't you have a look?"

At the time, Sunil was working with Air India in the COD department. Six months into the job, he was bored and disillusioned. Not just with Air India but the aeronautical industry as a whole.

"When I graduated I came to know that the aircraft industry is not as exciting as it might seem. Boeing, for example - has its own maintenance manual. As an engineer I would be conducting non-invasive testing procedures. As your experience grows, your ability to certify goes up and that's how you progress."

Not exactly challenging - or creative. IIT seniors were already frustrated.

"I too had an offer from Boeing but they wanted me to start right away, and work on a visitor's visa which I refused."

So Sunil too was looking out for 'something to do'; exploring various projects.

"At that time powdered metallurgy caught my fancy. The automobile industry in India was so far behind that I could sense, in the near future, we'll have lot of catching up to do. And then there will be tremendous spurt in demand for powdered metallurgy products."

Powdered metallurgy certainly sounds more worthy of an IIT

"Marketing involved a lot of common sense, a lot of sensitivity. Facial hair is embarassing, that's why we always said, hair creates 'shadow' on the face."

graduate's technical skills than cream bleach - but Sunil had no such hang-ups. When Sunita suggested he look at her idea he thought, why not.

The metallurgy project was complicated, capital intensive and linked to the success of the auto industry. The bleach project was relatively simple, required little capital and was consumer oriented. Most importantly, it served a need which was not being met.

"I literally forced this idea of bleach down his throat." is how Sunita remembers it but it was really a rational decision for Sunil. One that 'made sense'.

Well, that's how he saw it although an IIT engineer spending the next two years of his life formulating cream bleach did not make sense - to anyone else. Including the family.

"My father found it ridiculous. He said, 'What *malham* are you trying out'?"

And yet, he supported them - simply by not interfering or questioning. Just letting them be.

"When Sunil said he wanted to do something on his own, my father never said no, you have to go and do a job. Or that you are an IITian, you have to earn at least so much."

Perhaps he was simply too busy to get too involved, but ultimately it was about trust. "I trust you know what you are doing... go on."

Brother and sister did know what they were doing - but not how.

There was one cream bleach in the market by the brand name Jolen. It was smuggled into the country and retailed for the princely sum of Rs 400. But surely there would be many more takers for a locally made product - equally good - but at a better price.

The question was - how to make it happen?

Sunil had BSc level knowledge of Chemistry, thanks to the foundations laid at IIT in the first two years. Sunita herself was a chemistry graduate. But organic chemistry in the college laboratory is one thing, producing a cosmetic quite another.

"We had pharmacists, but no cosmetologist," recalls Sunil. And nothing you could pick up from abroad and just duplicate or replicate easily.

"We got formulas - from seniors working overseas. But if your formula has twenty ingredients, those should be available here, no?"

Raw material was a problem, suppliers weren't standardised and importing, a nightmare. So it had to be an indigenous solution, lots of trials, lots of error. The laboratory - Sunita's own kitchen! It took two years of experimentation in a mixie and trials on friends and neighbours to hit upon the right formulation.

"My father bought a small place at Andheri MIDC and we started manufacturing there. When we started, we used to call the workers once in two weeks to make a batch and then I would go out and sell that batch."

The strategy was simple: give a demo. There wasn't enough awareness about bleach, and what it could do. So the best thing was to show them.

And it worked like this: Get a group of women together, give a small patch on each hand and actually bleach two faces. Any woman who said her skin was sensitive and any woman who said she wanted to make her skin fairer.

Fem insto-bleach was a new concept. But the results were so dramatic, so visible that it took off immediately.

"It caught on really well from the first demonstration onwards. People immediately noticed the difference between bleached and unbleached skin. Hair was camouflaged, skin became 2-3 shades fairer and a little softer as well."

A great product is half the battle won. The other - often tougher part - is getting your product on the shelf. And here again, Sunita used a simple strategy - common sense.

"Suppose I had demonstrated in Walkeshwar, I would keep the product in 4-5 shops in that area. In fact I would give them a xerox copy with the names of the outlets where it was available for their next purchase."

And thus, demo by demo, area by area, Fem conquered customers and shelf space. It took a year to get distribution in place in Mumbai; another in the rest of India. But meanwhile more and more customers were getting educated - and exposed - to the product.

"We used the term 'insto-bleach' to start with to convey the instantness of the product. We explained how you mix it, keep it on for just 15 minutes, and then wash it off."

Seeing was believing and demonstrators were appointed across India, to spread the gospel.

"We also participated in exhibitions - Living in Style, Home Well, House Beautiful. Wherever ladies would be there, we would be there!" laughs Sunita.

There was this *josh* and this *junoon* of doing something, the excitement of demonstrating from morning to night.

"There were days when we had six demonstrations at different, different colonies, *mahila mandals*. round tables, what have you. And I was constantly training girls to demonstrate."

"Today if you ask me why did I do what I did I have no answer. It just happened, and I went with it."

From the very first demo, people took to the product and it was priced just right - at Rs 19. There was no looking back.

"The first invoice on 12th January, 1982 was for Rs 13,500," recalls Sunil." That was the day Antulay quit the government, that's how I remember."

The turnover for the first year was Rs 1.1 lakhs; the next year it jumped to Rs 11 lakhs. As demand grew, so did production. From once a week, to two times a week, then thrice a week. And finally, batches were churned out everyday!

Success spawns many imitators; soon there were a number of insto-bleaches in the market. So Fem stopped using the term 'insto-bleach' and became a 'fairness bleach'. Packaging evolved from tube to jar, and the company reinvested practically all the surplus it earned - into advertising.

There wasn't too much money - so the ad had to be simple yet memorable. It was Sunita who came up with the one liner: *Bas pandrah minute mein gori gori. Fem Fem se.*

"I couldn't say anything about hair - upper lip hair, chin hair, or you have extra hair that you need to camouflage and you shouldn't be looking like a man."

These were embarrassing facts that no one wanted to hear.

"The only side effect of bleaching was that you turn 2-3 shades fairer. So that was what I emphasised."

Besides the ad ran for just about ten seconds.

"There is a girl in front of the mirror - Sonali Bendre - and she says, "Fem bleach makes my skin beautiful." By the time she turns the ad is over!"

Luckily this was in 1980s, when there were just a few programs such as *Chhaya Geet, Yeh jo hai Zindagi* and *Hum Log* with super-high viewership. So any and every ad got eyeballs.

"Brands were made at that time because there was no surfing. I guess we got a little bit of *gori, gori* into people's heads since it is still remembered and recalled so many years later. But I wish we'd had more money..." she says wistfully.

Fem fairness bleach had clearly made its mark - what next? It had to be a product that was 'first in the market', not a me-too. And the product they chose was liquid soap.

"At that time there was no liquid soap available. Except for Homocol which you saw in metal tumblers which went round and round in theatres!"

Thus India's first liquid handwash - Fem soft and gentle soap - was launched in 1987. It had a unique coconut oil formulation and in what was another first for the Indian market, Fem introduced 'refills'.

Like fairness in 15 minutes, the liquid soap had a simple USP: a one touch, one drop soap.

"We used to demonstrate how you cut fish, your hands were stinking. Then you rub the same stinky hands on to the soap and the soap starts smelling. But with one pearly drop of Fem the stink is gone."

So far so good - again came the question, what more? By this time Fem was approved by the FDA and could manufacture shampoos, soaps, creams - anything it wished to. But that served no purpose, felt Sunita.

"The important thing was not what we could make but what was needed by the women. We had our ears to the ground because we

"The whole philosophy of Fem was to manufacture products *wanted* by women but not available, not what we could produce in our laboratories."

> "Everything at home was looked after but I felt wasted... that despite the best education I am not doing anything with myself. That's what made me catch hold of Sunil and say let's start something."

were demonstrating to them. A lot of ideas were coming from them, and one of the things they constantly brought up was a better hair removal cream."

At that time Anne French was very popular, but it smelt awful.

"Everyone complained that if you start using the hair removing cream in one room, the whole house got to know of it. So we developed a key ingredient and tried to de-odorise the cream as much as possible."

The viscosity of this key ingredient was also managed so that it went deep into the hair root and dissolved it.

"Regrowth of hair occurred much later than with Anne French. And we smelt better. So when we launched the cream in 1989, it just caught on- without much advertising."

Three products, launched in the early years, which were pioneers in their category. Or a category all their own.

Then came liberalisation, and with that, multinational companies. The whole game changed.

Dettol approached Fem to start manufacturing liquid soap. The company needed a coconut oil formulation, otherwise it would be considered a shampoo and charged excise accordingly.

"Worldwide, Dettol did not have a coconut oil formulation. So we formulated the coconut oil soap for them and started manufacturing it for them in 1990-91."

By this time, with three products of its own and the Dettol contract, there was a terrible space crunch. At MIDC, Fem had already expanded from one to five galas. Ultimately, in 1993, the company shifted its manufacturing base to Nasik, in a 25,000 square foot facility.

Now, of course, there is a second facility spread over 50,000 sq feet at Baddi in Himachal Pradesh. A location that's attractive because of excise exemptions from the government.

The three factories are, in a sense, milestones in this entrepreneurial journey. The first ten years - in Bombay.

The second ten years - in Nasik. And then, the shift to Baddi.

At each stage there were challenges - a dirt path from where you had to make your own road.

Take something as basic as working capital.

"My father funded our factory premises but we went to SBI for capital to roll over. Till the limits were low, they gave us. When we needed more funds, they started acting very pricey at which point of time we went to my husband's bankers - NKGSB (North Kanara Gaur Saraswat Bank)."

The family had been been banking with NKGSB for over a decade.

"We had very good relations so they took over our account and it was smooth sailing till about 1997, when we shifted to Corporation Bank."

In 1994 Fem also took the public issue route and raised Rs 6 crores by selling a chunk of equity. Sunil says this was the 'biggest mistake' of his life. Why?

"Because we had to share our earnings with 34% other who don't do anything. And for what.. a paltry sum of Rs 6 crores!"

The truth is, a growing company can never have enough capital. Apart from taking a modest salary, whatever money accrued - it was promptly ploughed back into the business. But it was somehow never enough...

Until one day, Fem decided it was time to change the rules of the game.

"The real breakthrough came in 2001-2002, when we started this Cash & Carry system and then we stopped needing working capital. We took limits, but we didn't utilise them."

Cash & carry is simple - you take the money first and then supply product to the stockist.

"We collect their cheques and demand drafts before we ship them any goods. So at any point of time our collection is much more than our sales!"

An ideal situation for any company, but surely it can't be that simple to implement? Credit is the oxygen of the business ecosystem. 'Cash and carry' means gasping for air. So why would retailers agree to it? Because Fem had a brand name, a position which could not be ignored.

"In three categories we were very, very dominant - no cosmetic shelf was complete without our hair removing cream, liquid soap or bleach. This gave us an immense sense of power and we started demanding money upfront."

Fem was actually taking a cue from Procter & Gamble, which started cash & carry in 2001.

"Of course Lever's had cash and carry long ago. But after P & G, smaller companies also started doing it."

There were initial hiccups. Stockists warned that Fem would lose market share.

"Who has money to park in your product? Kam order karenge", they said.

Okay, said the company. Let retailers order only as much product as they can sell.

"The first month we had a huge setback - people ordered only what they could sell, not just to fill up their shelves. But after 2-3 months, we again saw orders increasing."

The logic was simple. Once I stock your product by paying upfront, I want to get rid of it as fast as possible and recover my cash.

"People started pushing our products and that's how our sales went up", exults Sunita.

The extra cash coming in - every single rupee - was utilised to advertise and push up demand further. It was a calculated risk, but it paid off.

At this point, in 2001, Fem sales had crossed Rs 25 crores. Eight years later turnover has quadrupled - to Rs 100 crores*. And despite the onslaught of multinationals with advertising budgets the size of a banana republic, Fem has managed to hold its own.

"Till date, we are either the leaders, second or third in the category. In bleach we are No. 1, we have 90% of the market. In liquid soaps we are still No. 2 - it's Dettol, then Fem, then Lifebuoy. And in hair removal we are No. 3 now, Veet has gone ahead. It's Anne French, Veet and then Fem."

Are there any regrets about helping Dettol become No. 1 in liquid soap, by manufacturing for them?

"None at all. We knew they would overtake us at some point - they had the money to really hammer their advertising on every channel, every 5 minutes."

And much the same happened when Veet entered the hair

---

* Bleach still forms 60% of Fem's sales. Company turnover of Rs 100 cr also includes sales of pharma products of Rs 21 cr in FY 08-09

removal market.

"Every space is filled with MNCs today but in these three categories, because of our quality and personal touch - we're able to hang on, stay in the top three."

So, Fem has never felt threatened by MNCs?

"Oh, all the time," laughs Sunita. "Thank God the Chinese don't have hair, otherwise they would have come and annihilated us."

But there's another simple chink in the MNC armour, working in favour of Fem. The fact that it is so niche.

"Multinationals never generate products of their own, they will bring to India the same range they sell abroad. And they don't sell bleach. So hair removing cream and liquid soap are endangered. But bleach, which is our crowning glory, is still safe."

Maybe fair skinned Americans or Europeans don't need bleach. Or the market itself is too small to be attractive to a very large company.

"Bleach is used once in a year or once in six months when you are going for a wedding or on a special occasion. It's not a daily use product like a soap or toothpaste - it's a niche."

A niche Fem has worked hard to nurture and grow.

"Today also we are doing demos but in remote places. Not in the cities, or A class towns where everybody knows what bleach is. But B class onwards they need to be shown, they need to be convinced before they buy."

It's more expensive, more difficult, but it's important - to expand the market.

And although Fem has not introduced any major new product since 1989, the company has improved upon its core offering - bleach.

"We developed 'Oxy' which is a very, very superior bleach. Oxy was popularised only through beauty parlours for the first two years, then it was launched in the market."

A different strategy, but one that worked. Fem also exports its cream bleaches to the Middle East, Far East, some African countries and even as far as Trinidad.

"In those markets we don't need to advertise much. It's mainly in-store - shelf strips, pamphlets. Apart from Jolen there is a bleach by Sally Hensen, which is very mild - it does not work on our types of skin or hair at all!"

**"We never made a loss but it took 10 years
- 1982 to 1992 - to become comfortable.
And after another 10 years to became
debt-free and worry-free."**

The one me-too product launched by Fem - an anti-ageing cream called Botanica did not fare too well.

"Correct... our anti-aging cream was beautiful. Better than Garnier in every way. But the thing is we can never advertise like Garnier. Today, you have to shout out your message..."

Sunita recalls the many times they would have an ad but not enough money to air it.

"I had to wait for the next season for money to come in and then telecast the ad. So we worked very hard to keep the ad making expenditure to the minimum.. working with *chhota mota* agencies and copywriters of bigger agencies on freelance basis."

Ingenious but was it sustainable? How long would Fem be able to dig in its heels and retain the 1-2-3 position in its categories?

Many a promoter would simply give up and sell out - cash in on 25 years of blood, toil and bleach. Fem too had that option.

Like an attractive girl who kept getting asked for her hand, the company had numerous suitors over the years. And turned them all down. But in November 2008, the founding partners accepted a buyout offer * from Dabur.

"We realised that if we want to grow this company from Rs 100 crores to Rs 500 crores - the kind of inputs it requires, we don't have. Nor can we ever have."

The original idea was to divest 15% of the equity and bring in fresh capital but Dabur pitched very strongly and offered a price that "we could not refuse."

"Dabur is mainly into Chawanprash and Hajmola. They want to enter skincare but as of now, they have only one product called Gulabari (rose water). Fem was the name they really took fancy to because it gave them class, it gave them great packaging, it gave them shelf space."

Add to that the money power brought in by Dabur and the fact that

---

* *Dabur acquired 72.15% of Fem for Rs 203.7 crore in an all-cash deal in Nov 2008; additional 20% stake was acquired through open offer for Rs 54 crore.*

Fem is a listed company. And it was a match made in heaven, from both sides.

"They are not duplicating our facilities.. our people are unique.. they don't have a talent pool like ours," adds Sunil.

Despite being a small company - a start up - over the years, Fem has been able to attract highly skilled professionals.

"There were a lot of M&As in the pharma space. Many individuals who had taken retirement, taken severance pay - they were looking for employment and did not demand very aggressive salaries. So we could get some high calibre professionals at a reasonable cost - and take the company forward."

Fem was thus able to put in systems and production norms used by MNCs.

"We have pharma guys who treat this not as a cosmetics company but a pharma company. As a result our manufacturing practices are excellent. Our factory is excellent. Our products are totally standardised. You will not find any difference between our products and any MNC products in the market."

Quality Control, state of the art R&D and some of the best skin testing equipment - Fem has it all in place. The one thing the company did not have was a succession plan. For the simple reason that none of the kids in the family are keen to carry on the business.

"Both my daughters are grown up. One is married and settled in Washington. The other has completed her MBA in Finance & Systems and is a research analyst. Both of them are really very independent minded..."

Just like mom.

But it couldn't have been easy - all the years when they were young, and so was the business. How did Sunita manage to juggle her many roles and responsibilities - keep all those balls in the air?

"We had just started working on the idea of the bleach, when I was got pregnant with my second child. My daughter Tejal was born in September 1981, and Fem was launched in January 1982. So literally, I gave birth to two babies... at around the same time."

Living in a joint family was a great help. So was the fact that the office - at Nariman Point - was very close to home.

"I used to take a one pm to three pm break everyday - whatever happened. That's when the kids came back from school, so I would give them lunch, put them to sleep, and then come back here. In the evening they went down to play and by the time they returned I would be home. So it was not so bad!"

During exhibitions, the kids would often come over and visit. An unmarried brother in law who was very fond of children was like a second parent. But, it was not a bed of roses. The thorny issue of 'why do you have to work' did come up from time to time.

"The point is in my generation it was like your in laws were doing you a big favour by 'allowing' you to work. But my husband Ajay was totally supportive and that's all that really mattered."

Ajay was in the printing business at that time, but over the years he was roped in to manufacture the liquid soap. So it was 'all in the family' but certainly each one, doing what they were best at.

"Sunil managed all the manufacturing, purchase, labour, sales tax, excise *falana falana* and I managed the distribution, marketing, sales promotion, the advertising, exports, CSD (canteen stores department) everything in marketing and sales."

It worked beautifully for 27 years, but on 30th June 2009 this chapter ended. And a new one began.

Sunita will be doing what she loves best - building another brand.

"Fem had a 25% stake in Mitchell Group, a Florida based company which manufactures whitening products for African-Americans. Dabur was not interested in this, so I bought the stake from them."

Sunita will open up markets for Mitchell in Dubai, UK and Africa. Meanwhile, her husband will continue to manufacture soap - for the next five years.

Sunil will take over the specialty chemical unit as Dabur was not interested in that portion of the business

It's been quite a journey. And one that a spunky housewife and equally spunky IITian decided to take without knowing what lay ahead of the next bend in the road.

"I didn't expect the business to keep me so busy; I didn't expect it to grow so much. I had bargained for a small business with a bit of pocket money coming in... But everyday we had new experiences, new learnings and we just grew with it."

And sometimes that's the best way. The only way. The way that leads you where you were meant to be.

ADVICE TO YOUNG ENTREPRENEURS

Sunita Ramnathkar

If you want to start a business, I would say find out something which is not available and which people want. A hunger, a need for any service or product. Then go out to satisfy the need, in the best way possible.

You need to be educated thoroughly in that line or in general. Then go all out and satisfy, delight the person with fulfillment of that need. Grow that niche, and then when you have the money, the world is at your feet. You can do anything, in that line, or in a different line.

I'm quite an average person, if I can do it, I'm sure every person can do it. In my times there were hurdles like family hurdles, in-law hurdles. But this generation is equipped with much more understanding parents and in-laws, an enlightened society where men and women are equal or at least treated equal. Take advantage of that. You can leap into bigger horizons, bigger boundaries. You can leap higher than this.

Sunil Pophale

The good thing about an entrepreneurial job is that it is constantly changing. I cannot imagine being in a fixed job where the specs never change. That way I must say I am lucky.

I must also say that I made sure that I was lucky. So must you!

FOOD
FOR THOUGHT

M Mahadevan,
Oriental Cuisines

He gave up the 'prestigious' job of a professor in Madras University, to set up a Chinese restaurant. But his knowledge of cost accounting was equally handy in the kitchen. Today, M Mahadevan runs a food empire stretching across cuisines and continents.

You may think the restaurant business is about food.

M Mahadevan knows, it's really about *people*.

We are meeting at the Le Meridien hotel in Chennai. Sunday *ka din hai*, the coffee shop is empty. But it's not the ideal setting for an interview.

I adjust my handycam several times. but the table is too small. Try as I might, Mahadevan appears in the viewfinder - minus the top of his head.

A young steward notices our predicament. He walks up and offers to shift us to the bar area, which is quieter and 'more comfortable'. We gratefully accept.

Visiting cards are exchanged and the steward's eyes light up.

"Oh, you are the owner of Zara!" he exclaims.

"Call me sometime," Mahadevan smiles.

The unspoken offer of a job - if you ever want it - has just been made.

As we dive into Mahadevan's story I think, *he* was that young man - 30 years ago. Going that extra mile to make a guest happy.

And going many many extra miles to make an outlandish dream, inspired by an Arthur Hailey novel, come true.

FOOD
FOR THOUGHT

M Mahadevan,
Oriental Cuisines

M Mahadevan comes from the 'deep South'.

"I grew up in a very small town called Udulampet in Coimbatore district. My father was a doctor from Kerala - Palakkad. Later we moved to Tamil Nadu."

With older siblings qualifying as doctors, it was expected Mahadevan would follow suit. But this young man had other ideas. After completing his BCom and MCom Mahadevan moved to Chennai, where he got a job as an assistant professor in the University of Madras.

The turning point came one day while he was reading Arthur Hailey's *'Hotel'*.

"I was enamoured by that story, and said: 'Wow! I want to be a hotelier'!" The cool thing is, that feeling did not pass. Mahadevan decided to *do* something.

But how could a young professor in his twenties keep his dream alive? Mahadevan made a start by moonlighting. He applied to work as a management trainee at Hotel Sudarshan, which had just been taken over by the Ambassador group. By day, Mahadevan continued to teach. By evening, he worked as a 'night manager'.

"I liked this job, I liked meeting people," he says, animatedly. Mahadevan had a flair for hospitality and enjoyed the job. But his family was less than pleased.

"As I was the youngest child in the family, my mother was extremely affectionate. I would never do something without taking her permission. It was very difficult for me to convince that I wanted to switch to the hotel industry, because she thought teaching was the best, most respectable job in the world."

She said, "From being a professor, you want to become a HOTELIER!! Have you gone mad?"

In those days, working at a hotel - even a five star - was not very acceptable. Besides, holding two jobs could not have been easy!

"You worked morning and night?" I ask.

"Yes, morning and night."

"It wasn't strenuous?"

"It was. But even today, I can work for 14-18 hours non-stop. Even if I get five to six hours sleep, it is enough."

Mahadevan's routine went thus: College from 9 am to 4.30 pm.

Quick shower.

Hotel duties from 6 pm to midnight.

Then, back to college at 9 am.

And despite the double workload, every night he would get home and put in a couple of hours - preparing for the next day's classes.

"I was handling post graduate accounts and management papers. I made sure that I gave a good presentation to my students."

Besides, Mahadeven never found the hotel job to be 'strenuous'. He knew he was there to get trained in the business. After a year Mahadevan was promoted to night manager, which was more about supervision and planning.

"When you enjoy doing something, you don't feel the strain. But when you are forced to do something you don't like, the stress level builds up. When I look back, I feel it was a cakewalk!"

This phase lasted 3 years - from 1980 till 1983. At that point Mahadevan decided to quit and start a small business of his own. Why? No grand vision or plan to change the world. This young man was fired up by a simple idea. The idea of 'making more money'!

"Everyday I saw people walking into the hotel, and spending so much!" In one night a businessman would blow up Rs 2000 on Chivas Regal and a few chicken *tikkas*. That was more than Mahadevan earned in a month - from both his jobs.

"So, I looked at it, and said, 'I want to be an entrepreneur'!"

There was a fire, a fire to lead a better life. And it's nice to hear someone admit it, so candidly.

"People will say, oh, I wanted to be an entrepreneur for this reason or that, but my goal was, 'I want to move up in life, I cannot be sticking around like this for ever and ever'!"

Business might seem riskier than a stable job. But let's not forget that most of these jobs led precisely Nowhere. An increment every three years, a promotion every decade. That was not good enough for Mahadevan.

In 1983, the young professor quit his night job and started a Chinese restaurant with capital of Rs 60,000. Half of that came from his Provident Fund, the other half from a partner. But see how he went about setting up shop. See, the power of 'thinking different'.

Mahadevan approached the owner of a successful Indian restaurant, located on the main road, right opposite the Taj.

He said,"Listen! I don't have much money, but I will build my kitchen. And I am doing Chinese, which you are not. I can't pay you rent, but I will pay you everyday. 20% of what I make is yours, 80% is mine."

The restaurant owner thought, "OK, in any case he is opening Chinese in one corner, and my profit in Indian food is 20-22%. So, for doing nothing, I am getting 20%."

He agreed.

Rs 60,000 thus went into putting up a kitchen and a billboard. Brilliantly located premises came 'free'.

The years at the Ambassador had taught Mahadevan many tricks of the trade; he applied all he knew to make his tiny venture work.

"We emphasised on two things - good food, and good price. We served a bowl of soup for 9-10 rupees, and take away in sealed packets, which kept the food hot."

What's more, *China Place* had a spanking clean, glass kitchen - open to view. And chefs who wore hats and gloves.

"I got this culture from a five star hotel, because I said, we will not do a run of the mill kind of a thing. Let us tell people that for ten rupees, I can give hygiene, quality and good value for money."

Mahadevan had no experience in the kitchen side of the hospitality business. But he had learnt all he could - by observation.

"I was a night manager, but my fascination was food. Even today, I can't cook, but my tongue is sharp! I can look at a fried rice dish and tell the chef, 'Too much soy sauce!' He knows I know what I am talking about and respects that."

Ultimately, you have to *know* the job, it is not as if you have to *do* the job. A principle Mahadevan put to work with great success.

Initially, the professor kept his day job. Hence *China Place* opened only for dinner. Yet, it did spectacularly well. With items priced at just Rs 10-12, the restaurant managed a turnover of Rs 5000 a day or Rs 1.5 lakhs per month.

20% of that went to the owner of the premises, but rent and electricity were 'free'. Mahadevan only had to manage the cost of food, packing material and salaries of four chefs. But he kept an eye on every penny.

"I was a 'cost man'," he declares. "After all I was teaching cost accountancy!"

Mahadevan believes success in the restaurant business centres around one simple philosophy. I eagerly await enlightenment...

"Income minus Expenditure = Profit."

I blink.

"That's it."

Right... that *is* it. And you don't need to do an MBA to figure it out!

"Absolutely," says Mahadevan. "For a while I also ran an agency for Nestle, a kind of side business. That's when I got acquainted with the Nadars. One of the sharpest, most enterprising communities in India."

Mahadevan would meet the owner of a small tuck shop. The man would pull out a small notebook with a record of *everything*. What was supplied last year, at what rate, at what discount. And heaven help, if you try and charge him a paisa more this time.

"I learnt that this mantra of numbers is very important." And that lesson remains etched in the DNA of the company Mahadevan built, even today.

China Place prospered, turnover was growing. One fine day, a customer called Mr Reddy came up to him and said, "Mr Mahadevan, down the road, I am building a nice complex. The basement is available. Would you like to come and operate?"

Just like that?

"Well, he was impressed because every evening, I was there. Hands on. I was talking to customers." The passion and joy with which Mahadevan operated his little business was clearly, infectious.

Reddy offered to put up 70% of the capital. Mahadevan put up the

"I earned Rs 800 per month, so every rupee mattered. But I saw people coming and blowing up amounts equal to my entire month's salary in a single day. I said, 'This is ridiculous!' That fire egged me on..."

rest - part savings, part loan. And, he decided it was time to move on from *China Place* and focus fully on the new venture.

To the owner of *Tic Tac* - the Indian restaurant - Mahadevan said, 'The kitchen is yours...Why don't you give me the money I put in to build it'?"

The man agreed and Mahadevan invested that capital as well into his new place.

At this point he realised one important thing: "I need to be different." No more red and green Chinese restaurants!

Mahadevan decided to get Parmeshwar Godrej to do the interior decoration. But how would he reach her? She was a celebrity - you couldn't just walk in to her office!

Well, as luck would have it, one of Mahadevan's customers at *China Place* was M F Hussain.

"M F Hussain used to live in Chennai in those days. I went up to him and requested him to introduce me to Parmeshwar Godrej. He graciously obliged."

She said, "Listen, I don't travel much. I will come down only twice, and these are my fees."

It was a rather large amount but Mahadevan agreed. "I knew that my food is good; I wanted my decor to be equally good."

He asked Parmeshwar to design something clean and classy, and she delivered a pleasing white and blue colour scheme.

"I still remember the turquoise sofas - a day one hit!" he smiles.

The restaurant was called *The Cascade*. It was a fine dining place and began with an investment of Rs 11 lakh. Of that, Rs 10 lakhs went into fixed assets and decor, and Rs 1 lakh was the 'working capital'. But it was more than enough.

"You see, we buy on credit, and sell on cash. I already had my suppliers from *China Place*. They looked at my new restaurant and said, 'We want to work with you!' because I used to give immediate cash. And I used to build trust - that was very important."

So essentially, food is a business where you can 'trade on other people's money'. That's the good part. The difficult aspect of the food business is the licensing. It took one and a half years to get the various permissions in place.

But, the opening of *Cascade* was a turning point from which there was no looking back.

"It was 1987 - I started with four people. Today, I have over 3000 people working for me, in India and across 16 nations. I could do this because I looked at opportunities, and cashed in on them."

Like?

"I picked up concepts which was saleable. *Cascade* was not just Chinese but the first pan-Asian restaurant in Chennai."

But more importantly, Mahadevan smartly picked out items that would *sell*. So there were Malaysian noodles and chicken curry (always popular). As well as dimsums and spicy soups, which Indians simply love.

The idea was not to be authentic but yet bring something new to the table. "We Indians love *kebabs*, so I put yakitori on the menu!"

The moment *Cascade* opened, Mahadevan quit his job at the university. He'd cut down on his teaching commitments but now the time had come to make a definite choice. It was not a difficult one.

"*Cascade* was doing very well; we were breaking even from the first month. We were profitable from the second month, my partners were very happy."

A restaurant is a risky business but if it clicks, there's instant gratification. You can expect to recover your capital in less than two years time!

"In the variables, the only thing you have to watch is the cost of food. The cost of coffee in a five star hotel is 18-20%. But in a standalone restaurant, we are not that expensive. If I sell you a bowl of noodle for 100 rupees, my cost in it is about 35 rupees. The chicken, the noodles, the stock, the fuel that goes into it."

The fixed costs are the same - rent, salaries. So, again, Mahadevan emphasises that you have to watch what you spend on ingredients. You have to stay within the *laxman rekha*.

After the success of *Cascade*, Mahadevan could have started yet another fine dining restaurant. Maybe in a different location. But he had other, more radical ideas. The alert mind always keeps its antennae up. Because inspiration can come from anywhere!

At that time many exotic ingredients were not available in India. For example, Kikomon soy sauce. Or even Ajinomoto. "Those days I used to personally go and shop for these items in Singapore and that's when I saw this concept of a see-through bakery."

Mahadevan said to himself, 'This is going to be the in-thing in India!'

And thus was born *Hot Breads*, in 1989.

The uniqueness of the business model was this: traditionally, bakeries would operate from a central kitchen and then deliver finished goods to various shops. At *Hot Breads*, goodies were baked and sold at the same place. And the customer could literally see - and smell it happening."

"We brought the best of the machines from France and sent our chefs to Singapore," recalls Mahadevan. The total cost of the project was Rs 14 lakhs. How was it financed?

Well, Mahadevan had Rs 3-4 lakhs reserves from the *Cascade* operation. Interiors could be offset through revenues coming in over the next year. Still short of Rs 8 lakhs, he decided to approach the Tamil Nadu Industrial Investment Corporation

"There was a panel of five people who asked me questions. They saw my track record - that I was a professor, I was educated."

But there is this thing, even today, that if somebody is eating bread in South India, people wonder, "What is wrong with you? Are you sick?" This is a land where the cook brings hot *idlis* and *dosas* in the morning for breakfast!"

So it was that one of the members on the panel asked, "Mr Mahadevan, are you going to sell to hospitals?"

Mahadevan said, "Sir, I am not going to make Modern Bread. This is like snacks, just as we sell pizzas and burgers, we will sell curry puffs, we will sell black forest cakes."

But first, Mahadevan had to sell the idea to that panel. And he did that by giving them a 'total pictorial write up' of 'this is what I am going to do'. Luscious pastries and puffs - good enough to eat!

"They were convinced, that, "Yes - this is something different." And the younger generation was opening up in Chennai, and they said that eight lakhs is not much."

Besides, the value of the machinery was also exactly eight lakhs.

"If your feedback is sensible, then people will like you, respect you, and take you as a leader. So, you have to *know* the job, it is not as if you have to *do* the job."

"Will you hypothecate the machinery?" they asked.

"Yes, sir", he assured.

The next step was getting an import license. And that took four and a half months. Remember, this was 1988 - you had to go and apply to the Ministry of Commerce.

The ministry objected, "How can you put up a bakery in 800 sq ft? It is not an industry! This is cheating!"

Mahadevan said, "This is the plan - we produce and sell at the same location, it is compact." Again, he took a video he'd shot of a bakery in Japan to get his point across.

If the Japanese could manage in small spaces - why not Indians?

After putting his case forward three times, somehow Mahadevan convinced the concerned officials. They need not have worried. *Hot Breads* was a 'sell out'.

The chain introduced many new concepts such as 'curry buns', a snack with chicken filling. With so much demand, the bakery went in for rapid expansion. In six months there were three outlets of *Hot Breads*; the first two years were fantastic.

"I opened in Delhi, in Calcutta, in Bombay."

By 1991, *Hot Breads* had seven outlets and had even set up shop in Kathmandu. By this time the bakery chain was doing a roaring business of Rs 2 crores annually.

Then, there were queries from Dubai, and Mahadevan went there to understand the opportunities abroad. This was a turning point.

"I started concentrating abroad and neglected India. Dubai was booming, there was so much growth, so much demand."

Mahadevan put up a series of food ventures in Dubai on a franchise cum ownership model. His own investment in each business was limited to 20%. From there, he went to Paris, and then, the US.

So what was happening to *Hot Breads* in India? Well, it was on an auto-pilot mode. Expansion was happening - but through the franchise route. *Hot Breads* sprang up in Bangalore, Cochin, Hyderabad...

"But franchising was a mistake... a BIG mistake."

"Why?" I ask.

"Because people did not respect franchising. The minute they learnt the business, they wouldn't pay royalty.!"

What's more, they would deviate from the bakery's basic template. In Chandigarh, for example, *Hot Breads* started selling dosas!

The franchisee said,"Mr Mahadevan, *dosa* is also a 'bread'. It is a South Indian bread."

Mahadevan said, "No, this doesn't work!" But he did not have monitoring, or effective controls. And in India, the law is not on the side of the franchise owner.

"If somebody is using the *Hot Bread* name without permission, then I have to file a civil case. I need a battery of lawyers... and the case will drag on for years and years."

Problems, problems. Franchising may not have been the right format, but one thing Mahadevan knew for sure - you cannot grow rapidly, if you 'go it alone'.

And so he was always on the lookout for partners who would team up with him, whose *dil maange more*.

Thus it was that in 1993, Mahadevan started *Copper Chimney* in Chennai, as a joint venture with Sunil Kapoor of 'Blue Foods'.

"He invested 50%, so I still pay him 4% royalty," he mentions.

And I think, a lesser man might be tempted to create his *own* fine dine Indian food brand; stop paying royalty. But life is a web of relationships. If you're greedy you will - in the long run - be a poorer man.

Not all partnerships work out, of course. In the year 2000, Mahadevan sold 50% of his stake in *Hot Breads* to Shamit Bhartia (son of Shobhana Bhartia, owner of the *Hindustan Times* group). A new company called B & M (Bhartia and Mahadevan) was formed. Each partner put in Rs 1.5 crores as working capital.

"Shamit had just come to India, and found that Hot Breads was very popular in Delhi. They had already taken the franchise for Dominos in India, they wanted to do something big in the food business."

However, while Dominos has gone from strength to strength, *Hot Breads* has actually contracted. What went wrong?

Well, small things and big things. The management was unable to shut down rogue franchisees. And their own outlets set up in Delhi were poorly located, poorly managed, and had to be shut down in a year's time.

In a JV situation *Hot Breads* became 'nobody's baby'. In 2009, Mahadevan decided to buy back his original 50%, because *abhi bhi, idea mein dum hai.*

The 13 *Hot Bread* outlets run under Mahadevan - all in Chennai and Pondicherry - were notching up sales of Rs 11 lakhs a month. The plan is to take curry bun magic across India, once again.

Well, this is an impressive enough story. But what Mahadevan has told me so far is just the tip of the foodie iceberg he's created over the last two decades!

Despite success with *Cascade*, Mahadevan realised there was a place for a mid-priced Chinese restaurant chain. And thus he created *Wang's Kitchen* which now has nine outlets - in Chennai, Dubai and Toronto.

The foreign locations, on royalty or profit share basis with a local partner.

Mahadeven had still more bees in his bonnet, so in the year 2000, he set up the fine dine Thai eatery *Benjarong* in Calcutta and Bangalore. Next came a Kerala cuisine restaurant by the name of *Ente Keralam*. Later Andhra and Chettinad items were added to the menu and it was rebranded as *Kokum*. Currently, there are three such outlets - in Pune and Chennai.

And an entirely new business model came up in 2002, when Oriental ventured into food courts. The first foray was known as *Planet Yumm* and was set up at the Chennai Railway station.

"Planet Yumm is about 1400 sq ft, and we do sales of Rs 5.5-6 lakhs a day. Highest per square feet turnover in the entire country!" says Mahadevan, with obvious pride.

"Most of my restaurants have a glass kitchen. The moment the chef knows that the customer is looking at him, he will try to keep it clean, he will never put his fingers in his nose!"

Food courts, in fact, are more about real estate than they are about food. You take 40,000 sq ft and divide it into ten counters. Oriental puts up the coffee shop, Chinese, South Indian and offers the rest to a McDonald's, KFC or Pizza Hut.

"You make higher profit in fine dining. But if you look at the volume of business, it will come from food courts and coffee shops."

Scalability is high, the money is easy and yet, Mahadevan will not put all his eggs in any one basket. Fine dining, he says, has its own charm.

At this point Mahadevan mentions another chain he's started in 2006 called *Noodle House* - a very trendy restaurant with low seating and 'one bowl meals', like in Hong Kong. And a coffee shop called *French Loaf* which opened in 2008.

"It is similar to *Hot Breads*, but upmarket. The prices are 30-40% higher."

I am reeling under information overload by this time. Mahadevan's food empire is like a vast buffet where one can't quite keep track of the many delicious items.

"Why so many different brands?" I can't help asking. Most people concentrate on one or two and let them grow. Mahadevan has a different view. He sees his company as a 'string of pearls'. Something he learnt by observing Azim Premji.

Besides, there is a method to the madness, he explains.

"We have only three verticals," he says. "One is Food Courts. We have nine of them, two more are opening shortly. I have a professional who heads that business and looks after it.."

"Then I have Chinese and Oriental Food. Except for Kerala food which is really because my mother is from Kerala and I had a passion for that cuisine."

And then there are verticals like a bakery - with multiple brands,

> " I always tell my boys, "I want you to carry a smile!" The minute you wear your jacket, your personal life is out. You might call this a plastic smile, but you have to smile. You have to greet people."

each catering to a certain set of customers.

The high end brand French Loaf imports flour from Germany and sells multi-grain bread, enriched with omega-3. This bread will sell for Rs 75-80 per loaf. *Hot Breads* is mid-range, with items priced between Rs 12 -20. Then there is a cheaper range which sells in supermarkets, by the name of *Bread Lite.*

So it's all quite logical and sharply defined.. And yet, 'focus' is not a *laxman rekha*, At times, Mahadevan will step out of the zone he's defined - for practical or sentimental reasons.

Take Oriental's most high profile venture *Zara* - a name that truly ushered in the idea of 'nightlife' in Chennai. It was born, not out of choice, but compulsion.

"The government built a bridge in front of my *Copper Chimney* and *China Town* restaurants. Business went down by about 80-82%. So, I sat down and thought, the only way to bring back business is to get into beer."

But how? At that time in Chennai, only hotels could have a pub and serve liquor. But then, the plot behind the restaurant came up for sale. Mahadevan bought it, built a hotel with 20 rooms and 40 beds, and opened *Zara* in 2002. Sales skyrocketed!

The Mahadevan philosophy is, keep trying. Something new, something never done before. You don't sit still and just keep the cash registers ringing.

So Oriental is soon opening a chocolate shop in Dubai by the name *Maple Leaf.*

"But the trials were happening here in Chennai. This is home, so mistakes don't cost me much!"

It's also about keeping your eyes and ears open, and learning from wherever you can.

"Just last week, I have taken over a bakery in California," he says, with a twinkle in the eye. "They are developing 'sourdough bread', which is made without yeast. My boys in the US will learn how to to do it, then they will come and train everyone here."

Great stuff but surely, somewhere down the line the good professor must have made some mistakes? Yes, he admits. But he knows there is a formula, and if you tweak it and adjust it - things usually work.

"Number one - location. Number two - product mix. Number three - general acceptability."

> ## "70% of restaurants close in the first year. If you continue into the second, and survive the third, then it is set. That's the goal we work with, anywhere in the world."

After all, it's all a matter of taste.

"Absolutely! If I go to Dubai, I don't make Indian pastries, I make Arabic pastries. At *Hot Breads* in San Fransisco, we do a lot of *vada pav* for the Indians. It is a sell-out. We also make chutney-cucumber sandwiches. The whites love that."

But how does one customise for many different tongues? Simple - you give free trials.

So in Paris, where Mahadevan runs two Indian restaurants exclusively for the French, spice levels have been reduced drastically. And that is not the only attention to detail.

"I have two exhausts working in the kitchen, because the minute the curry smell hangs on his coat, the Frenchman will never come back. It is an office going area where people come for lunch."

But can one really do *so* many things at once, is the recurring question. The answer is yes and no. *Cascade* was one of the ventures which Mahadevan let go. Essentially, life is about making choices and Mahadevan chose to become an NRI.

"From 1994 I have been a non resident Indian. My foreign and Indian operations are completely separate. The money I make there I do not bring back here, and vice versa."

International operations are controlled from Dubai, which 'is an easier place to work'. But life is a circle and with India booming, Mahadevan is once again putting his energy into expanding in this country. And this time, he has a cheerleader and taskmaster in the form of private equity firm Peepul Capital.

In 2007, Peepul bought a 50% stake in Oriental Cuisines for $20 million. But did Mahadevan really need the money? After all, the food business is all on 'cash sale'.

If your restaurants attract customers you have no need at all of working capital. However, if you want to scale up rapidly - yes, you do need all the money you can get! I can't say if Mahadevan's heart is really in empire building mode... There is a definite ambivalence.

"At times, I really get frustrated and I wonder...why did I take an investor on board? Because when someone puts in money they of course want the company to grow, grow and grow."

In 2008, Oriental Cuisine had a turnover of Rs 20 crores. By March 2010 it is expected to touch Rs 70 crores. For 2010-11, the target is Rs 100 crores.

"That kind of a speed is not in my blood," says Mahadevan. Thus, like many a wise founder, he has stepped aside and handed over the show to professionals.

The new CEO at Oriental Cuisine is Vishwadeep Kuila - a 1989 batch MBA from IIM Ahmedabad. And he is 'in charge'.

"I am on the periphery, just watching. I come in to help, when the CEO calls me. Because in my line, there can be only one captain."

But the transformation from entrepreneur-led to a professional set up, brings with it the occasional heartburn. A third of the workforce has grown with the company, risen up the rungs. They must now adjust to a new boss, new ways of working.

It is a delicate, balancing act.

While Mahadevan is hands-off in almost all respects, the one area he is personally involved is costing. Through email and SMS, he keeps track of 'food sales' on a daily basis. Now that operations have expanded, Oriental uses SAP as well.

"My key concern is that food cost must be within 35-36%. If not, you don't know where your capital has gone!"

However in this growth phase, for the first time, Oriental is running at a 'loss'. And that is difficult for the good professor to digest! He exclaims, only half in jest, "Every morning, I ask 'Vishwadeep, tell me when you are turning Oriental around'!

And he shares a concern which every company faces, as it spreads its wings.

"If you give people what they need, they will come back to you. I still hear of people driving down from Bandra to Nariman Point to get a *paan* from a particular fellow."

"As we grow, we have brought people on high salaries. From 11% to 14%, the salary bill has suddenly gone up to 22%! And sales are not reflecting that much... yet!"

Despite capital, and the best talent money can buy, Mahadevan is well aware that growth never comes easy.

"When we have grown like this - boom! - there are bound to be mistakes. When you are doing on a large scale, it is like painting on a bigger canvas, you tend to spill something somewhere."

Investor compulsions apart, today Mahadevan is not motivated by making more money or putting his brands in the limelight.

"Each unit I open, sixty guys get employment. I am not talking like a politician, but personally I feel, that is what keeps me going now."

Today, restaurants run by Oriental Cuisines employ around 2000 people in India, and around 1200 abroad. And Mahadevan is always on the lookout for more.

"Whenever I meet pleasant people, I always want to enroll them!"

It is more difficult to retain employees today, of course, but Mahadevan has devised ways and means to keep them motivated.

"10% of the proceeds at our fine dining restaurants goes to the boys who are running it. 10% out of *sales*, not profits, mind you!" And this includes everyone, down to the guy washing the dishes.

Like most other operational details, the restaurant managers define and implement such schemes. What then, does N Mahadevan do from day to day? Although he remains emotionally and morally anchored to his business, he now spends much of his time to 'give back to society'.

Thus Oriental now runs 'Winner Bakery' in Chennai's Loyola College, along the lines of an NGO. The corporation provides the building, the bakery runs like a normal business, but the profits go to municipal schools. That was a sum of Rs 30 lakhs last year! The money was used to build toilets for girls, provide spectacles for poor children and train teachers in Montessori.

But that does not mean 'Winners' is a cheap brand. No sir, even the Park hotel places orders here!

Another pet project is the bakery school which trains young people from rural areas and makes them employable.

"In the interiors of south India, there are boys who really need a break. So, I bring them, I accommodate them, I give them Rs 1500 rupees stipend, plus I train them as bakers and confectioners."

So far, 300 students have passed out and have been employed by Oriental and other food businesses.

Mahadevan's next venture is a barista training centre. He has opened a small coffee shop inside Loyola College and installed imported machines there. Two Italian baristas are now training boys from the local slums in the art of making cappuccino, café latté and French press coffees!

The latest in Mahadevan's employment-cum-income-generation efforts is at Chennai Central Jail. Mahadevan convinced the DGP of Prisons to give him some space. Labour and electricity is free, while Oriental pays a nominal rental..

"I brought my imported machines worth 22 lakhs there. Rotary Club will be giving me a truckload of flour every month. The convicts will work to convert that flour into bread, and distribute it through various orphanages, municipal schools and NGOs like Banyan."

All absolutely free of cost.

Currently the prison bakery is running two shifts - with 10 workers each. Over 300 prisoners applied for the jobs - so there is tremendous potential to scale up.

When it comes to charity, Mahadevan works with any party, any cadre, any organisation. But his belief is: "Never give them fish, teach them how to fish!"

And like a true fisherman Mahadevan believes there is an ocean of opportunities. He is glad to serve as a lighthouse for fellow entrepreneurs whom most would eye as 'competitors'.

"I have taken many Indian restaurants abroad. For example, Anjaper, a south Indian brand, which is famous for Chettinad food. Then there is a restaurant run by a husband-wife team from Calicut which I helped to start in Dubai. Every day, there is a 45 minute queue outside that place!"

So are these business dealings, or investments? Not necessarily.

"Numbers are very important for me. I operate in 16 countries and my email every month only talks about what are the sales, what is the cost."

Mahadevan is a widely connected man and is happy to use his network for the benefit of others.

Many expat Indians say to me, "Mr Mahadevan, do you know of any restaurant where I can put in money?" And Mahadevan will put two and two together, to create five. He will even advise on the best locations in cities he knows and loves - to give that new venture a fighting chance.

It takes a very big heart to do that.

"The minute another Indian restaurant comes up in Dubai, the lives of 30-40 guys will be better. If they are getting Rs 8000 here, they will get Rs 18,000 there!" For Mahadevan, that is return enough.

And despite the many balls he is juggling in the air, Mahadevan balances his work and family artfully. "For one month every year I take off with the family and no one can reach me - whatever the emergency."

His school going son and college going daughter may or may not join the business.

Mahadevan does not know yet, and it is not a big concern. He's lived his life the way he wanted, and surely he will allow them the freedom to do the same.

"I travel, meet people - do the things I enjoy the most. Tell me, how many people are blessed to live like this?"

Many more, I silently hope.

ADVICE TO YOUNG ENTREPRENEURS

Income minus expenditure = profit. It's one simple line which you should never forget!

I always say- "Do your homework" And we have a policy- 'Measure twice, cut once. Don't measure at all, and you keep cutting, cutting.'

So if I am developing affordable teppanyaki, I must know how much is the duty to import sake (rice wine). You have to know what you are doing; if not, join hands with someone who does.

And you have to have that fire, I don't accept defeat.

If you get into the food business, remember the main thing is hygiene, which you cannot compromise. When I brief my chefs in 116 restaurants and bakeries in 16 countries, I say, "These are not my assets. My assets are my son and daughter, who are sitting there. If they can eat, then Mrs Ambani can come and eat here as well.

Buy by the day and sell by night. Don't stock up much, don't give stale food. The customer will always come back to you if he or she feels, "I had my fill, my money was well spent." You have to build a relationship.

And remember, never get complacent. In this line, ten times the customer gets a good meal. The 11th meal, the *kebabs* are not good. But you will only talk about the 11th meal, you will forget the first ten good meals. That is human nature.

So never let down your guard, never compromise!

THE HUMAN <u>TOUCH</u>

Hanmant Gaikwad,
BVG (Bharat Vikas Group)

As an engineering student, Hanmant Gaikwad took tuitions - to support himself through college. Today, he runs the Rs 300 crore Bharat Vikas Group (BVG), a facilities management firm which not only has the cream of corporate clients, but maintains Rashtrapati Bhavan.

Hanmant Gaikwad sits in a very big office behind a very big desk, under the watchful gaze of Swami Vivekanada. The placard in front of him states, "I like people who can get things done."

I like Hanmant because he is exactly such a person.

Like millions of Indians, he had no bank balance, no godfather, no special privileges available to the upper class. But, he found opportunities everywhere.

The seed of the business he planted to support himself through college has grown into a mighty multi-faceted organization. With an annual turnover of Rs 300 crores.

Yet he is extremely humble, even diffident. As he recounts his early struggles, Hanmant refuses to meet my gaze. As the story progresses, he is suddenly more confident, in command.

It's like I am witnessing the journey from the buffalo shed to BVG House - right before my eyes.

Bharat Vikas Group is a commercial success but is about bigger things as well.

Dignity of employment.

Dignity of labour.

Dignity of human relationships.

Because the mightiest of trees is only as strong, as its roots.

THE HUMAN
TOUCH

HR Gaikwad,
BVG (Bharat Vikas Group)

Hanmant Gaikwad was born in Koregaon in Satara district.

"My native place is Rahimatpur, around 10 kms from Koregaon. My father was a clerk in the court and we lived in a small, rented house."

Hanmant was a brilliant student, especially good in mathematics.

"Since first standard I was getting prizes in Mathematics. In class four I got a scholarship. It was around 15 rupees per month."

When he was in class six, the family shifted to Pune. They lived in Phugewadi near Dapodi in a tiny one room house. 10 by 10 feet. At this point Hanmant realised the difference between himself and those who had money.

"I started thinking, *'Unke paas bahot paisa hai, ameer log hain.'* We are poor."

The situation was made worse because Hanumant's father was chronically ill. He had to be admitted to the hospital for two-three months a year.

"My mother pawned all her ornaments, to somehow get money for his treatment."

She also started working as a teacher at a municipal school and took up some sewing jobs.

Hanmant was then studying at Modern High School. He needed one rupee to buy a bus ticket to and fro everyday. Even that was hard to come by.

"My mother used to ask the ladies who came to pick up their stitching "Hanmant needs one rupee to go to school today." *Iss tarah se hamare din nikle.*"

Despite the hardships, Hanmant secured 88% in class 10. The only guidance he got was from the headmaster of his mother's school.

"Your son has got good marks, put him in Diploma."

In Diploma, all the bright students take electronics - and that's what Hanmant did as well. He joined the Government Polytechnic in Pune.

"First year, I got 74%. Second year, I got 72% and third year, again I got 74%. In second year, I lost my father to a cardiac attack."

The year was 1990.

Hanmant completed his diploma and joined Philips as a trainee. But he wasn't happy with the work he got there.

"They used to throw jobs to me and say, "Check this, check that." *Mujhe jamaa nahin.*"

What, then?

"It was father's dream to see me as an IAS officer. I decided to try for it. But first thing I need a degree. I need to do my graduation."

The natural choice for a diploma engineer is to go for a BTech. But engineering colleges charge hefty fees. At the time, the family's only source of income was a teacher's salary of Rs 2300 a month...

Hanmant's mother took a loan of Rs 15,000 from Pune Municipal Co-operative Bank and got him admitted to Vishwakarma Institute of Technology (VIT).

"And then I decided to also do some earning. *Khud ka kamaana chalu kiya.*"

Hanmant and his friend Yogesh Atre started taking diploma classes. In the first month, they earned Rs 3200, which they split 50: 50.

"I started another set of classes where I managed to make Rs 5000. *Lekin bahut jhamele chalte the.*"

The teacher was ready, students were ready, but no one was ready to give the space. Eventually, a good Samaritan offered his garage free of charge for classes.

Meanwhile Hanmant also took up painting jobs and quickly discovered it was an excellent business.

You need 4-5 painters, and little or no capital. A two BHK job with oil-bond painting would bill Rs 7000-8000. If the owner went in for lustre painting, it could go upto Rs 15,000.

And the profit margin was a healthy 40%!

Hanmant arranged for painters from his viilage. A four member team could complete one job in 10-12 days. After all expenses, that meant a cool Rs 5000 profit per flat.

"*Aise do flat toh mahine mein ho jaata tha.* So I started earning around Rs 10,000 per month," he recalls. "I never asked my mother for a single rupee since then."

The young engineering student paid his own fees from third year onwards. But his lifestyle remained frugal.

"The distance from the college to my house was 21 kms. So I used to do up-down on cycle everyday, 42 kms."

Around this time gratuity of Rs 80,000 due to his father also came in. The family bought a 2000 sq ft. plot in Sanghvi and with a little help from relatives, constructed two additional rooms in Pune as well.

Life was getting better, but Hanmant had his sights set higher. In the final year of engineering, he was attracted towards the writings of Swami Vivekananda.

"I felt *ki kuch alag karna hai.* What I should do, I did not know but in 1993 I formed an organisation - Bharat Vikas Prathishthan."

Bharat Vikas Prathishtan collected small amounts - Rs 10, Rs 30, Rs 50 - and started giving 2-3 poor students a small monthly stipend.

"We chose students who were on their own, who were not getting opportunity like me to earn..."

A really big opportunity knocked when Hanmant was in his final year of engineering, And he was ready and waiting, to open that door.

Hanmant heard that there was work going on at Balewadi stadium for the upcoming National Games. He approached the Lama Agency, landscape and garden consultants to the project. And somehow he procured a contract worth Rs 3 lakhs for concreting the pathways.

"I was little bit knowing about Civil engineering because we had just constructed our house. I knew one *cementwala.* Some sand suppliers."

> **"Swami Ramdevji *kehte hain, 'Karm hi dharma hai, karm hi pooja hai... Aaram haraam hai. Jis aadmi ne yeh samajh liya, woh aadmi badaa ban jayega'.*"**

Hanmant was confident he could handle the job.

"I always do calculations. *Paanch logon ki team kitna kaam karti hai din mein?* How much cement does it take? How much sand? I had understood all that."

The work would take about 7 days and money was promised in 15 days. The profit margin was a fat 50% and it all seemed very straightforward. Hanmant accepted the contract and what's more, he even completed the job in the stipulated seven days.

And he did it by "motivating" the workers.

Back in 1993, daily wages were Rs 50 for ladies, Rs 100 for gents.

Hanmant thought to himself, "The work has to be completed in seven days, and I am making Rs 1.5 lakhs in profit. So why not pay a bit more? They will be happy and work with more enthusiasm!"

While the going rate for a *jodi* was Rs 150 per day, Hanmant paid Rs 250. In addition, he brought them *wada pavs* in the mornings, and country liquor in the evenings.

So far so good - problems started *after* the project was completed.

There was an earthquake in Latur, hence the Games were postponed by six months. Then came the rains and the pathways Hanmant had built were flooded.

"We did not level the ground properly before concretising... *is liye jagah jagah par chaar inch paani khada ho gaya.*"

The payment due to Hanmant was suspended.

Tension mounted.

At home uncles cursed the day this foolish boy decided to get into this *jhamela*.

Hanmant would sit in Balewadi from seven in the morning till very late at night, trying to find a way out. And he did. The same labourers whom he had earlier paid Rs 250 came up and said, "You have been good to us. Now you are in trouble - we will help. *Aapka kaam ho jayega.*"

"Mujhe lagaa ki labour ko khush rakhenge toh woh aur achha kaam karenge."

They brought in materials.

They pitched in their time.

The original job took seven days whereas the repair work took two months.

But it got done and the payment was released.

"I was absent for the first semester exams - all papers. I had to make up for it in the second semester. But I was able to complete the job and earn a one lakh rupee profit."

It was quite a learning experience.

In 1994, Hanmant completed his BTech and joined TELCO - the Tata Engineering and Locomotive Company, now known as Tata Motors - as a graduate trainee.

"Wahan bhi bohot mehnat kiya."

Not just hard work, but smart work. Far beyond what was expected of him.

With the help of Ganesh Limaye*, his counterpart in the Ancillary Development Department, Hanmant converted old cables lying as scrap from years together into usable material. This resulted in a saving of Rs 2 crores for the company.

With so much spirit, so much enterprise, why work for someone else? And why accept a salary of Rs 7000 when you can earn far more every month doing all kinds of contracting jobs?

One simple reason: Social Standing.

"A job with TELCO was very prestigious. People said it will be easier for you to get married," he adds.

In fact people would come from Hanmant's native village thinking he was a 'big man' in the company. That a word from him might secure them a job.

Now a graduate trainee is M1 - the lowest grade in the management cadre. He moves up slowly - from Senior Engineer to Assistant Manager to Deputy Manager. Then Manager, Senior Manager, Divisional Manager, AGM, DGM, GM, VP…

---

* Ganesh Limaye is Director (Purchase) at BVG India while Yogesh Atre, Hanmant's partner in the tuition class business , is Vice President (Marketing).

A very long and very strong hierarchy indeed.

While Hanmant couldn't get people from his village a job with TELCO, perhaps he could get them *some* form of employment?

"*Mera painting ka kaam toh chalte hi the.* I had a team of four who kept that going and earned an additional Rs 10-15,000 p.m."

If only he had more jobs in hand, he could form more such teams. Hanmant approached his manager in TELCO.

He said, "*Saab*, I have 7-8 people from my village looking for work. If you give me some job I can employ them."

The manager said, "Since you are an employee, we cannot give any job to you. You need to form a trust or society formed for purpose of social work."

Hanmant said, "We have already registered a trust - Bharat Vikas Prathishtan."

On 22nd May 1997, Bharat Vikas bagged its first housekeeping contract for 8 people.

"The job was to clean the Indica plant, which was coming up at that time. Four people in the paintshop, two in Safari and two in H block."

And the person responsible for supervising their work was not Hanmant but Umesh Mane, who had quit his job four months earlier, to work full time with Bharat Vikas.

"Umesh's family and mine - we have relations for last three generations. BVG *ke total success mein Umesh ka bahut bada haath hai.*"

In January 1997, Hanmant mentioned to Umesh that Telco might give Bharat Vikas some housekeeping work. The very same day Umesh quit his job .

"*Maine resignation de diya bank mein*," he declared

"But why!", exclaimed Hanmant. "*Kaam milne waala hai.. mila nahin hai ab tak.*"

"*Bas...aapne bol diya, maine resignation de diya.*"

Umesh was the first person to believe in Hanmant, and his vision for Bharat Vikas.

The two arrived at a simple working arrangement.

"*Main kaam leke aaungM. Paise ka main dekhunga. Kaam Umesh sambhalega.* Till today, we are doing the same thing. Marketing is handled by me, finance is arranged by me. Umesh looks after the operations, and he is the Vice-Chairman."

In its very first year, Bharat Vikas achieved a turnover of Rs 8 lakhs. The next year that jumped to Rs 56 lakhs. Upto this point Hanmant was still working with Tata Motors.

"In 1999, I got married and then I also decided to leave the job. I started BVG as a full time activity."

The first thing he did was change the name of the organization from Bharat Vikas Prathishthan to Bharat Vikas Services. Then, Bharat Vikas got its first ever mechanised cleaning contract, once again for the Indica plant.

"We bought ride-on sweeping machines, and other equipments worth Rs 60 lakh. Tata arranged for the loan through Tata Finance."

Hanmant went from plant to plant, marketing this new idea of mechanized cleaning. And he quickly realised one thing.

"Companies wanted a complete solution. They did not want to buy a machine unless some contractor could supply people to use that machine. Ultimately they were only interested in one thing - cleanliness."

Bharat Vikas got an enquiry from GE Power in Bangalore. Would they be willing to come down and take up the job?

"*Karenge, koi dikkatt nahi hai*," replied Hanmant.

"Ten of us piled into one Sumo. Umesh, myself, eight workers… the machine was tied on top of the vehicle."

The party left on Friday from Pune and arrived in Bangalore on Saturday. Monday was the inauguration of the factory; the team got to work immediately.

Meanwhile, Hanmant went in search of rooms - *koi rukne ki jagah*. By evening he had a place on rent.

By Monday the entire plant was spic and span. The manager was happy with the quality of work and recommended the tiny company from Pune to a friend. Bharat Vikas got a contract from a 100% export oriented unit of Himmatsingh group. In no time, they had 7-8 clients in Bangalore.

Enquiries came from Chennai, then Hyderabad.

"Chatrapati Shivaji was an ideal for me. *Aaj bhi hai*. When we started getting work in south I felt like it was *dakshin pe sawaari*."

Thus little by little, Bharat Vikas 'conquered' the South.

At each new location, the company employed a standard formula.

"Bachpan se aadat main kisi ke saath competition nahi karta. Jitna mehnat kiya, utna mujhe aana chahiye. Company ke liye, main jitna mehnat karta hoon, utna aana chahiye. "

"Every city we had one trusted person - a boy from my village - as the supervisor. 30% of the workers we send from Pune, 70% we take locals."

It cost a little more to put up the Maharasthtra boys, provide them one meal a day. But the benefit is that BVG is able to maintain a fine balance.

"Paanch-sau, hazaar rupaye ek ladke ka kharcha padhta hai... lekin long term mein there is no strike, there is no union, there is no *jhamela."*

The locals cannot hold BVG to ransom. This is especially important because the kind of services BVG provides are 24 X 7.

"For railway stations or airports, there is no holiday... no Dussehra, no Diwali. For those kind of operations, you need to have a proper system of working with people. *Woh system humne develop kiya hai."*

And all this activity was co ordinated from a makeshift office in a buffalo shed - *a bhains ka tabela.* Rental: two hundred rupees a month.

By 2003, Bharat Vikas had achieved a turnover of Rs 4 crores a year although profit margin was not very high - 10-12 % after tax. And then the company got a big break. The contract to maintain the library of Parliament in New Delhi.

"One Mr Srinivasan was the chief engineer there. He wanted to give the job to a reputed agency and to do the job you needed to purchase equipment worth Rs 40 lakhs."

No agency was willing to take the risk because Srinivasan was willing to grant only a 6 month contract.

"If you perform well, then I will continue, otherwise I will throw you out," he said.

Bharat Vikas stepped forward and said, *"Hum karenge."*

"I did it because I was confident that we will deliver."

And they did. The contract was extended by another six months.

In 2004, BVG bagged an even more prestigious job: the mechanised cleaning of Parliament House i.e. the Lok Sabha and Rajya Sabha buildings.

"We won the tender. And here security people created some problems. That how can a private party be allowed inside Lok Sabha and Rajya Sabha chambers?"

For one month BVG maintained the public portions of the building. The job was done so well that MPs started asking why the same standard could not be maintained inside the chambers

The Hon. Speaker intervened. He said, "I want the same contractor to take care of the entire building."

And thus BVG entered the inner sanctum of Indian democracy, by invitation.

Next, BVG was asked to take a look at the Prime Minister's residence.

"There was a red stone walkway, of around 200-300 metres, where the PM takes his morning walk. *Woh pura kaala ho gaya tha.*"

BVG was asked, "Can you clean this up?"

"We said yes and made it *ekdum chakachak.*"

Not surprisingly, BVG soon got a housekeeping contract for the entire residence of the PM. This was followed by the crowning glory: Rashtrapati Bhavan.

Simultaneously, business with the private sector was also growing.

Tata Motors asked, "Will you work in Jamshedpur?"

Hanmant said, "*Karenge.*"

"Rudrapur?"

"*Karenge.*"

The faith of its first client has reaped rich dividends for BVG.

"Our first billing from Tata Motors was Rs 12,000. Now, the billing in Pune itself is Rs 1 crore per month - for various sevices."

Bajaj, Mahindra, Ashok Leyland, Hyundai. Volkswagen, FIAT - the who's who of the auto sector are BVG clients.

Apart from mechanised cleaning, BVG diversified into housekeeping, landscaping and gardening. Anything a customer requires - from electrical to civil maintenance - BVG is ready to provide.

ONGC, ITC, Hindustan Lever, Accenture and even Indian Railways are just a few of the other big names that Bharat Vikas works with. And the way it gets business is simple: satisfy one client and he will bring in several more.

"We never had many people in marketing. Our philosophy is to do the job well. *Jab kaam acchha karoge to customer khud aapki marketing karega*."

And this formula has worked for BVG when dealing with the government as well as the private sector.

"If you are a hardworking, dedicated person, there is a lot of work available. Only difference is now we are talking big contracts."

At one time a contract worth Rs 10,000-20,000 per month was a big thing for BVG. Now, he looks for a commitment of minimum Rs 1 crore per month.

"We have just got a big contract from state government to clean all their hospitals across Maharashtra. It is around Rs 4 crore per month, Rs 48 crores per annum. So like this, things are happening."

The annual turnover of BVG is now over Rs 300 crores.

"We have a branch in Guwahati, we have a branch in Chennai, we have a branch in Baddi. We have branches in 22 locations and 12 states." 60% of the company's business comes from the private sector; the remaining from the government. In all, BVG works with close to 300 organisations, including some completely non commercial ones.

"We maintain Patanjali Yogpeeth (Baba Ramdevji's ashram). Also worked for Sri Sri Ravishankarji's ashram. As a social commitment I have also taken up the cleaning of six temples in Maharashtra, free of cost, on daily basis."

This includes Alandi, Pandharpur, Tuljapur - temples visited by the common man.

It is a truly heartwarming story, but I cannot help wondering how Hanmant manages this complex operation. How does BVG ensure the highest quality standards in hundreds of locations?

Part of the answer lies in setting up the right systems.

"Achha kaam karenge toh aur kaam milta hai.
It is a cycle and you have to keep it going."

"At every stage, we have monitoring, quality systems and numerous check-lists. Before starting any work, we plan it down to the last T."

That is how BVG successfully managed the difficult task of shifting entire plants from one location to another for Fiat and Tata Motors. Including portions of the Nano plant from Singur.

Bharat Vikas Group now employs 16,000 workers. "We take in those who are 7th fail, 10th fail as workers and pay them Rs 4000-5000 a month starting salary. We also provide ESI, PF, bonus etc."

Graduates are taken in as supervisors and paid Rs 12-15,000. Assistant Managers, Managers, DGMs - Bharat Vikas now has an entire professional cadre. And even an expatriate!

"Earlier we would think a hundred times before paying someone Rs 50,000 as salary. Now we do not think twice if we find the right person."

Human resources are *the* most valuable asset for any company. But how much you value people as human beings is the question most CEOs fumble to answer.

For Hanmant Gaikwad, it's about doing 'whatever I can' for the maximum number. Whatever it takes.

As a result of his efforts, the central government has recently sanctioned a scheme to provide 13,000 low cost housing units in Chinchwad. 600 of these will go to BVG workers.

"For the first time in the country there is a scheme to give houses to common people - like our workers. They will get a 500 sq ft house at the rate of Rs 300 per sq ft. The house will cost them only Rs 1.5 lakhs." Whereas the market value of the property is anywhere between Rs 12-15 lakhs.

"Now those 600 people who are getting a house worth around Rs 12 lakhs in Rs 1.5 lakh rupees - they will always be dedicated and motivated for BVG. Do or die situation *mein woh kuch bhi karenge*."

"*Toh* whatever limited resource is available with me, whatever relations I have... I am trying to give best possible to my workers. And things are happening."

"Do rupaya kharcha kiya, toh teen rupaya maang ke lene ka customer se."

Till last year, no one had heard of BVG, *koi zyada poochta nahi tha.*
Today journalists want interviews. They ask Hanmant, "Which
management books have you read?"

He replies, "I have not read management, I have not studied
management. It is in my blood."

His fundas are simple:

"If I spend two rupees, I must get three rupees from the customer."

"Do your job as well as you possibly can."

And of course, there is destiny.

"I am happy that Bharat Vikas - this name I thought of in 1991, it is
going along the right path."

That is exactly why banks are now queuing up to offer money,

"I remember when I wanted to buy my mother a washing machine
and fridge, when I first got job with TELCO, the bank would not give
me loan of Rs 30,000."

Today when BVG applies for a Rs 130 crores loan, banks are ready
and willing.

"They are not asking us for 50% collateral - only Rs 10 crores."

But back when BVG was an unheard of entity, it was the faith of a
few individuals in Hanmant Gaikwad, which made all the difference.
One such person was Eknath Thakur, Chairman of Saraswat Co-
operative Bank.

"Eknath Thakur is a visionary person. I remember he told me, 'I
don't believe in collateral.. that is *saahukari.* I do banking'."

In 2002, when BVG needed a loan of Rs 1 crore to purchase
equipment, it was Saraswat Bank which offered the money. Without
margin money or collateral.

"I could not even offer my house against the loan - it was an
unauthorised construction. Eknathji believed in me and released the
money, regardless."

Hanmant also fondly remembers Mr Vaze of Bank of Maharashtra
and Mr Bongirwar of IDBI. For helping him through the uncertain,
early days.

The vision of BVG is now reality, but this is just the beginning.

"I have just crossed 36... running 37... so time is there and people
are supporting me, even investors are supporting."

Support has also come in the form of valuable advice.

"In 2005, I met Anish Jhaveri (then Director, HSBC Securities) who explained to me concepts like 'valuation' and PE multiplier."

Anish advised, "Do not save on taxes by taking cash out from the company. Pay taxes and see how people multiply your profit by investing in you, helping the company grow faster."

And that is exactly what happened. Anish introduced Hanmant to a clutch of investors*, who put in Rs 6.5 crores into BVG. Last year Kotak also took a small stake, for Rs 30 crores. The company may divest more equity soon, given Hanmant's extremely big plans.

"My vision is to achieve Rs 3000 crores turnover in next 5 years' time. As Ramdevji says, "*Badi soch, kadi mehnat, pakka iraada.*" (Big vision, hard work and determination) If you have these three qualities, you can do anything."

Housekeeping still forms the bulk of BVG's business - upto 60%. But Hanmant sees the company moving beyond - into areas like power, electrical infrastructure and waste management*.

"I have got one plant, wherein I convert waste plastic to fuel. Cost of converting is barely Rs 12-15, while I sell at Rs 30. So there is good profit."

Hanmant is constantly seeking new business, new opportunities. That means working Sundays, holidays, Diwali, Dussehra.

"Now gradually, Umesh and I take one day off.. weekly. But it is not fixed." Hanmant's wife and two daughters Adita (age 9) and Arya (age 5) are understanding.

"*Kuch karke dikhana hai...* I have not inherited anything from ancestors. I am not a Tata or Birla."

But this is how Tatas and Birlas are made, I think to myself.

Apart from business goals, Bharat Vikas continues to have social objectives. Next year Hanmant is planning to create a trust of Rs 50 crores, generating interest of Rs 70-75 lakhs. With this, he plans to provide monthly scholarships to 3000 students starting from class 7 upto graduation.

"I will do this activity with my personal money, I will raise the funds by selling some of my equity. We may go for IPO next year."

There are many miles more to sweep; promises to keep.

And miles to go before I sleep, miles to go before I sleep...

---

* Kirti Doshi & Gagan Chaturvedi (Antique Securities), Girish Kulkarni (TDA Capital) and Raj Misra (Indea Capital).

ADVICE TO YOUNG ENTREPRENEURS

Basically *kya hai ki*, one thing is there that hardwork, dedication, quality of work, there is no substitute for this.

If you say, "I will work from home, I will wake up at eleven in the morning..." No, it will not work.

Kuch karna hai, toh marna padhta hai..

But if you do good work, you will get more work - I guarantee you that.

There are so many businesses with a lot of potential. Take painting.

40 lakh people stay in Pune, out of that suppose 20 lakh stay in good localities. If on average five people live in one house, that means there are 4 lakh houses.

A house needs to be painted once in 5 years. That means every year around 80,000 houses need painting. That is the scope of the painting business and remember the owner gives you an advance plus you have a 40% margin.

Dhandha karne ke liye bahut paise ki zaroorat nahin hai. Sachhe dil se, imandari se kaam karo and you will be successful in whatever you do.

SHINE ON CRAZY
DIAMOND

Ranjiv Ramchandani,
Tantra T-shirts

Ranjiv Ramchandani studied microbiology, but hated it. He joined advertising, but hated the hierarchy. Ultimately, he became his own boss with Tantra - a company which prints wacky and uniquely Indian t-shirts. And, he's lovin' it!

The first thing I notice about Ranjiv Ramchandani is, "He's not wearing a Tantra t-shirt."

He shrugs - no big deal.

Ranjiv does not need to advertise his t-shirts - you see them wherever you go. People proudly sporting the 'Om' symbol, the all-terrain auto rickshaw or even the Taj Mahal. Bearing the legend 'Via Agra'.

Tantra has done to the t-shirt what Karan Johar did to boy-girl romance.

Made India *desi desi* cool cool.

The man behind the mad idea started life as an average guy, with average dreams.

Doodling on the side.

But he kept searching, kept striving, keep seeking that creative kick.

The search took him to advertising, and then far far away from it. To a place where ideas came to life - on a 't-shirt'.

Tantra t-shirts carry messages.

The message of Ranjiv's life is, you can have your cake and eat it too.

Be creative *and* make good money.

Be crazy *and* successful.

Dream it. Then do it.

Be happy.

It's a good life and I wish it for all of you, everywhere. Whatever you do...

SHINE ON CRAZY
DIAMOND

Ranjiv Ramchandani,
Tantra T-shirts

Ranjiv Ramchandani was born in Colaba, the 'spiritual hub' of Mumbai.

"I studied in Xavier's School, Dhobi Talao - not ICSE but SSC. Both my parents worked with the government. It was as middle-class as middle-class can be "

Ranjiv was an average student. Not amongst the top ten. Not in the last ten, but comfortably anonymous, somewhere in the middle.

"My 10th standard results were average - I didn't have the marks to get into a posh South Mumbai college. Luckily, my parents used their Sindhi connections to get me into Jai Hind College."

Ranjiv bumbled through the next five years, finally graduating with a degree in microbiology. Protozoa and bacteria didn't quite fire him up, but the company he kept sure did.

"I think college opened my mind a bit, I had friends who were not in the regular mould. Even the music we listened to – like Frank Zappa, and the books we read like *'Hitchhiker's guide'*…were very different from what everyone else was doing."

Around that time, Ranjiv, inspired by MAD magazine, started cartooning. He walked into the Mid-day office one morning, to show his samples.

Two days later the editor – Anil Dharker – called and said, "You're on!"

The strip was called 'Twist and Shout' and appeared in the Sunday Midday under the pen name 'Joran'.

One thing led to another and soon Ranjiv started another strip in the popular magazine *Business India*. This one was called 'Like father unlike son' - a lighter look at a father-son duo running a family business.

Despite this creative streak, Ranjiv stuck around with the microbes. After completing his bachelor's, Ranjiv stumbled into a clinical pathology course at Sophia Polytechnic.

"It was terrifying because there were just five guys in the whole campus and we had a tyrant of a headmistress there - one Parsi lady - who was Adolf Hitler and Josef Stalin rolled into one."

Ranjiv hated the course, hated the idea of examining urine and stools for a living. Then why did he persist?

"The thing is, you don't want to be a loser. I had spent three years studying microbiology and this seemed to be the logical thing to do."

Besides, he had no idea what else he could do.

"Some people discover who they are and what they want to do at 18, others discover the answer at 26. Still others never figure it out all their lives. We all germinate (or fail to) at different times."

Ranjiv is candid enough to admit how clueless he was. He recalls applying to an ad of British Airways which said 'Stewardess required'.

"I didn't know the precise meaning of 'stewardess' - I even sent a 'full-size' colour photograph! They replied back saying, "Thank you for your application, but we're looking for female candidates..." so that was rather embarrassing."

Ranjiv then took a shot at hotel management, with the Oberois. He went to Delhi for the final interview, but it didn't quite work out. So Ranjiv completed his pathology course and joined Bhatia Hospital as a laboratory assistant. He worked there, in a dungeon-like basement, measuring urine samples.

"One fine day I looked myself in the mirror, wearing that lab coat, and asked myself, 'What the *hell* am I doing?' I should be into something I enjoy, something that gets me going and that's when I thought of giving a shot to advertising."

Why 'advertising'? Because it seemed to be full of crazy people who did fun things like write witty slogans and draw funny pictures. A place for artists and cartoonists, poets and entertainers...

So Ranjiv quit the hospital job and took up a part time course in creative writing at KC College. There, he met someone who was

"The great thing about my parents - which I still thank them for - is that they were very non-interfering, very relaxed, not very ambitious themselves. They just let me be."

working with an agency at Nariman Point.

The guy said, "I can give you a job."

Ranjiv said, "OK - I'll take it!"

Even though it was client servicing, not copywriting.

"I was paid Rs 1900 per month and had this Marwari, pan chewing, safari suit wearing boss," he recalls with a grin. "Not quite the creative hub I'd imagined - it was more like a government office!"

There he was, a young man wanting to change the world with his ideas, doing the job of a lowly client servicing executive. Humiliating, but part of life's experience.

After a year (and an 'increment' of Rs 100) Ranjiv decided it was time to knock on the doors of professional ad agencies. So he walked into a couple and gave a 'copy test'.

"I got into two agencies at the same time - one was 'Karishma Advertising' right here at Nariman Point. The other was at 'The Edge' in Worli - which to me seemed like halfway across the world."

Ranjiv decided to meet the bosses at both agencies before taking a final call.

"I really liked Sheila Sayed - she was a fun, spontaneous, and a great mind. So even though I had to change two BEST buses to get there, I joined 'The Edge'."

Ranjiv had done so well in his copy test that he was mistakenly hired as a senior copywriter. What's more, one of his cartoons was published on the cover of *Business India* magazine and suddenly he was the 'cool young punk' in the agency.

The guy with *talent*.

"They paid me some Rs 2500 per month, but that was not important - I was finally in a 'real' agency."

One fine day, his boss Sheila Syed threw a big party for all the employees. There, she announced she was quitting 'The Edge'. In fact she and her husband Munnawar Syed (then MD at Everest Advertising) were starting a new agency called Triton.

And so, along with many of the employees at the Edge, Ranjiv too moved to Triton.

"I worked at Triton from 1991 to 1997. The office was on the famous Pherozeshah Mehta Road, in Fort."

Triton was a steady, secure place - not a rockstar agency which won awards and accolades. Business compulsions dominated, client servicing called the shots. Good ideas were killed off early...

"Of course they did send me to Cannes, and to conferences in Singapore and Paris. They took good care of me moneywise, gave me a car. It was all quite comfortable!"

But that did not stop Ranjiv from being the 'troublemaker'. The guy who asked tough questions of the establishment.

"I remember being asked to write the agency's official brochure. I refused. I said, 'I don't believe in what you want me to say. It's bullshit!' That got me into a bit of trouble with the bosses."

Being part of the system was not working for Ranjiv. In search of a creative kick, he started a weekend experiment.

"One afternoon four of us friends were in a bar, having drinks and all conspiring to conquer the world. We decided to 'do something', work for our own vision, rather than somebody else's."

The idea was 'India on a t-shirt' and it had been with Ranjiv since a trip he made to the UK in 1991. There, he came across a range of t-shirts based on the peculiar culture of Scotland.

I said, "Wow! This is like creating a wearable poster - *you can use the t-shirt to say anything!*"

Back in India he found there was nothing remotely similar. But it took another six years for Ranjiv to act on the idea.

"The name we chose was Tantra - short, strong and something to do with India. And it had an underground kind of feel to it."

Just like the project itself.

The modus operandi was simple. The comrades in arms would generate some designs and then figure out how to get it printed.

"There was this senior art person called Sanat, he created our first three prints - 'Khadi, 'Kali' and 'Goa'."

But it's one thing to sketch something on paper and quite another to translate it onto a t-shirt.

"When we started I didn't know nothing about fabric, or printing. The first supplier I went to said, "This is never going to work! Six colour, eight colour printing is not possible."

I said, "OK - but you've got to try again!"

Now in advertising the colour 'red' means 18 different kinds of red.

"When I didn't get my shade of red I screamed at the supplier."

Terrified, he said, "Take it, take it free!"

Ranjiv then went to a company called Dawn. There too, he got into a scrap with the owner. Dawn was actually in the business of making *banians* - and that's what their samples looked like.

"Coming from advertising you can throw lots of attitude because you are working *for* somebody. The system protects you. When you're on your own you have to work with your wits."

Ultimately Ranjiv managed to produce around 500 pieces of the first 2-3 prints and these were sold through informal channels. And this whole t-shirt business might have remained a weekend pastime had it not been for a run-in at the agency.

"I used to value my Saturdays and Sundays. But that doesn't mean I wouldn't work if I was called on Saturdays. The trouble was this client servicing guy came up with a half-baked brief and wanted me to produce an ad by Monday morning 10 am."

I said, "This is not possible, unless you give me more meat! So the rotten fellow went and complained about my 'attitude' to the boss."

On Monday morning Ranjiv got a curt note from the boss saying, "Let me know if you are interested in being here."

Enough was enough; Ranjiv decided to go on long leave and just never come back!

Next stop: Kurla station, on the way to Tirupur, the t-shirt capital of India.

"I had some contacts so I decided to go there and place a bulk order."

'Bulk' at that stage was around 2000 pieces, in 4-5 prints. Total investment - Rs 1.2 lakhs.

So far, so good. But how does one actually *sell* so many pieces?

Ranjiv knew the customer would buy from day one - no question. All questions were only in the mind of the retailer, because Tantra was an experimental brand. Nothing like it had been seen before...

> **"When you go along the wrong path it's like you've eaten something and it's not agreeing with you; you need to be aware internally, talk to yourself and figure out what the matter is."**

"In advertising, it's called 'disruption'. Tantra was not just a t-shirt, it was about communication. Even our tags 'spoke' to the customer!"

A great new product needs an evangelist. Tantra found its first believer in a hard-nosed, hawk-eyed Sindhi shopkeeper by the name of Mr Hathiramani, bang in the middle of Colaba Causeway.

"Our initial prints were all touristy, so his location was perfect. He agreed to keep 10-20 pieces. They sold out overnight !"

He called promptly, the next morning and said, "*Aur paanch sau piece bhejo* !"

So what was the magic? Location was one factor, but Ranjiv feels that Hathiramani also had the 'right heart' and the 'right spirit' for the product. Soon enough other stores realised '*maal bik raha hai*' and orders started building.

"Initially people came all the way to Colaba to buy our t-shirts. Then, shops in Bandra and Lokhandwala also started keeping it. Tantra became popular not just with tourists but with the local crowd, especially college students!"

Because he was sourcing from Tirupur - where large volumes were the name of the game, scaling up was not difficult.

"Tirupur is essentially an export-oriented zone. In the initial years they used to treat local buyers like shit. In fact they have a very funny system - when you you enter the factory they will first garland you and perform aarti. Then they ask, 'Which company are you buying for? American? German? French'?"

If you reply 'local', they actually snatch back the garland!

Ranjiv quickly learnt some of the tricks of the trade – like staying at the right hotel.

"There is only one 5 star hotel in Tirupur and they send out the guest list to all the suppliers in town. So we booked ourselves there and soon started getting calls from people looking for orders."

"In 1991, I visited the MAD magazine headquarters in New York. I just went there and knocked; this guy invited me in and took me on a tour. I met the William Gaines, Angelo Torres and saw some of Al Jaffee's original artwork. It was mindblowing!"

Of course, quantities were modest initially - 3000-4000 pieces a month. Ranjiv would dream of the day he would hit 10,000 pieces a month.

"We didn't know the concept of 'margin'. The idea was to make Rs 30-40 per t-shirt sold and make about as much as I would as a creative director in an agency..."

Except that here, Ranjiv had to be creative, client servicing and chief execution officer - all rolled in one. And every little thing about the garment business had to be learnt, from scratch.

"I remember we approached a department store in 1997 and there was this lady in charge. She asked us what is the 'shrinkage'. We were really naïve and did not know you had to test the t-shirt fabric in a laboratory!"

What Ranjiv did was soak a red t-shirt overnight in a bucket and collect the water in glass bottles.

"We didn't actually get to meet the lady... One of her juniors saw us carrying those bottles and they probably thought we were a bunch of idiots!"

Eventually this store did start stocking Tantra, though this incident extended that process by a whole year. But it was a learning experience, and Ranjiv tried a different approach with another modern retail outlet. He calls it the 'magic letter'.

"Every year I send out a few letters with the full intention of 'getting through' to that person in terms of content, in terms of positive spiritual energy. And 9 out of 10 times it works!"

The letter to this retailer gave 10 reasons why they should stock Tantra and each of the 10 reasons was very powerful.

The marketing manager called and said, "OK - can you come over and discuss it?"

"He was a real tough customer, even the deputies sitting on either side of him had this tough and angry look. I wonder whether the corporate types do all this to psyche us little guys out!"

He threw margins and numbers at Ranjiv.

"All of which I didn't understand ('I was always bad at maths you know!'). Finally I agreed to some crazy bargain and when we later got into Shoppers Stop, Globus, Pyramid, I had to offer them all the same wafer-thin margins..."

But the visibility definitely helped in building the brand.

In garments, as with most other businesses, there is the concept of wholesale. But it was the direct-to-retail model which worked for Tantra, in the initial years.

"We did appoint one distributor in Mumbai but most shopkeepers preferred to order directly from us. And that lazy distributor guy wasn't getting us any incremental business!"

Speaking of 'us', what about the four other guys in that bar? The gang which produced the first set of visiting cards?

"Out of the four people, one guy refused to leave the comfort of Triton. They offered him a big increment and he just stuck on there. Sanat – the artist who made the first few t-shirts - wanted to work freelance. The third guy he did join me. But..."

It was not a happy partnership. The two parted ways in less than a year and the chap launched his own rival t-shirt brand.

"I thought initially it was unethical because he would go to the same stores with the same kind of product we were selling. That's life," he shrugs. "But it didn't dent Tantra's sales."

Ranjiv managed the show with a skeleton support staff, in a small office behind Strand Cinema in Colaba.

"There was this kid from Jai Hind College who just turned up and said, "I want to work with you" and I instantly hired him. I also had a junior accounts person but she swindled me while I was on a trip

> **"As an employee you are working for somebody else's dream and that person's dream may be just to make money. So you are always left wanting for more."**

abroad, which I discovered only six months later. Of course I had to ask her to leave!"

Things were crazy upto 2000-2001.

"Shopkeepers from Goa and Delhi would just turn up at the office and say, "We want your t-shirts." And they would all be shocked at the tiny little place we operated from."

By this time Tantra was selling over 10,000 t-shirts a month.

All well and good, but what about the creative part - the *soul* of the business? Anyone could pick up a funny line and print it on a t-shirt. But there was something special about Tantra. Something different.

First of all, the quality of talent. Hemant Morparia - the well known cartoonist - is just one in a long list of creative minds who's contributed designs. As did ordinary folks, fans of the Tantra brand of t-shirts.

"An Air India pilot emailed us and asked if he could send his ideas. We turned one of those ideas into the 'Auto rickshaw' t-shirt which is still selling!"

In fact, coming up with *ideas* is not the issue. Choosing the right ideas - the ones which will sell more tshirts and maximise your profit - is where the trick lies. And for that you need not just a creative mind, but a trained mind.

"It's 100% gut feel, actually."

Neither does Ranjiv believe in creating 'options'.

"I remember at the ad agency there was one approach, there was an alternative and there was an alternative to the alternative. I used to find that so dishonest! You have to *believe* in something, and just go with it."

If the concept is fundamentally strong, Ranjiv might improve upon the design in terms of typography or illustration. But that's about it.

"If it's good enough people will buy... if not, they won't... that's the cold hard fact of the matter," he says.

However, at Tantra sales aren't *everything*.

"We enjoy the prints which sell less because after all, they're all are our babies!"

Sometimes Ranjiv will stand at Narisons in Colaba - where an entire shop window is devoted to Tantra t-shirts - and just watch customers.

"I think an MBA would have coloured my mind, told me 'that's not possible'."

"I love it when someone looks at one of our very obscure prints - which 99% of the junta would not understand. But if this one guy is laughing and he buys it, it's still worth it."

The point is to never 'dumb down' the brand - let it remain quirky!

In the last 12 years Tantra, has produced over 2000 designs, although not all are on shelves at any given point in time. What's more, Tantra has spawned sub-brands as well as a parallel brands which go by the name 'Barking Dog' and 'Line Maro'. Aimed more at the local market, with edgier lines and no 'India' focus.

"If I am going to give one store the Tantra brand to stock, then what about the guy next door? Better I create my own me-too brand and double our sales. In fact, I think we should even make our own fakes and put it into the streets - but maybe that's too radical!"

The other area Tantra scores in is the quality of its t-shirts. Unlike most brands Tantra actually get better with each wash. The secret, says Ranjiv, is higher 'gsm'. Or more threads per square inch.

"So you decided right at the beginning not to cut corners?" I ask.

"No," he replies. "We were just ignorant!"

Well, ignorance paid rich dividends and after initial skepticism people were saying. "Hey, we didn't know this idiot had any potential - look how well he's doing!"

At this point - in 2001 - Ranjiv roped in his brother-in-law Vimal Mariwala to handle the manufacturing and marketing side of the business. Vimal was pretty fed up with his job and happily accepted the offer.

"Vimal is better looking, he is taller," jokes Ranjiv.

The truth was doing *dhandha* was taking its toll on the creative soul. Malls wanted to meet every week, which meant travelling all over town. Westside and Provogue asked Tantra to produce an in-house line of t-shirts. The idea of going back and selling ideas to someone did not excite Ranjiv.

"My whole thing about coming out of advertising was that I wanted to sell only to my customer. So Vimal and I divided up the work. He

"Every human being wants to get up and say look - this is who I am, I count in the grand scheme of things."

doesn't get too involved in the creative side and I don't bother much with the rest of the operations."

Production is Vimal's baby - an intensive exercise with one factory alone running 4-5 different orders in a staggered manner. As one yarn goes into knitting, the other one is already into dyeing and a third batch is being cut and printed.

Each batch generally consists of 30,000-40,000 pieces, and within that Vimal will decide how many colours, how many sizes, how many styles - based on orders.

Tantra does not own any production units - it has outsourced the work to 2-3 different factories. However its own staff handles the quality control aspect.

"The bulk fabric is pre-tested and the garment goes through a range of QC tests, before it is packed."

So how many t-shirts does Tantra churn out annually? My guesstimate is over 100,000 pieces a month. At that volume the company's turnover would be Rs 25 crores a year - give or take some.

For a reasonably large operation, Tantra has a pretty small number of employees. Around 25 people in a smallish Nariman Point office, another 25 in warehousing and 20 odd overseeing operations in Tirupur.

Meanwhile, Tantra has a strong national footprint and retails through a variety of formats. In fact 30-40% of sales now come from malls. A place Ranjiv was not sure he wanted to be, initially.

"I felt the minute we go to malls we are no longer underground as a brand. But I realised that malls bring volumes and if I don't, some other brand will capture that space..."

The Sindhi in him ultimately prevailed!

At the same time, however, Tantra also opened up EBOs or Exclusive Brand Outlets. There are 20 odd EBOs now - in Delhi, Jaipur, Mumbai and even Guwahati, Shillong and Shimla. The EBOs are run by Tantra's distributors.

"Exclusive outlets are important for a brand like ours, which has strong mindshare. Once a customer steps in, he gets the full-on experience. He cannot walk out without buying *something*!"

Which is why EBOs contribute 25-30% to Tantra sales.

What's more, Tantra has grown and diversified beyond the classic round neck t-shirt.

"We do a lot of winter merchandise - fleece, polo necks, plains, long sleeves... We even do some clubwear! In fact, what we want to do now is start a t-shirt supermarket, if somebody can finance me..."

Not that Ranjiv is really looking for investors. In fact, Tantra is still run as a partnership firm. Another hard-to-believe fact: In the last 12 years, Tantra has not borrowed a single rupee from any bank.

"Actually, it would be very easy for us to scale up 100 times, but we don't want to do it because it would just bring stress and high blood pressure."

Right now, Ranjiv is 'enjoying the ride'.

"It's so much fun and it makes decent money - what else does a human being need? You should be able to afford your *daal-chawal* and you should be able to enjoy what you enjoy. Like a movie on DVD, maybe with good surround sound!"

And quality of life; freedom to just be. Which Ranjiv certainly does.

"My day is very flexible - often I go home at 3-4 o'clock in the afternoon. The other thing I love about doing my own thing is I can come to work the way I am. No need to pretend, no need to shave if I don't want to!"

And no one to stop you, ask you to be 'sensible'. In fact back in 1997, when Ranjiv was still single, he had the idea of putting his own matrimonial ad on the tag of Tantra t-shirts!

"It's crazy, isn't it! I mean you can do anything. In fact we are not breaking the rules as much as we should be because we are bigger, a little bit institutionalised..."

"Tantra is an honest product. We never go on sale because we've already priced it as low as we can without going out of business!"

Which is not necessarily a bad thing.

"Something could happen to me, it could happen to anyone! So I am trying to institute a system, a design cell. We will create a bank of people who understand what the brand is and what kind of work we need to do."

The real challenge is to keep Tantra fresh, cool, relevant - both to the loyalists and to the next generation of t-shirt lovers...

But I can almost hear Ranjiv's response, "What, me worry?"

Not a chance.

ADVICE TO YOUNG ENTREPRENEURS

Doing your own thing is better than sex.

Having said that, I believe there are two kinds of people on this planet - those who want to work for somebody and those who want to do their own work. Among those who want to start their own enterprise, some are deluded and some are actually talented. Do first figure out if you've got talent!

If you've got talent then of course work hard, hang in there, make it happen.

If it doesn't happen in the first two years, maybe it isn't meant to happen.

People say, "Oh! If you start a business you are going to get screwed, you don't know what's out there ..."

I say to them, "There is nothing out here - it's all plain and simple. Nobody knocks on your door everyday and says - pay up!"

I think there are limitless possibilities, whichever business you are doing. You need to explore and be creative in every field, do things in a way that has not been done before.

The product should touch you. It should press some button in you which hasn't been pressed before...

Doing your own thing makes you more at peace with yourself. You're following your own DNA, your own rhythm, your own pace in life. You are connected to your inner self, your soul.

Our mission in life is not to reach sales targets. The purpose of life is to be happy. That's what Dalai Lama says... In fact that's what our next t-shirt says!

KARMA
COMPANY

Suresh Kamath,
Laser Soft Infosystems

This MTech from IIT runs a software firm where programming jobs are open to all - not just engineers. Suresh Kamath believes that social responsibility and sound business can go hand in hand - and his company is living proof of it.

Suresh Kamath's first words are, "Thank you for coming here and spending time with us today."

His words are soft, and very sincere.

Just like his company.

Laser Soft is in the business of software but it is not what you'd expect of a 'software company'. There are no glass towers, Cafe Coffee Day style canteens or oh-what-a-cool-ID-card employees.

In fact when the cabbie first entered Valasaravakkam, I was sure he'd taken a wrong turn.

This is no IT park but a middle class residential area. Suddenly we spot the board of 'Laser Soft' on an ordinary pista coloured cement building.

The head office is further down and that's even less impressive. But when Suresh explains why he chose this location; why his company does not want to be the next Infosys, it all makes perfect sense.

Suresh Kamath believes that ordinary people can do extraordinary things.

That growth cannot come at the cost of quality of life.

And that software should be 'affordable'.

He is a David among Goliaths.

Pygmy among giants.

But he stands tall.

Suresh Kamath believes that business has a deeply social purpose and it's not the size of the company which truly matters. It's the size of your heart.

KARMA
COMPANY

Suresh Kamath,
Laser Soft Infosystems

Suresh Kamath was born in Mysore, in a lower middle class family. "My father used to work for a billing company. My mother has studied only till 8th standard. I am the eldest of five children."

The single most important influence in young Suresh's life was Swami Vivekananda.

"There was a Sivanand Ashram very close to my home in Mysore. Everyday there were discourses, people talking about philosophy."

Suresh was curious. Someone lent the lad a few books on Swami Vivekananda's life and he was fascinated.

While Suresh didn't understand much initially, he was struck by one thing. Most thinkers and philosophers are focused on one aspect, but Swami Vivekananda was different. He spoke about patriotism, religion, spiritual quest - everything combined.

"*Jnanalok* was very inspiring...I thought, 'I should do something for our country'." At the time Suresh was 12 years old.

What this meant in practical terms was that he started working very hard. "I started doing better academically."

Suresh's dream was to become a doctor and serve society. However there were very few medical colleges at the time and reservation ruled the roost. So he ended up doing BTech instead - at National Institute of Engineering (NIE) in Mysore.

Suresh excelled in studies and secured the gold medal. He then completed an MTech in computer science from IIT Madras. After graduating in 1982, he did a 3 month project with Patni computers, where Narayan Murthy was also working at the time.

At the end of three months, Suresh had a permanent job offer with Patni in Bombay, as well as TCS in Chennai. But, he was clear about two things.

"I had decided I would not go abroad at any cost. And eventually I wanted to start my own company, somewhere in South India."

Suresh took up the TCS offer with the idea of 'learning something' and in 3 to 4 years time, striking out on his own. He gained much in experience, but was unable to save much.

"I had to send Rs 500 p.m. to my father, Rs 500 was my house rent and Rs 300 my monthly budget. I was not able to save more than 5 to 10 rupees every month." Over 4 years, Suresh saved Rs 200. This was the 'capital' for his start up.

Not much, even by 1986 standards! Goes to show that money - or lack of it - is never a good enough reason to keep sitting on the fence.

Now most software companies back then (and even now), specialise in services. Suresh took the opposite stance. "I wanted to make a company which focused on products."

People said, "You are a fool. You will close down within 4 to 6 months."

I said, "Let me find out for myself..."

Nobody believed him, except his father, who said, "You will succeed, do it!"

Suresh accepted the challenge and started his own company on 1st May 1986. The first thing he did was hire five people at a salary of Rs 1000 per month. All working out of his tiny flat.

"The first 5 people, I couldn't approach engineers. So, I went to NIIT. Some BScs, some BComs, they didn't know anything of programming." Suresh then trained these people and yes, the first few months were difficult. But it was surprisingly easy to find clients.

Suresh went cold calling and approached the biggest bank in the city - the State Bank of India.

At the head office someone said, "There is a problem in one of our branches, can you solve it?"

Suresh replied, "We will do it, but we don't have computer. Can you give me permission to work here in the night?"

> **"The IT industry has assumed that it has to grow at a breakneck speed, but I beg to differ. If the company grows at break neck speed and the employees are stressed, and they break down, they burn out, I don't think it is worth it."**

The branch manager agreed.

Thus in the day time, the team hung out at the branch and learnt about banking. In the night they all went to work on SBI computers. In just about a month the team developed a product which did the trick.

At the time SBI had an operation called "DD" which created a lot of backlog. It went like this: a particular branch handled the account of the Madras Fertiliser factory. This company received payments from farmers all over the country in the form of cheques. State Bank purchased these cheques and gave money to Madras Fertilisers immediately. Now, the bank was left with the tedious job of collecting money by sending cheques to various branches.

It was a manual process handled by just 4 to 5 people. The volume was enormous, so cheques would be lying around for days!

"We automated the entire process", beams Suresh, recalling the first blush of success. "Within 2 weeks the backlog was cleared up."

The interesting thing is no one on the team knew the first thing about banking. But they were willing to learn - from books, from observation, from anyone and everything. And, they were determined to prove themselves.

SBI was pleased as punch and gave the company more work. In fact, other SBI branches purchased the "DD" product as well.

"We made the first sale for Rs 4000 and then we had to work really hard for the month. Subsequently, we sold the software to other branches. Then they came up with other problems. So, we gradually went to other areas of banking."

The DDRR system, general ledger, current accounts, exports - Laser Soft started automating various operations.

Meanwhile, Suresh had also approached Apollo Hospitals. Again, the team studied the processes and became familiar with healthcare terms. In 10 months, Lasersoft was able to computerise the entire hospital's medical records.

Two big clients trusted a young company, just like that!

By the end of year one Lasersoft had a turnover of Rs 64,000. For the next five years, the company continued its focus on banking and built up a formidable reputation.

"By '91, we had worked in 52 areas of banking. Also, we got used to handling volumes, because we were dealing with the largest bank in the country."

Armed with this experience, Lasersoft approached other banks like Indian Bank and Corporation Bank. "At Corporation Bank, we developed a cash management system for corporate customers. We developed the product in a month's time, in the second month it was live, and in 15 days they had backed up the entire records."

This project became a huge moneyspinner for the bank. "They made hundreds of crores of profit in that. And they are using that software, till today."

The great thing with a product is that you can sell it to different customers. But of course, you customise.

"Every bank is different. They have different processes and accounting methodologies. So, if you don't customize, it is not efficient for them."

Initially the customization was very high - nearly 30 to 40%. After working with different banks, Laser Soft figured out the differences and provided parameters within the software itself to take care of the issue.

The company also extended its clientele in the health sector with customers like Manipal Hospital and Bombay Hospital.

All customers came in through one route only - word of mouth. And so it was that in 1991 Lasersoft bagged a most prestigious contract. To computerise an entire branch.

"State Bank had a branch in Chennai, called the overseas branch. It was the biggest branch for the bank in those days, making maximum profit." But there were some basic issues.

"Exporters used to come in with documents and bills, to get finance from the bank. The staff would handle 25 bills per day, after that they would actually turn the customer away and say "come tomorrow." After the automation the branch could handle even 200 bills."

Little wonder that profits doubled overnight.

Laser Soft's work got noticed and, enquiries poured in from export-import branches across the country. For Lasersoft, the contract was a 'milestone moment'. At the time the company employed 40 odd people, and had a turnover close to Rs 30 lakhs. This was a chance to take a giant leap forward.

"Delhi, Calcutta, Bombay, Indore, Cochin, we went to so many places. I think 65 cities in all!"

This work would keep the team busy for the next 3-4 years. Meanwhile, the economy was opening up. The reforms brought in by finance minister Manmohan Singh had an impact on banks.

"Export-import changed drastically and a lot of opportunities opened up for us in that period. 60 to 70% of our income came only from these branches."

Laser Soft's USP was that it understood banking from head to toe. And hence could design software which was more robust. Design is critical to good software and Laser Soft was able to create products which were flexible. They could adapt and deal with change.

"We had worked four to five years understanding, very patiently, how a bank works. That helped us hugely when it came to designing software for them."

By 1998, the company employed 200 people and the turnover was 'a couple of crores'. And this is where what could have been yet-another-Indian-software-success story deviates from the script. Suresh Kamath did not really care about size, about scale, about global footprint. For this entrepreneur business is not an end in itself, it is a means to accomplish other things.

Matlab? Laser Soft is not a company which undertakes CSR activities - it is a socially responsible corporate.

"Till now we have not paid a single paise of bribe to anybody," says Suresh." And that's one reason we have gone this far." Hmm, but that's the line which made Infosys famous.

Usme kaun si nayi baat hai?

Well, there's more to come. Laser Soft, says Suresh, could have been a much bigger company in terms of turnover. "But we believe software should be sold at 'affordable prices'." He explains it thus:

"In the world of commodities, suppose this phone costs 2000 rupees, they will sell it for a 50% mark up at best."

"In IT what happens is, if this phone is Rs 2000, they will say it is made by IBM, which is the biggest company in the world, the

> **"In the software industry after 8 or 9 years you stop programming and become a manager. That is wrong. We still write programmes, we still work in technologies. The experience of the seniors is used to develop better products."**

technology is complex and so on so forth. Ultimately the phone will cost Rs 2 crores!"

Suresh quotes an example specific to Laser Soft. "We automated Corporation Bank's central banking system, where the entire bank and its branches are connected. ATM also. And this we did it at a cost of something like 20 crores. Out of that 20 crores, our software price was Rs 3 ½ crores, the balance money was for the hardware, the networking, and other hardware devices."

"If you go to a larger company, they will do the same thing for Rs 500 crores. See the difference!"

Laser Soft earns a fair price but nowhere near what the 'market rate' is. Because it believes the market is fleecing the customer and this is an injustice to society.

"See... suppose a cement company buys software, that becomes one of the production costs for them. If the company pays more money for software, then the cement price goes up. Similarly petroleum, everything goes up. The common man gets affected."

To put it bluntly, because software is somewhat esoteric to the common man, there are companies selling a 'Maruti' at a price equal to Mercedes Benz. Now this is the first time I have heard such an argument but it has a ring of truth to it...

It also explains why, despite having so much going for it, Laser Soft remains relatively small and unknown. From Rs 2 crores in 1998, the company has grown to Rs 40 crores and an employee base of close to 700. In any other industry that might have been an achievement. In software, you remain a pygmy.

But Suresh being more than a little *pagal*, sees it more in terms of David competing with Goliaths.

"We make products and compete with Infosys, TCS and all the biggies in the field. We are a small company but we are giving them

> **"We sell software at the right price. Despite that, we have made money every year, paid our taxes, paid PF, given a good salary to our people. I think this is the right model."**

a run for their money... "

"But unlike an Infosys or Wipro, nobody knows about you!" I exclaim.

"You go to any bank... they know me."

General public?

"Yes, nobody knows about us. We don't do any publicity about our work."

And Suresh does not care. What he does care about is issues like employing 'differently abled people'. Which is nothing short of a mission at Laser Soft.

It started like this. In the early '90s, the company was small, but stable. Suresh decided to hire differently abled people to work - starting with the reception. Word spread and one fellow called Parthasarthy turned up. He was afflicted by polio.

The Laser Soft office required him to climb a flight of stairs. Parthasarthy found it difficult but somehow made it.

"I felt very bad that I made him climb up to meet me. I said, 'I am very sorry to make you climb, I would have come down'."

He said, "No, I wanted to, because I need to know if I can come daily to work."

I asked, "Can you climb this staircase daily?"

He said, "Yes."

Suresh hired him on the spot. A man so keen to work would definitely be successful - and he was.

Parthasarthy did extremely well. He only had some training at a government computer institute when he joined. But he worked his way up from programmer to software manager and now heads several teams.

"Parthasarthy has worked for so many foreign banks, he has travelled abroad. He got married, he bought his own car, now has two children." Suresh then actually buzzes Parthasarthy to join us. Meeting him is an emotional moment.

100 of the 700 employees at Laser Soft today have stories like Parthasarthy. Every time a vacancy is advertised, hopefuls turn up from all over the country. As far as Delhi,and Gujarat.

"We started hiring people from different communities. One class is this polio affected people, they are a large class. Then we started taking people from the deaf and dumb community. Initially we took a few people, because communication was difficult, training was difficult. They use sign language which none of us knew."

But once that hurdle was overcome, these employees became trainers for others. Today Laser Soft employs about 20 people who are deaf and dumb.

The company runs a whole training program called 'Light', only for the differently abled. Trainees are paid a stipend of Rs 5000 per month and given extensive classroom instruction. After 6 months or a year, they take an entrance test. All those who qualify are absorbed. And most do!

"They work so hard, their commitment levels are very very high."

At Laser Soft, differently abled means not just people with physical disabilities. The company also takes in people who are not considered 'smart enough' to be hired by the software industry. And not out of charity.

"Today most software companies only hire engineers... Totally wrong thinking."

Suresh's argument is simple: Engineering graduates are not readymade programmers - they have to be trained for 6 months to a year. So why can't you also train non-engineers?

"We have people who are not engineers - who are just 10th pass - and they have done extremely well. In fact engineers work under them. But there are some engineers who are very bright also. The whole generation is so bright, their IQ is very good - whether engineer or non-engineer."

At Laser Soft, even if a driver wishes to become a programmer, he is encouraged. "So, many people have come as drivers and now they are programmers. They are from very poor families. When they come here they can't even speak English properly... They totally get transformed."

It is a *leetle* bit difficult to digest.

"You are saying that anyone can become a programmer if they have the dedication and willingness, you don't have to go through an engineering college or course?" I ask.

"Yes."

"So, you don't find any difference in these trained engineers, and somebody who does not have any technical background . They can perform equally well, if they get the correct guidance?"

"Yes."

"Education qualification is not the criteria, it is what the person can do," he adds.

If only more employers thought like that...

It is actually a win-win situation for all concerned.

"These engineers and MCAs, brilliant boys and girls, they also like the company's social motives, they also support, so whatever we do is not one man's effort. They are so dedicated to the company - even if somebody offers them a better salary they won't go."

And there are other reasons for this strong loyalty as well. In 1998, Laser Soft was looking for a new office and like all software companies considered moving to the 'IT corridor'. But then Suresh decided it made more sense to keep the needs of the employees in mind, especially the differently abled.

"When we were in Nungambakkam, people had to come from different parts of the city. Transportation was so painful for these people, the buses, so horrible. So I thought why not move to a place where employees can be provided housing somewhere close to the office."

And thus it was that Laser Soft moved to Valasaravakkam. Low profile, but the employees simply loved it.

"In 1990, a house on rent here cost just Rs 1000. Today it costs Rs 3000 - still very cheap." The company took a lot of these houses on rent for employees and enabled them to work more, simply because they live next door.

"No one wastes 2-3 hours a day on transportation", smiles Suresh. "They can go home whenever they want, come and work whenever they want - that flexibility is there, it really helped us. So, we started doubling, from that we grew very fast."

And yet, the idea is not to grow so fast that you lose out on everything else.

"The general perception is that we are doing charity. I say it is a business model. Needy people are getting jobs, we are making profits every year, we are paying dividends - where is the question of charity?"

"I wanted to create a healthy atmosphere where people can learn, excel in their work but not be under stress. They should have a good quality life... stay healthy. We do good work, and no stress at all, no pressure, there is freedom for people to perform. Freedom means innovation. People innovate and do fantastic work."

And yes, with all this they hardly have the incentive to leave. Loyalty is high, so much so that from the first five employees, four are still with the company!

Wonderful. So here we have a company with 20% year on year growth, no bank borrowings, no liabilities, satisfied, happy employees - and absolutely no outside funding! Well, therein lies another instructive story.

"We did take funding in the year 2000 from ILFS. People convinced me that you should take capital, you must go public, grow."

ILFS valued Laser Soft (which then had a turnover of Rs 5 crores) at Rs 30 crores and bought a 16% stake. But three short years later, ILFS wanted to exit by selling the company. Now most promoters in the IT industry would jump at this chance and cash out - but not Suresh. He wanted to sustain and grow the company further. Besides, the new buyer might certainly not share the vision and mission of Laser Soft in the social sense.

Why was ILFS in such a hurry? Was Laser Soft not growing fast enough?

"We were growing, but they wanted to make money out of that investment." There were many suitors - among them Siemens and I-flex - who wanted to not just buy the ILFS stake but the entire company. And it was not a happy experience.

"While this was going on we were not able to work, not able to focus. There was a lot of wastage of time, lot of worry for the employees. If the company is sold what will happen to us?"

"IT companies project an image of being rocket science or doing something glamorous. It is not. To make products, we don't need to be in a fancy campus."

So I decided one day: We will not sell.

The only way out was to buy back the ILFS stake. In 2006, Suresh did just that. Pooling in promoter capital, contribution from employees and funds raised from the bank, Laser Soft pulled it off.

"We bought back the shares from ILFS at the same rate offered by I-flex. All the employees contributed - from as little as Rs 5000 to Rs 1 lakh - whatever savings they had. I am still paying back the loan... about 4.5 crores.."

The journey so far has been fascinating - what lies ahead?

"Five years from now, we should be somewhere like 2500 people. And we should be worth at least Rs 130 crores."

70% of Laser Soft's customers are in India. The rest are in Europe, the Middle East and Africa. "Now we want to work in the US as well," says Suresh.

But how will this small company battle it out for business with the Big Boys of Indian IT? Suresh believes Laser Soft *has* a technological edge.

"We are the only company in India - even perhaps in the world - which has developed a banking system in Java. And we have developed the software in such a fashion, that it is very scalabale. So, it is ideal for reducing costs, ideal for mass banking."

In the last two quarters of 2008, Laser Soft attracted business from 35 to 40 new banks. The slowdown has, in fact, benefitted the company.

"Banks have suddenly become wise, they want to reduce costs. That makes our software - what it can do, and the pricing itself - very attractive."

Marketing has become more important than ever. And it was a weak area for a company that believed in telling it like it is - talking straight. Suresh has therefore roped in the former MD of State Bank of India - Mr Venkatachalam - to join as Chairman.

"He has the knowledge, the vision, and he is a man whom I respect very much. A very ethical, inspiring person for all of us. So, I requested him, "Sir you come and become our chairman, not just for namesake, you please run the entire strategy, the finance, investment, marketing - everything."

Under the chairman's guidance, Laser Soft has built a professional marketing team. And the difference is visible. "People go abroad, pick up a lot of orders. We now have clients like Mashreq Bank in the Middle East."

Going forward, Suresh sees huge potential for more products in banking, especially related to treasury, mutual funds and forex. And there's also much to be done in healthcare - Laser Soft's other core expertise area. And, fundamentally, in software connecting different sectors.

"In the future, all enterprises are going to talk to each other. We are making software for retail, for distribution, for banking, for healthcare, but ultimately everything will get connected through the mobile phone." And Laser Soft is creating products which it believes will help bring about that revolution.

"Our goal is *always* to do something which nobody has done before." For example, Laser Soft harnesses the idle computing power of desktop PCs in banks. A simple idea which reduces hardware requirements considerably.

And technical details aside, this sounds like a man still excited at the thought of waking up every morning and coming to work!

"The technology is so challenging that we feel almost... addicted. New things keep coming up. So, at times we spend about 18 to 20 hours a day working! But we also balance it out - take breaks, have fun time with the family."

Suresh has two teenage daughters and a supportive spouse.

At the end of the day it all boils down to love.

Love for the people you live with.

Love for the people you work with.

Love in what you say.

Love in what you do.

Love for all humanity.

Making no distinctions.

"I believe only ordinary people can do extraordinary things. If people think they are already extraordinary, they will do ordinary things. The attitude, the focus on work comes by thinking we are not great. Because it is all about team work."

So, is this the Jnanayoga of Swami Vivekananda - manifested in the form of business?

"Yes, absolutely."

As I exit the Laser Soft office, a young man afflicted with polio strides past me on crutches.

I smile, and think to myself, "What a wonderful world."

Post-script: *Six months after I met Suresh Kamath, there was a surprising development. On 15th Oct 2009, Polaris acquired Laser Soft Infosystems in a deal valued at Rs 52 crores.*

As of now, Laser Soft remains an independent entity.

One day David will probably be subsumed by Goliath. But I hope - when that happens - the sweetness of the small company with a giant heart, will flow in the veins of a Software Giant.

<u>ADVICE TO YOUNG ENTREPRENEURS</u>

I enjoyed every minute of whatever I did in the last 23 years. And even today I have the same energy as when I started.

Start businesses in areas which you really believe and like to do. You should do something different, and don't believe what people say. People say business cannot be run on ethical ways, you have to be dishonest. That is wrong - we can do everything in the the right fashion and still be successful.

Have the the motivation to do something for the country, for its people. There are a lot of needy people, lot of things to do. Take up the challenge and do it! You are definitely capable of it.

Spread happiness among people. Ultimately, that's the most valuable thing. Whatever amount of money you have, if you do not have peace, it is of no use.

LOOK MA, NO HANDS!

Raghu Khanna,
Cashurdrive

Raghu Khanna is 24 years old and started a company right out of college. Cashurdrive is based on a simple idea which required no capital, no office, no fancy technology. His story shows that experience is over-rated - there is no better time to start, than now.

"He's way too young," I thought when I first met Raghu at an entrepreneurship summit. "And he's just gone into business!"

I mentally crossed him out of my 'people I would like to interview' list.

But then I heard him speak. And I realised that Raghu has been an entrepreneur not just from August 2008, but all his life.

In school, in college, in his choice of career - Raghu struggled against the odds, and beat them. Whether it was getting the branch he wanted at IIT or an internship abroad, he used his brains, his boyish charm and his ability to bluff.

To live his dreams.

In the 16 months since he started his own company Raghu has turned a simple, easily copied idea, into a proprietary business.

"Give me any car, anywhere in India, and I can wrap your ad on it," he declares.

Raghu is a living, breathing example of *jugaad*.

Ki no matter what the situation, 'I can wriggle out of it'.

Because deep in his heart he knows, if you apply your mind, stretch your spirit..

You will find a way, to do *anything*,

LOOK MA, NO HANDS!

Raghu Khanna,
Cashurdrive

Raghu Khanna was born, brought up and 'spoilt' in Shimla.

"I did my schooling from St. Edward's School, Shimla. My dad is a professor of political science in HP University and my mom, a housewife."

When Raghu was in class 5, he had a crazy idea. He got together with some friends during Diwali and started selling pots.

"I caught hold of a guy who made gamlas and asked him to make small lamps. Then we went house to house and sold them."

Each customer was even provided with a 'bill' - a small piece of paper stamped 'Matka House', with Raghu's signature scribbled alongside.

"We used to buy the lamps for Re 1/- each and sell for Rs 1.50. The money we made was blown up on ice cream or buying cricket balls."

For most of his school life, Raghu was a backbencher. More interested in dancing and extracurriculars than studies.

When Raghu was in class 6, he failed in history by two marks. His housemistress called him aside and said, "I can give you grace marks but *tumhe iski aadat lag jaayegi*. Why don't you start studying harder?"

Raghu took the advice to heart and stopped fooling around. He managed to stand 3rd in class 8.

"That was the time I realised that I can do anything!"

After completing class 10 with flying colours, Raghu went to Chandigarh to live with his naani. And prepare for IIT JEE. It was a very competitive place, full of toppers. Raghu scored a zero in the very first test at his physics tuition - but continued to fight.

His heart was firmly set on joining IIT.

"People appear for JEE, then they settle for CET and finally they take admission in NIIT... What keeps people from dreaming big is fear of failure. I already knew what that was like, it did not bother me."

Raghu managed to secure a rank of 3689. But the best he could get was admission into the Bachelor of Design program at IIT Guwahati.

"You know what my problem is, I never ask God for the exact thing I want in life. He sent me to IIT, but did not give me the branch of my choice!"

Raghu did join IIT Guwahati, but after a couple of classes, realised design was not his cup of tea. He tried for a change of branch, but it was not allowed at the time.

"I spent a lot of time with my seniors in the first semester. I used to ask them, "This is something that I really don't like - what can I do about it"?"

One of them gave Raghu the book: ' Who Moved My Cheese'.

He advised, "This is life - accept it."

But Raghu just couldn't. In January 2004 he packed his bags and returned home. There were just 3 months left to prepare for IIT JEE once again, and he had to start from scratch.

"There was no Physics, Chemistry, or Maths in the design course, so I had lost touch. All batches of tuition classes were full, but somehow I found a Physics professor, Mr B M Sharma. I used to go to him late in the night to clear my doubts."

It was walking through hell, but something inside told him: keep walking. *Tension mat lo* - this too will pass.

Raghu secured an AIR of 1040 in the JEE screening test, but in the mains his rank slid to 2559. His AIEEE rank was 1610, which meant he could have his pick of local colleges or NITs. But having tasted life at IIT, he was not willing to settle for less.

With a rank of 2500, Raghu could opt for textile engineering at IIT Delhi, or architecture at IIT Roorkee or an MSc Geology. Raghu decided that Civil Engineering was his best bet and landed back at IIT Guwahati.

His mother said, "Are you sure you'll be able to adjust once again?"

"I'd completed two internships in Europe as a student so I had no craze to go abroad. I had already travelled and seen the world!"

Raghu replied, "I have to do something, I had to prove everyone wrong!"

Back on the IIT G campus, there was general confusion. Some thought he had failed, while others thought he was from the preparatory course.

The good news was that IIT was now permitting change of branch. Raghu studied hard and managed a CGPA of 9.14, which allowed him to switch from Civil to Electronics & Communication.

"I was the happiest person. I went to Goa to spend my holidays and had a good time there. But when I came back to IITG I had to face 2 'discos' i.e. discipline committee actions."

One was for a verbal argument with someone while he was a student of design. The second related to a 'wild party' which the Deputy Director happened to gatecrash.

The professors were confused, there was one file for Raghu Khanna, '2nd year student' and one for Raghu Khanna, '3rd year student'.

"I had to explain that both Raghu Khannas were one and the same. I have three different roll numbers and three different ID cards in IIT Guwahati - one in design, one in Civil and one in EC. Somehow I wriggled out of that situation."

Meanwhile Raghu noticed friends in the third year going abroad for internships. He asked himself, "Why can't we go in the second year?"

So he took a senior's CV, reformatted it and sent it off to a professor in Italy. Along with the CV Raghu included a 'larger than life' presentation about IIT. Including names of some of its illustrious alumni such as Arun Sarin, then CEO of Vodafone.

"Toh basically aapne tukka maara?" I ask.

"True - *zyada se zyada* I won't get it. No harm in trying *na*? I had another internship offer from IIT Bombay in any case."

As it happened, Professor Dalessio from the University of Roma Tre called up immediately. He sponsored the air tickets, arranged for accommodation and offered a stipend of 350 euros.

There was one small problem: Raghu's CV stated he was proficient in Java as well as C ++. But he had never studied either language!

"If I really need to, I'll figure it out," he reasoned. And that is exactly what he did.

"I made Rajat Gupta my ideal. See, he left ITC, went to Harvard, then joined McKinsey and look where he reached. I thought, we IITians - we can do anything. *Dimaag to hai na!*"

The codes were in Italian - but translated into English by a PhD student. Raghu's job was to debug the programs, but his main project was to design a software which would help handicapped people use the computer, by tracking their eyeballs.

The concept of *jugaad* worked not only in the lab, but in the kitchen. When Professor Dalessio wanted to try some Indian *khaana*, Raghu obliged with r*aajma chaawal.*

"Actually, I used chicken masala because that's what I found in an Indian store. I knew the professor had never eaten *raajma* so as long as the food was spicy, it would be considered 'Indian'!"

And that was not all. Raghu learnt to manage his funds, to stretch his tiny stipend as far as it could go.

"I used to get the best and cheapest air tickets and travel all over Europe," he grins.

How?

"I had to search! And I learnt that when you buy things in bulk it is much cheaper."

Take something as basic as vegetables. Raghu would find ten people near his apartment who needed tomatoes, buy 5 kgs at one time and manage to save a good amount. Enough to eventually buy himself an iPod.

He even managed to borrow a tux to enter the world's oldest casino in Venice - without paying the 250 euro deposit. By working his charm on the bouncer.

"I started with just 50 cents and made a 3 euro 'profit'. But it was a great experience."

Raghu returned to IIT Guwahati, but the project he did in Italy kept him thinking. Could his software find some other application?

"I read about an accident where the driver got drowsy, and lost control of the car. And I said this is it!"

What he needed to do was extend his program to calculate the blink rate, so you could figure out when a driver was becoming drowsy. He found there was a great deal of interest on this subject from companies like BMW and Volkswagen.

Raghu worked on a 'drowsy driver detection system'. He entered his idea into the IIT Guwahati business plan competition and won the first prize. That gave Raghu the confidence to enter the Philips 'Simplicity' challenge.

He flew to Mumbai for the finals, where 19 others pitched their 'million dollar' ideas. There Raghu happened to chat up one of the judges - Alok Kejriwal, founder of Contests2win.

He asked Alok, "How did you get the idea of starting this company?"

Alok replied, "I was sitting on the sofa... when it came to me!"

Raghu realised that an idea was a powerful thing - it could be converted into a cash cow.

The moment he was back on campus, there was an interview with Schlumberger - one of the most coveted companies on campus. Raghu had already cleared the first round, so his chances were bright.

The interviewer asked, "If we don't take you in Schlumberger what will you do?"

Still on a high from the Philips challenge, Raghu replied, "I will start my own business."

"Then why do you want to work with us?" he persisted.

"So I can earn enough money to start my venture," replied Raghu.

That wasn't the best thing to say in a job interview... Schlumberger *haath se gaya*. Now what?

Raghu finally managed to get recruited by Samsung but meanwhile he decided to apply for an MS - both in his core branch and in finance which he had always found interesting. And studied as an elective at IIT.

"Each application costs about Rs 7-10,000 but I took the risk and I got through for MS in Finance at London School of Economics as well as Georgia Tech (Masters in Financial Engineering). I thought *ki ab to future set hai...*!"

In the fag end of his fourth year, Raghu got hepatitis and went home to recuperate. On the way down from Shimla to catch a flight to Guwahati, he noticed the back of a truck. It had something interesting written in Punjabi.

"That would make a good jingle," he thought.

And then it struck him.

"Why can't ad agencies use cars and trucks as a *medium* for advertising?"

Back on campus, Raghu discussed the idea with friends but most were skeptical. Would car owners agree to put somebody's advertisement on their vehicles? A couple of friends suggested, "Start a community on orkut and find out!."

And Raghu thought, why not!

The 'Brand on Wheels' community on orkut simply asked the question: "Would you like to get paid to put a sticker on your car? If so, register here!"

Raghu had no idea what *kind* of sticker. But he had heard of the term 'permission marketing' and 40 odd people said,"Yes, we give you permission."

Meanwhile Raghu graduated from IIT Guwahati with a job in hand from Samsung. But his heart said 'further studies', and he was all set to join Georgia Tech.

But a couple of casual conversations got him thinking. A cousin's friend, who had studied in the US and was now running a startup said, "*Tu bahar jayega, Master's karega, tujhe yehi lagega... ki India aa kar business shuru karoon.* Why not start off now itself?"

There were a couple of months to kill, so Raghu decided to continue working on his *gaadi par advertising wala* idea. He created a rudimentary website and decided to do some 'publicity'.

"I made up a small press release talking about the plans I had for this venture. Also mentioning of course my IIT background. Then I went personally to different newspaper offices.

One fine morning Raghu got a call from Ravi P Tiwari.

"*Main Hindustan se bol raha hoon,*" said the voice at the other end.

"*Hindustan se to main bhi bol rahan hoon,*" quipped Raghu before he realised this was the Hindi newspaper *Hindustan* published by the *Hindustan Times* group.

Tiwariji printed the news with the special brand of mirch masala Hindi journalists are famous for: "*Business ke dhurandharon ka*

> ## "When I meet brand managers they have all kinds of crazy ideas. If I say, '*Sir yeh nahin ho sakta hai*" they reply,' I am the client, I can demand anything!"

naya idea."

The article then explained how cars would 'earn' money for their owners and for good measure, printed Raghu's cell number.

"I was still asleep when my phone began ringing. People wanted to know what is this scheme, how they could earn money. And some small advertisers - jewellery shops, real estate agents etc asked about placing ads."

Within 3 days the Brand on Wheels website got 1500 registrations from car owners and 22 companies seeking advertising space. Tiwariji promptly printed this news as well.

Meanwhile a reporter from the *Economic Times* in Chandigarh got in touch with Raghu. She introduced him to a 'venture capitalist' from South Africa.

"This is great, I thought. He will fund me or better still buy out the idea and I will go and study further!"

After one meeting with the VC Raghu realised it would not work like that.

"*Woh banda Bunty-Babli bana raha tha* - all talk, no substance. And then I realised *karna hai to khud hi karna hai*. Because no one will be as passionate about it as I am."

Finally, Raghu took the call to stay back in India and get into business.

"Whatever happens, happens for the best," said his mother. "*Jai mata di kar ke khol do!*"

On 23rd August 2008, Raghu officially launched 'Brand on Wheels' as a private limited company. At this point he asked the four friends who'd been 'helping out' if they would like to join as partners.

"I told them it involves some amount of risk. But they were all comfortable in their campus jobs and said 'no thanks'!"

Raghu put in Rs 20,000 of his own and built a new, professional looking website.

A couple of weeks later someone asked him. "Are you the same as 'Brand on Wheels' from South Africa?"

Raghu decided there could be a copyright issue and changed the name of his venture to Cashurdrive. Even as he built an inventory of car owners interested in the concept, Raghu got his first client: Bonn Bakery, based in Ludhiana.

"A lot of small shops and businesses had approached me but I wanted to work only with good brand names. However at that point I had no idea how the advertising system worked, so I thought let me go step by step."

At Bonn Bakery, the owner was the sole decision maker. And since hoardings had been banned in Shimla, he was willing to give this new medium a chance.

Order to mil gaya - now to actually find a way to execute it. When Raghu went to purchase vinyl, he found prices ranged from Rs 6 to Rs 200! Then there was the question of car sizes. And most importantly, who would actually do the sticking?

"I got in touch with the boys who put sun control film on cars. But they had never done anything like this."

And their charges were exorbitant. So Raghu observed how they went about the job and tried to do it himself. It was a terrific flop.

"I had no idea how intricate the operation is. There were so many wrinkles and bubbles in the application, it looked awful!"

And somewhere in all this, he forgot to take into account the door handle. That's exactly where the client's logo was situated and it had to be cut!

Things were looking a bit bleak for the new venture, when Raghu's cousin had a brainwave. There was a gentleman in Shimla whom all the young boys took their cars to, for fancy stickers. Maybe he could be of help?

Subhash Sharma - or Panditji - as he was better known was absolutely the right person for the job. He had 30 years of experience, and was precise, and dedicated to his craft.

"Using the proper instruments he showed us one sample application and we were relieved to know that yes, it is possible!"

Working day and night, the Bonn Bakery order was completed and the cars put on the road.

Raghu still remembers the exact figure on that first cheque: Rs 1,23,000.

Operating from home in Shimla, with a cellphone, laptop and a cousin coaxed into becoming an intern, Raghu sent out another set of press releases. Coverage in *Business Standard* brought Cashurdrive to the attention of numerous brand managers.

In October 2008, Raghu bagged the first of the big brand names he had been so keen on.

Reliance Mutual Fund booked 75 cars for a duration of one month. Close on its heels, Tata Indicom booked 125 cars over 3 months. Both campaigns were in tier 2 towns of North India - Chandigarh, Shimla, Patiala and Ludhiana

Registrations from car owners poured in. Cashurdrive was paying out an average of Rs 2000-3000 per month per car, making it an attractive proposition... But not enough advertisers were signing up.

In December 2008, Raghu realised he would have to shift to Delhi if he had to grow the business. With the help of one boy who had some experience in ad sales, Raghu went about evangelising his idea.

"I had to generate leads, meet new clients, get their campaigns. The most difficult thing actually was getting appointments!"

Raghu learnt that the two most important people he had to win over were the guard, and the receptionist. He also learnt the art of sending 'proposals' and of coming up with innovations which would hook brand managers.

"I realised that unless I provide value addition, no one would be interested."

For Adidas, Raghu suggested an 'L shaped creative', made to look like a guy playing football with the tyre.

Meanwhile, Meru cabs approached Raghu - could he sell ads on their cabs? He also got a call from Autographics Digital in Bangalore, a company in the application business.

"Autographics introduced me to many more brands. Their interest was in wrapping more cars!"

By January 2009 Cashurdrive had registered 12,000 car owners, and venture capitalists began showing interest.

"They would come, drink coffee and go away. I felt they were wasting my time! Should I put my energy in making business plans or simply get more business?"

Raghu decided it was more prudent to focus on his operations at that stage. If revenues were coming in, investors could always be brought in at a later stage.

"I wanted to be in a stronger position - *abhi to jo wo keh rahe hain karna padega...*"

Another big break for Raghu was meeting Mr Vimal Ambani* along with Guido Alvino, President of Mactac. This company produces the vinyl sheets used on Coke and Pepsi truckbacks. Cashurdrive became a local partner, responsible for wrapping the vehicles.

More than mere business, Mr Ambani became a source of inspiration for Raghu. And a mentor of sorts.

By April 2009, Cashurdrive had notched up revenues of Rs 21 lakhs. And it was no longer a one man army - there were six employees, including two applicators and two part-timers in Bangalore and Chennai.

The trouble was, business suddenly dried up... but there were salaries to pay. Raghu remembers this as the worst crisis he's had to face - so far.

"I literally used to google names of brand managers and make cold calls at their offices. I remember I made the pitch for Adidas while the marketing manager was on a cigarette break outside the building!"

Cashurdrive got that campaign, as well as a mandate from Lays chips, Pepsi, Pizza Hut and DoCoMo, among others.

"People advised me not to be stuck on big brands as they take time to give a decision. But they give good rates and pay on time, whereas local companies and start ups would ask for barter."

Perseverance paid off, in the longer run. By December 2009, Cashurdrive had completed campaigns for 21 brands and revenues stood at Rs 86 lakhs. Raghu expects to close March 2010 with revenues of Rs 1 crore.

"The profit margin varies because we pay a dynamic sum to car owners. Application and printing cost also fluctuates but yes, we do make 20-30% on average."

The lure of 'easy money' spawned many copycats such as 'Cash ur ride' and 'Cash ur wheels'. But the secret sauce lies not in the idea but in the execution. In that one driven individual called Raghu Khanna.

"I will come down to Mumbai for a single meeting, and I will

---

* *Vimal Ambani is the nephew of Dhirubhai Ambani; the brand Vimal was named after him.*

convince the brand manager - I will give options which excite him."

Raghu is now looking to 'scale' up. To move from 30, 40, 50 car campaigns to a 1000 car contract at all-India level. And to execute campaigns in rural India.

"People ask me, 'What is the scalability of your business?' My answer is there is no definition of scale. It depends on your capabilities, on your selling skills."

And that's something Raghu has always had in plenty.

"I never bought a train ticket but always managed to get a berth!" he grins.

Success is as much about *choosing* the right business, as doing business right. Of aligning your passion with your unique talents.

Raghu is young, and has tasted success early. What if he simply gets bored of doing this?

"I am sure there will be bigger and better opportunities," he says, with a twinkle in his eye.

To be Raghu is to be fully alive - bee in the bonnet, spring in your step.

———————————————

ADVICE TO YOUNG ENTREPRENEURS

Today entrepreneurs run after funding at a nascent stage. If you have any small idea you go to google and start searching for VCs who can give you half a million dollars. *Ek do saal lag kar kaam karo,* you will earn that much, I say!

Internet ki duniya mein sabse bada fayda hai free of cost facility. Anyone can use it to get in touch with anyone else. But you need to have a knack -getting people to notice you takes *dimaag.*

People say it's better to have work experience but that's not really true.

When your idea is new, no one knows any more than you about how to make it happen. You simply have to figure it out along the way. So the earlier you start, the better!

JUNOON

Some entrepreneurs are driven by a particular idea, or passion. Something which is different, ahead of its time. These ventures are about making that dream, a living reality.

KITABI
KEEDA

R Sriram,
Crossword

Sriram did not have the burning ambition to start a business - he simply wanted to immerse himself in the world of books. Yet, this college dropout went on to build India's largest bookstore chain, and spread the 'reading' virus far and wide.

R Sriram is most unlike any other 'Sriram' I have met.

He is a college dropout, an atheist, and does not believe in the traditional institution of marriage.

'Log kya kahenge' never bothered him, as he charted his own alternate path.

No, he did not know exactly what he wanted. But he kept looking and asking questions.

Searching for purpose, for something that ignited his passion.

That something was his love for books.

Out of this passion was born an enterprise. This enterprise brought people back to bookstores; it made reading cool for a new generation of kids.

Sriram became an entrepreneur to make this dream come true. To make a difference, to add meaning to many lives. To put books like this into your hands...

As he shares his long and exciting journey, I whisper a silent 'thank you'.

KITABI KEEDA

R Sriram,
Crossword

R Sriram was born in Madras, in a traditional Palakkad Brahmin family.

"I am the eldest of four children. My mother died when I was 3 years old, my sister was about a year younger than me. My father then remarried."

Sriram was a happy child, although somewhat introspective. He discovered books quite early, thanks to the 'library' class in his school. He then began reading anything and everything he could lay his hands on – mostly secondhand books.

At the same time Sriram was very active outdoors.

"I still have early memories of my friends coming home, waking me up. We would play for a couple of hours and then go to school!"

He went on to represent his school and college in track and field.

Sriram's father worked with BHEL - Bharat Heavy Electricals Ltd – and did very well for himself. But he could not progress beyond General Manager because he was not an engineer. He was keen to see Sriram become one.

Sriram was not particularly studious but managed to be in the top 5 ranks throughout his school life. But as he neared class 12, he started asking himself, "Do I really want to do engineering?"

"I think one of the things reading does is it gets you to start looking at yourself, reflecting and helping to face who you are, what you want to do, what you are passionate about."

In fact existential questions had been bothering him even as a child. Sriram was in class 7 when he first wondered, "Who am I? Why am I here? What is my *purpose* in life?"

"I grew up in a very religious environment but was always the skeptic, always asking questions.

I had to experience things for myself for them to be real, for them to be something that...I could decide whether to accept or not."

And Sriram could not accept that the world of careers began and ended with medicine or engineering. He wrote the IIT entrance exam for his father's sake but his heart was not in it – he did not get through.

Sriram joined Loyola College for a BSc in Mathematics but at the end of his 1st year also joined the diploma program in visual communications. It was an evening course which exposed him to creative writing, copywriting, photography and art.

At the end of it he was offered an apprenticeship as a trainee copywriter with Ogilvy, Bensen and Mather. A position which paid no money but offered a wealth of experience.

"In the third year my attendance really fell off as I was working. So I dropped out of college in the last semester - I never completed my BSc."

The idea of earning a 'degree' simply lost its importance. Of course, this was not taken kindly by his parents.

"My father tried to get me to write the bank exam, enroll for ICWAI classes. He said, "If you don't like this, then find something else!" Of course, he cared about my welfare, I understood. But I didn't appreciate the choices that were available to me."

Sriram dabbled at various things, but that 'something' remained elusive. He tried his hand at journalism, and then at market research. Although he did not make a career out of it, the market research stint was a valuable learning experience.

"I was never the most talkative person in a group, the kind who would start a conversation, or speak to strangers. Working with IMRB forced me to learn how to approach people and hold their attention."

It was small things – like ringing the doorbell in a pleasant manner, what distance you should stand at, what tone of voice to use.

"I must say that laid a very strong foundation. I learnt how to listen to people, and later I used that in dealing with customers!"

> ## "I have to be passionate and involved and engaged with what I am doing. If I am not, I cannot put energy and effort and discipline into doing it."

The IMRB job did not pay much - but it was enough at the time for *chhota mota* personal expenses. This went on for a couple of years and then in 1987, Sriram joined Apollo hospital, in the back office.

"I had a circle of friends who were anxious for me – one of them got me this job. I did not enjoy it and quit in less than six months."

Sriram then joined a sister concern of Apollo, a software firm. Here, he worked as a technical writer but within two months he knew this was not what he wanted to do with his life.

"For me when you get up in the morning if you don't feel inspired to go to work, then there is something wrong."

In January 1988 came a turning point. Sriram heard about a bookshop called 'Landmark' which had just opened in Madras. *This* was the kind of place he had always dreamt of working at.

Sriram simply went up to the manager and said, "I would like to work here."

There was a ten minute conversation about books and literature and the manager said, "You're hired! Can you start tomorrow?"

There was no formal training or orientation, Sriram was simply given a section of the store to manage. This meant attending to customers, helping them find what they wanted and also providing inputs to the buying team on what books the store should order.

But on the very first day Sriram realised it was hard to find a particular book. He would first have to put the shelves into order.

"I had spent a lot of time in libraries like British Council so based on that I put my own simple system in place. Because I did that myself I could easily locate a book for the customer. And of course because I loved books, I could recommend titles as well."

Within a month customers would come specifically to talk to Sriram. And he would actually open books, quote passages and even read out poetry. Sriram's section of the store started doing extremely well.

Meanwhile, Sriram was constantly bugging Hemu – the owner – about titles missing from the store, titles they should be keeping. One day Hemu said, "OK, enough of complaints, now *you* start buying!"

The back end of the book business was a revelation. In a dusty old distributor warehouse Sriram spotted a bunch of great books collecting dust.

Hemu asked, "Will they sell?"

He confidently replied, "Yes!"

The books did sell and Sriram soon discovered another goldmine – catalogues. Now he could directly place orders with publishers. Taking into account the tastes of customers – whom he met on the shopfloor – Sriram was able to source relevant and interesting titles.

At the end of six months, his salary was doubled to Rs 1500. While handing him the cheque his manager cautioned, "Don't let it go to your head."

He need not have worried. The rolling stone was finally gathering moss – and loving every moment of it.

"Making a difference to a customer's life gave me a charge. The more you do, the better you do it, the more the pleasure!"

One of Sriram's loyal customers was Markos Vellapalli, a lawyer from Kottayam. He was looking for something to gift to his young daughter. Sriram recommended a book to him titled '*Mr. God, this is Anna*'.

A few months later he stopped by and sought Sriram out. He shook his hand and said, "I want to thank you, Uttara loved the book!"

Many customers thus became more like friends. People of different age, background and experience but bound by a common passion for books.

Around a year into the job, one such customer called Ram Prasad invited Sriram home. His father was a well known Telugu film producer and he was moving to Hyderabad, to help him set up a studio.

"I am a dreamer. I do a lot of things which people consider illogical but for me there is a very clear logic to what I do and why I do. I live by my convictions."

> ## "It is not like when you are pursuing something you love, it is a bed of roses - it is hard, hard work."

He said, "You know Sriram, the one thing I am going to miss is Landmark. Will you come with me to Hyderabad and help me to set up a book store?"

Sriram was flabbergasted.

"One part of me was very excited and the other part was very scared. I wondered how on earth will I be able to do it!"

After careful thought Sriram realised he had some knowledge, but not enough. He would need a couple of other people who knew parts of the business he did not. People with complementary strengths, complementary skills, but shared values.

One such person was Anita – a literature graduate from Ethiraj college who had joined a few months after Sriram and handled the children's section. The other was Sudarshan Reddy, who handled vendors and accounting.

Both of them agreed - and thus began a new adventure.

The three musketeers left Landmark in November 1989 for Hyderabad. None of them had a clue about writing a business plan, estimating cashflows or working capital.

"We did not ask for a stake in the company - we simply had no experience! But we were appointed as 'General Managers' and given an opportunity to build something. For us, that was remarkable and tremendous!"

The pay was better, of course but more importantly, Sriram learnt his fundamental lessons in retail.

Starting with how to identify a site for the store.

At that time the average shop size in Hyderabad was 500 sq ft in size; 1000 sq ft was a luxury. And a startup could not afford rentals in existing upmarket locations.

"We scouted all over Hyderabad and Secunderabad, and I realised how important it is to learn by walking around. You get tremendous insight by just being on the street, talking to people."

Sriram finally zeroed in on Sardar Patel Road, close to the Panjagutta area which was developing rapidly at the time. Walden became the first retailer on what would later become a popular high street – but back then it was a huge risk.

Another risk was naming the store 'Walden' – inspired by Henry David Thoreau*. But in the end it did not matter, because the store itself was so unique, so different.

"Walden was the first bookstore to stock a wide range of non-book items such as stationery, music, movies and toys. We wanted to make it a friendly place, an inviting place and not only for hardcore book lovers."

Years later, a book called *'Blue Ocean Strategy'* would advocate the same.

"I realise now that there are terms for all this. At that point it was just instinctive that we should focus on non-customers, or underserved customers. Even to the loyalists, we offered a dramatically different experience."

Walden opened in July 1990 and quickly became the dominant bookstore in Hyderabad.

"We were young and full of ideas. We worked non stop, seven days a week, with tremendous energy."

An energy which was contagious. Building on the Landmark experience, Sriram and Anita struck a personal rapport with customers. Entrepreneurs, intellectuals, politicians and bureaucrats frequented the store.

"I learnt a lot through conversations with people – although I did not realise it then!"

Another little trick Sriram learnt was how to distil wisdom from the crowds. It was impossible for him to read every book in the store but by talking to a dozen people you could get a good sense of whether a title was worth recommending.

"I had a CRM system in my head which kept track of which customers bought what books. The next time they came in I would ask, "Did you enjoy it"?"

Happy customers makes a happy retailer, but equally important is support from vendors. Sriram's credibility with distributors stood Walden in good stead. They knew that this man knows what he is buying, and he knows how to sell it.

Walden thus enjoyed 90 days of credit which is rarely available to newcomers. This helped to defray a significant part of the working capital expenses.

"We call the 'head office' the Support Office because we believe that our purpose is to support the business of the stores."

A year after Walden was established, Sriram started thinking – what next? "That is when I started dreaming the dream of establishing a chain of book stores."

Sriram realised that the excitement was in starting up. Once a store was established, it was basically management – and that did not charge him up. The trouble was Walden's owners had no interest in opening more stores; this was something Sriram would need to figure out on his own.

But setting up another Walden would cost Rs 18-20 lakhs. Where would that money come from?

The State Bank of India training centre was across the road from Walden; many senior managers were loyal customers. Sriram talked to them about raising a loan.

They said, "You will need to provide collateral."

"My father had this property which took him 25 years to save up for. There was no way I would go and ask him for it!"

Sriram realised another important truth at that point - asking the right question is more important than having the right answer.

"Instead of asking, 'Which bank will fund us', I should ask, 'Who stands to gain the most by funding us'?"

"The minute he asked that question, the answer was obvious. Somebody in the publishing business – either a publisher or a distributor - stood to gain the most by having a captive chain of book stores.

In those days, publishers and distributors were seeing single digit growth. And they were completely dependent on small shops with limited shelf space for sales.

Sriram made out a list of prospects; right on top was India Book House. The local manager was a friend and wellwisher who mentioned that the owner – Mr Mirchandani – was coming to Hyderabad in a month's time.

Over a few evenings Sriram learnt everything he could about the man.

"I got a very important insight, which was that Mr.Mirchandani had an attention span of 3 minutes. I had to get his attention in the first 2 minutes."

Mirchandani visited Walden and was impressed. Sriram made his elevator pitch in a crisp two minutes.

He said, "I have a proposal for you to open a chain of bookstores like this one. That's the only way you can generate sales and grow 20% or 25% annually."

Mirchandani was intrigued. He invited Sriram to meet him in Mumbai and share the details. Sriram consulted Anita and she was all for taking the gamble.

Sriram bought his first ever air ticket - to Bombay - with his new credit card. He managed to convince Deepak Mirchandani about the viability of the project with a small but impassioned presentation, and a two page business plan.

He said, "Ok, but there is one condition. We have this property - if you can use that, we will do it."

The property was on the first floor of a building near Mahalaxmi temple. Great for an office, but not a retail store! Sriram decided it was worth taking a chance...

"We'll do it!" he said.

The Mirchandanis were clear about two things: the biggest investment in a retail business are space and inventory.

"The patriarch Mr G.L Mirchandani - shrewd businessman that he was - said *property to hai hamara* and second investment is stock. Our warehouse is filled with books! So what do we have to lose? Let us say yes to this young couple."

Sriram was 28 years old, Anita was just 25. Remarkably young for the kind of responsibility given. Moreover in a trade where almost everyone at that time was in their 50s or 60s!

"So here we are two soft spoken South Indians, young no doubt, but with a lot of passion and we also said we don't want a salary, we want to be partners in the company."

Although they did not own equity, they had a share in the revenues/profits. And operationally, Sriram and Anita would call the shots.

"You see, we came up with the idea of Crossword and convinced them to invest in it. That set the tone of our engagement. We always felt like 'owners', not employees."

And when you have ownership of a project you don't ask for permissions or approval. You simply go ahead and do what you think is right.

The Mirchandanis got their first shock when Sriram said he would not only be selecting stocks from IBH godowns, but sourcing from rival distributors. He knew the store had to put the customer first, and offer the widest and most relevant titles – no matter what the source.

It was a convincing argument.

"The Mirchandanis understood the wholesale business; on the retail side they decided to trust our judgement."

While working at Walden, Sriram and Anita often discussed what they would do differently, given another chance. How could things be better?

"We were driven by the need to create a world class experience. At that time we had never travelled outside India, never seen what world class stores were. Our notion of world class came from the best books that we had read and loved."

And it was not just about selling books, but creating an experience. A warm, welcoming space which would attract not only *kitabi keedas* but anyone with a curious mind. Children, families, people looking to 'hang out' somewhere interesting.

It started with the naming of the store itself. 'Crossword' – simple, memorable, understood by a five year old. Then, came the layout of the store. It had to be big, really big. Because the range of books was going to be much wider than anything available at that time.

And customers would be encouraged to browse the shelves, even sit around and read books for free if they wished... All for a good reason!

At that time all bookstores sold books at a minimum discount of 10%. At Crossword, books would be sold at full price.

"Once we said we are not going to discount we had to create a compelling value proposition. So that the people say the discount doesn't matter, I love coming here, it adds so much to my life!"

That 'X' factor is what Sriram and Anita had to create – and luckily they had 6000 sq ft of space to work with. What could they do now, to draw people up that narrow staircase? The first step was hiring an architect.

"In those days people did not engage professionals to design retail spaces but we knew design was extremely important. We spent a lot of our time and energy looking at every small detail."

> **"Energy is a hallmark of anybody who wants to create anything. And you not only need to recharge yourself, you need to energise others!"**

Details like the height of the shelves. From an economic point of view, it made sense to put taller fixtures. Instead, Crossword decided no fixture would be more than five feet high.

"Why five feet? Because we observed an average woman is about five foot one. And we wanted to keep the fixtures such that anyone standing at one end of the store can see through till the other end."

Then, the books had to be classified properly; such that customers would be able discover the right book. Large departments like business management were broken down by subject. Books were alphabetically ordered, with 'shelf talkers' making it easy for customers to help themselves.

Small wooden stools and classic black library chairs, encouraged customers to sit down and enjoy books at a leisurely pace.

"And obviously if you are faced with a wide variety of books you need half an hour to an hour to browse through them, find what you want. In which case a toilet became a necessity!"

All this detailing did not come cheap - it cost Rs 50 lakhs in all, including the stocks. About Rs 800 per square foot, and completed in a record two and a half months.

The first ever Crossword bookstore opened on 15th of October 1992. Skeptics said *do teen mahine mein band ho jayega*. In fact, the store surpassed all expectation, within the first six months.

"Of course, word of mouth was very strong but we also promoted the store in new and interesting ways. Without any kind of 'advertising budget' as such!"

Thus began the tradition of free 'readings' on weekends, for children. Something Anita used to do informally at Landmark – for her customers. At Crossword, it became part of the culture, a way to say "I'm different" and stand out.

"Then, we realised that we had a very valuable resource which was the author himself or herself. We decided to actually bring authors into the store, to launch books and do readings. That brought us a lot of media coverage."

Another innovation was staying open on Sunday, when all other shops on Warden Road kept their shutter down. Within six months Sunday became the day of the week registering the highest sales. The store became a destination for families to spend quality time together.

Keeping this in mind, a good 20% of space was devoted to children's books. And 30% of the stock was beyond books – items like CDs, CD ROMs, gift articles and greeting cards.

"We actually had lower gross margins* on toys and stationary compared to books. But by keeping this assortment we were able to cater to the needs of the entire family."

Innovation is not a one time activity, it's work-in-process. And you need not have one big 'aha' moment. Just small insights, from talking to and observing customers.

For example, many customers carried a pile of books around, as they browsed through the store.

Why not design a basket for their convenience?

Crossword also became the first Indian bookstore to have its very own 'bestseller' list. People loved the idea and that led to the concept of a rack titled 'Sriram recommends'. Titles which the book-loving CEO personally vouched for.

In fact, the team had so much faith in its customers that it changed the standard line in all cash memos to read: "Goods and services once sold will be exchanged."

Less than one percent came back. Of that 90% of were genuine exchanges, received as gifts.

Then there was the the way books were displayed. Sriram and Anita improvised all kinds of interesting arrangements – much later they discovered it was called 'visual merchandising'.

But why take so much trouble?

"For a book to be a classic it needs to be the best and writers – great writers - strive to do their best. They never attempt to do just an average job. I think we were inspired by that, to keep improving, to keep striving."

And it was not just at the front end.

In 1992, all stores used manual cash memos. Sriram and Anita were convinced they had to use point of sale terminals. They commissioned a small firm to write a sales and inventory management software.

* Margins on toys is generally 18-20%; books is 20-40%

"What's the point?" grumbled the crusty senior Mirchandani.

"GL, come back tomorrow and I'll tell you why," said Anita.

The next morning Anita produced five different sales reports - sorted category wise, volume wise, value wise. The old man immediately saw the value...

"Knowing what was selling each day was our secret weapon. We were able to order things that were in demand!"

In less than two years Crossword was well established in Bombay and nicely profitable. Sriram and Anita convinced the Mirchandanis to open a second store in Delhi.

Finding 5000-6000 square feet turned out to be quite a task. Finally, they got the department store Ebony in South Extension, to give out its second floor. The store did extremely well but the book trade was going through a difficult period. IBH did not wish to expand any further.

Banks were still not lending to retail – but Sriram and Anita were convinced there was a need for a bookshop with a national presence.

"You might say it is a completely foolish idea but surprisingly, a lot of successful business has been set up in times of challenge, or even recession."

They began exploring the option of franchising. But was Crossword a business which suited that model? Was there a proprietary formula they had which made for a successful bookshop?

Even as they were pondering these issues, a young couple walked into the Bombay store. Gaurav Shah and his wife Supriya were passionate about books. Gaurav was an MS from the US and supplied airconditioners to Carrier. But the Shahs also dreamt of opening a small bookshop in their native city – Ahmedabad.

"Their aunt who lived on Napean Sea Road told them to check out Crossword. They loved it and wanted to meet the people behind the store."

One thing led to another and in October 1995, Gaurav and Supriya Shah took up the first Crossword franchise and opened the store at Mithakali in Ahmedabad.

Finding a large enough space was once again an issue. Explore unconventional options, suggested Sriram and ultimately the Shahs zeroed in on a basement. So far so good. But would the 'read any book as long as you like' ethos of Crossword work in Ahmedabad?

The Shahs were skeptical.

They duplicated the Crossword decor, the tables, chairs and arrangements beautifully. But they added a small black card which said: Please do not browse for more than 15 minutes.

But soon enough the cards disappeared. Within six months, Crossword Ahmedabad became a throbbing store with far more stools and chairs than prescribed under the franchise agreement.

"Gaurav would smile and proudly point out, "See all the children sitting there and reading!"

It was a leap of faith by the Shahs which paid handsome dividends.

Crossword quickly opened franchise stores in Pune and Baroda. Each store paid a royalty to the parent company and in turn, got everything from infrastructure and software support to the crucial sourcing of the right books.

By 1998, Crossword had seven stores and a turnover of Rs 16 crores, but it was not enough...

"I started feeling the need to open many more stores. And by then we had realized one important truth - going from Bombay to Delhi and then to Ahmedabad was not the wisest thing to do. We did not make a big enough impact in any one city, or really experience benefits of scale."

Sriram also realised the company needed to invest in better technology, and manpower. But how was he to go about it?

"I didn't know all of these things so again I read up, and I spoke to some customers – which is a favorite technique of mine. They were merchant bankers and advised me to go out and raise capital."

Sriram convinced IBH to divest a stake in the company and I got this mandate in writing from them. He then appointed merchant bankers SSKI to scout around for investors. There was a great deal of interest, with over 20 serious investors. After considering all offers, Sriram was inclined towards Shoppers Stop and ICICI Venture.

"We did have a couple of people willing to pay more but we felt it was important to partner with someone who had a commitment to retail and strength in real estate. Also we had a rapport of sorts with B S Nagesh, CEO of Shoppers Stop."

The deal was concluded in March 2000 as a 'slump sale'. This meant the entire cash balance of the company – including a crore in profits – went to IBH. 100% of the equity, the running concern and the brand name went to the buyer.

Sriram and Anita got a small equity stake.

IBH was pleased – they made 15 times their original investment. Besides, Crossword renewed the lease of the Bombay store for 5 years and continued buying stocks.

But things did not work out as well for the store itself. Shoppers Stop went through a bad patch. What's more the team at ICICI Venture which backed the deal left the company. The new team kept the transaction hanging for close to a year.

The money ICICI was to pay for Crossword was delayed. So Shoppers Stop 'lent' ICICI this money – and levied interest on Crossword!

"But meanwhile, our expenses had gone up. as we had expanded the corporate team - to grow the chain. We had to work really hard, stretching our working capital to the limit. In fact, we pretty much had to change our strategy."

Shoppers Stop offered space within its stores, which led to the 'shop in shop' concept. This was later extended to petrol pumps and multiplexes. Bestsellers were given more importance, because they freed up cashflows.

Sriram doesn't look happy as he shares this.

"I am not very happy about it... I had no choice. Yes, we managed to expand nationally, despite all the issues and problems but..."

The excitement was gone. Anita was the first to quit, in 2004. Sriram followed suit in 2006.

"It was very hard for me to do that. I took several years to think through and deal with it. But finally I knew that all my life I have done things out of passion. And if I was not enjoying this anymore, it was time to move on."

There were many lucrative offers to set up another bookstore chain but Sriram and Anita will have none of it.

"Crossword was not a job or career. It was an opportunity to build something interesting... to follow a passion, to realise a dream."

"Some of the best hires at Crossword were people who simply walked in and said, " I love what you are doing, can I work here?"

Sriram continues to be associated with the annual Crossword Book Awards but no longer holds executive powers or a position on the board. Yet I feel the spirit lives on...

"The purpose with which we live and build something is finally vital - that is the differentiator. And our purpose was to create a culture of reading - not just make money from books!"

Which is why some of the best hires at Crossword were those who simply walked in and said, " I love what you are doing, can I work here?"

And such were the people who took the *keeda* forward, even as Sriram wondered, what next?

"I realised I was passionate about several things. I wanted to help build businesses rather than running a business. And I was very keen to make a difference to the community."

Sriram now divides his time between consulting assignments and non-profit activities. He is co-founder of the firm 'Next Practice Retail', as well as on the advisory board of SNEHA and Pratham Books*.

In addition, he is President-elect of The Indus Entrepreneurs (TIE), Mumbai chapter and shares *gyaan* on life, the universe and starting up a business, at various B-schools.

And now, there is Kavya, who is almost five, and has opened up a whole new world for Anita and Sriram.

"We have adopted Kavya. That was by choice, because both of us from a young age wanted to adopt a child. We also have a niece – Radhika - who is 14 and stays with us."

In fact, Sriram and Anita lived with each other for many years, before they married six years ago.

"We don't believe in the institution of marriage, we don't think it is necessary. But then when you want to have a child... it is easier to do it as a married couple."

It's not about rebellion, but conviction.

"I do what I believe in and I think as long as your beliefs don't harm anyone else, you should live life the way you want to!"

Claim the keys to your kingdom and rule over your dreams.

---

* Pratham Books publishes low cost, high quality books for kids; SNEHA is the Society for Nutrition, Education & Health Action.

ADVICE TO YOUNG ENTREPRENEURS

I have lots of advice but I am not sure they should listen to me necessarily. I think you have to listen to yourself. You should hear what others have to say but finally find what is right for you and do what works for you.

The chairman of Starbucks once said, "To succeed you need to *care* more than others think wise. You need to *risk* more than the others think safe. You need to *dream* more than others think practical and you need to *expect* more than others think possible."

You need to care deeply about whatever you do and very often people might come and say you care too much but I think that is a common factor amongst people who have done anything in life.

You need to risk more than others think safe, you need to dream certainly even though often people will say, "Get real!"

Finally I would also like to echo the words of Dr Venkataswamy of Aravind Eye hospital. He says, "Intelligence and capability are not enough, there must be a joy of doing something beautiful."

I hope that people have the joy of doing something beautiful because then your life becomes truly blessed. I mean from the *inside*. So that is really what I am trying to discover.

At the end of the day I know that through my work, I have touched a lot of lives. Finally it's not about money or fame, it is the extent to which you are able to make a *difference* which makes the journey worth its while.

To use the words of Viktor Frankl, 'Man's search for meaning is really what provides purpose in life'. Create that meaning and everything else will follow.

VOTE FOR CHANGE

**Saurabh Vyas and Gaurav Rathore,
PoliticalEDGE**

Hostel ki *dosti* and a common love for politics gave birth
to this uncommon company. These two idealistic young
men are putting their grey cells to use, providing
research and consulting services exclusively for
politicians.

If two mint-fresh IIT graduates had to start a new business, you'd expect them to choose IT, BPO, consulting, green technology. Certainly, an idea executed neatly from the comfort of an a/c office.

You have to be *mad* to get into something which takes you to dusty, electricity-less villages in Uttar Pradesh.

Mad about politics.

Saurabh Vyas and Gaurav Rathore chose the truly rough road into the 'real India' when they decided to chuck their campus jobs and get into political research. That's right research for politicians.

In the semi-darkness of an open air coffee shop in shining Gurgaon, I see two very young guys. One growing a beard, I think, to create the impression of extra years. Not a bad idea, considering the client profile.

As one Gandhi *topied* prospect pointed out,"I have been in politics before you were born."

Yaane ki tum humko kya sikhaoge bachchon! Well, apparently a lot, going by the 250 + politicians they've done work for so far.

Gaurav and Saurabh's story just goes to show that age is no bar, experience is no bar - you learn what you need to. And then have fun, improvising.

Which is why you don't feel the bumps, as you turn the bend into that village with no roads.

The road *you* are paving.

VOTE FOR
CHANGE

Saurabh Vyas and Gaurav Rathore,
PoliticalEDGE

Saurabh Vyas is a small town boy.

"I am from Udaipur, although most of my schooling was in Jaipur. I'm a St Xavier's Jaipur passout, my father is a banker - he is a GM in Rajasthan State Co-operative Bank."

Gaurav Rathore is also a small town boy.

"I am from Kanpur, although I have lived all over UP as my father is an electrical engineer - he works with the state electricity board."

Like most small town boys with some aptitude for studies, Saurabh aspired to get into IIT.

"In Jaipur - in 1998 - there were only two options, either you become an engineer or a doctor. When you entered 11th, you had to decide where you want to go. I was strong at maths so I went in for engineering and if you are targeting engineering then IIT is the best place to go...."

Saurabh enrolled in Career Point - at Kota - and secured a rank of 1576.

Like every other IIT aspirant he wanted Computer Science, but ended up in Aerospace Engineering - a five year dual degree course.

"I think at the end of it branches at IIT don't matter at all. It is just about the 5 years I lived there - the experience, the knowledge. Not just from textbooks, but from everything and everyone around me."

Gaurav was one of them.

"We met on the first day, we were both in the same wing of the hostel, Hostel 2..." And in no time at all, *gehri dosti ho gayi.*

"Mine is a little different story because I didn't actually plan to get in to IIT." says Gaurav. "I had not appeared for any of the engineering exams after class 12 - I wanted to go to DU (Delhi University). But I was enrolled in UP board and the results came late."

The day for submitting admission forms passed; the DU dream was dashed. His father then asked, "What are you going to do for this one year"?"

I said, "Okay fine, I'll just write some exams, and I enrolled in a coaching class."

As luck would have it, Gaurav got through and with a pretty good rank of 1437. And once you get through, it's very hard to say "no - I don't want this!" So Gaurav joined IIT Bombay in the metallurgical and material science branch. And again, it was stuff outside the classroom that really impacted him

"I was always okay with academics, my CGPA would prove that... an average guy." Which, at IITB is a seven point something, the kind of student who's more into organising Mood Indigo, dramatics - all extracurriculars. But most of all, seniors interacting with the juniors.

"The year that we entered IIT Bombay - 1999 - was the year of the dotcom boom. We had seniors in our hostel rooms who owned companies worth crores... Everyone was gung-ho about life!"

Over the next two years, highs became lows as virtual empires came crashing down. As did the job market.

"The placement became really bad in 2001. 2002 and 2003 were the lowest points in the cycle and we faced the brunt of it," says Saurabh.

Gaurav wanted a job with HLL or ITC; he settled for Deloitte & Touche.

The office was in Hiranandani, right next to IIT, where Saurabh was completing his final year. So Gaurav practically lived on campus.

"There is a Pizza Hut at Hiranandani, where you know at 2 o'clock some *cyclewalas* come and sell coffee. We used to sit there till the wee hours of the morning discussing cricket, economy, life in general..."

But ultimately, every discussion would end in politics. Because the group was really passionate about politics, and that's where a hazy business idea took shape.

"We knew we can't enter politics or create a political party right. But

> **"We had seniors with successful ventures. Seniors who passed on information about what's going on, what's happening in the industry - those kind of things. That is what is missing at any other college."**

we thought *ki,* we can do something in that field."

Adds Gaurav, "In the '90s all the different fields were very unstructured and they got structured. But nobody thinks of politics - politics everyone says *chalne do chal raha hai.* So why not try to structure the way a political campaign or a party or a candidate works or runs his show?"

The 'opportunity' was identified way back in 2004, but talk did not translate into action.

"At that point, we knew *ki hum karenge is cheez ko,* but not immediately after passing out. It made sense to work for at least one year so we could build up some savings."

And so Saurabh took up a job after graduation, with a startup called Fractal Analytics.

"I always wanted to do statistical modeling - there was no other choice for me. So it was a dream come true."

Fractal Analytics - a financial analytics firm - was started by five IIM Ahmedabad graduates. Saurabh was the company's 48th employee and says it was an amazing experience.

"Fractal also started like a dotcom but later moved into financial analytics. I learnt a lot from the guys at the helm - the way they treated us, the vision they had for the company, the way they handled problems."

Meanwhile Gaurav was fed up of the work at Deloitte and shifted to Schlumberger. The company posted him to Sudan, which is a difficult place, but the upside was Schlumberger is an oil company and pays you a lot of money.

"I just worked for 5 to 6 months there but saved quite a lot of money," laughs Gaurav. Money which was to come in handy, in just a bit...

Now many a time having a job distracts a potential entrepreneur from his goal. Here, all the pieces actually started falling in place.

"Gaurav worked with the CRM practice in Deloitte; that gave us an idea about how to integrate and talk to the customers - the voter. I worked in analytics and learnt how data is collected, statistical modelling and all those things."

Says Gaurav, "It all happened, automatically, it's like you know once it happens it happens. Otherwise you can just keep on thinking about it..."

"We went on a Himachal trip just for fun and we decided, "*Chalo*, let's start!" That's it - it was a snap decision," says Saurabh.

Everyone came back, wrapped up things and *khatam hua naukri ka silsila. Shuru hui* life, as an entrepreneur.

No concerns from the family? Such bright, young boys, settled in good jobs, leaving it to do something vague. Something to do with politics?

But surprisingly, both families were very supportive. Although they did not really get what *bachchelog* were getting into!

"Luckily we were not *joining* politics, but yeah, there might have been some odd comments here and there."

"And we had no financial liability," adds Saurabh. Such as responsibility for parents, sister's marriage, *pitaji ka* operation *vagairah vagairah.*

And so, with one year work ex under their belt, two young men set out to change the world of politics. Not by becoming politicians but by becoming their eyes, ears and CRM support.

A business idea with a difference - but where does one begin?

"When we started, we looked at what was being done in the US and we figured out we can adapt some aspects - mostly on the technical side. But on the ground things are absolutely different here!"

In the US there is a lot of secondary data available. In India, there is no data - you have to go out and collect it. That means you have to build a bigger team, undertake fieldwork, and so on. *Kaafi jhanjhatein hain!*

"And more importantly the politician in India wants something different than a politician in the US. There, it is more of brand building you know - strategising, speechwriting and all that stuff. In India what they want is *gaon mein mera kya chal raha hai.* The basic grassroots stuff."

Didn't the idea of going village to village to collect data overwhelm them? After all, they had no experience doing such work!

"Well, we knew we were getting into a difficult field," says Saurabh. "Politics has to be grassroots and you *have* to go into the field. It's not easy for sure but our passion kept us going at every step."

Work started in May 2005, although the company was registered in June. Apart from Saurabh and Gaurav, there were two other partners.

One of them was Manan Chauhan, a batchmate who was doing his masters in Public Policy from the University of Chicago. The fourth partner was another IIT batchmate.

"We started working from our home in Gurgaon - a 3 BHK with a very large hall. Whatever savings we had, we pitched in. And then we kept pitching, and pitching, pitching for the whole first year!"

In one year that added up to around Rs 15-20 lakhs. Were they really able to save that much with five years of work experience between the lot?

"The time I worked for Schlumberger in Sudan." says Gaurav. "That was really how we could generate some funds."

In an operation like this, funds primarily go towards salaries. A small technical team and a small team collecting data - in the field.

"Totally around 10 to 12 people. There were 3 guys in the technical team and 7 to 8 guys who were the core of the research team. We built the numbers slowly, as we got projects from clients."

But how does one go about getting clients for such a specialised service?

"The whole idea of getting a politician to listen to young guys was difficult. We started by meeting a couple of young leaders initially, making presentations."

One such prospect was Milind Deora, the young, US educated MP from South Bombay.

"So how many phone calls did you have to make, to get that meeting?" I ask

"For Milind? One. Just one."

Really?

"Milind is a good guy and of course we never told him he was one of the first politicians we were pitching to. He still does not know that, actually!"

And what did they say to him?

> "The common man feels that 99% of politicians are frauds and they don't know anything, but we say around 40% are good. They are trying hard to do something, but there are constraints."

"The essence was that we want to bridge the gap between the voter and the politician by collecting information and channelising it into a software. We presented to him a software that actually enabled him to view things at the booth level in his constituency."

Using this software you can analyse your voter through various parameters - be it caste, development, or geography - and compare it with past election performance. Of course, you have to first collect data, analyse it and then the idea is to make a road map for the coming 3 years or so.

"Milind just kept on blasting, "Okay you will do this? Okay fine, what next, what next, what next"!" recalls Saurabh.

The presentation ended in exactly 2 minutes.

"He didn't even look at the laptop," adds Gaurav. "He said, 'Just leave it here and speak'!"

It was an important learning experience in how to 'sell'. And think on one's feet.

Milind did in fact become the firm's client and continues to be one. He gave them a small project, with the hint of more to come, if he was satisfied.

"Milind gave us some data and asked us to analyse it, using our software. Give him some insights into past election performance."

While Milind did act tough, he was interested in the concept *per se*. With seasoned politicians from the cow belt of India, it took a lot more convincing. In fact getting a meeting was a task in itself!

"The only thing we could do was make cold calls, to the number of the MLA or MP, listed in the public telephone directory. We had to convince them *ki ek baar miliye to sahi*!"

Once that meeting happened, most people appreciated the concept. But, they had doubts about the credibility of the team.

"We had to sometimes bluff our way through at times," laughs

Saurabh. But it worked and soon the company had a few more small projects from UP and the border areas of Nepal.

"In UP, we had to start from scratch - develop a questionnaire, do the survey, collect data. Recruit and train a team!" Despite numerous hardships and obstacles.

"I remember a place, a small place in Nighasan, one of the first few projects. It was very important also to put together a good team going and get the project done in a good way. There was no hotel, we had to take a couple of rooms in someone's house. Electricity would come between 6 and 6:30 am…"

Par apne andar ki aag ke sahaare, rasta dikhta raha..

"I'd taken a couple of people from my hometown, to start with. We picked up some locals. I coached them, *kaise kya karna hai…*"

Leading by example. The process was scientific but the approach was common sense.

"We used stratified sampling only but the idea was to collect data on both quantitative and qualitative aspects."

Now a politician knows how he has already fared but what he really wants to know is how will he fare - in the next election. What are the issues, the caste equations, the local political dynamics.

"And believe me, some of them said *ki, yeh humne apne ladkon se pata kara liya hai.* But if their own boys collect data they do not get honest answers. Whereas our data is completely unbiased."

And includes the 'bad stuff' which *chamchas* would hesitate to bring up. Gaurav provides an example to make his point.

"Suppose I am working for a Congress guy - Mr A. Now Mr B is also aspiring for a ticket. If Mr A gets the ticket, Mr B will be a sore loser and can definitely damage him. The party can't do anything about it."

Political Edge will pinpoint the areas where Mr B can cause

"When we started, we had to take our people to the villages and show them how to do a survey. We were not experts so we tried out different things. In fact, we didn't pick up any people who were already researchers."

maximum damage, so that Mr A can prepare himself for all eventualities.

The other important bit of advice Political Edge gives to politicians is what they can do - to make constituents happy. And increase their chances of getting their votes.

"Politicians spend a lot of money and put a lot of effort into managing the constituency, but they never had proper feedback on what to do for people, which would actually give them a 'return'."

Let's say an MLA or MP sanctions 50 handpumps. Great, but does he put any thought on where to locate them?

There are typically 200 polling booths spread over an assembly constituency. What happens is, the people close to the MLA will corner quite a few of these amenities. Even if there is no real *need* for an extra hand pump in the area near his house.

And the "*inke gharke bagal mein laga do*" style of operation damages the reputation of the MLA - without him even realising!

"The voter asks for something - you do it. For ideological reasons or caste loyalty he may not vote for you but at least, he will not be antagonized. He will never be able to badmouth you!" says Saurav.

And the image of a populist but effective leader is thus slowly built.

Which is great but how much are politicians willing to *pay* for this... And did they have to give their services for free to convince the first few clients?

"The pricing strategy evolved over time, but nothing for free. Never."

Although as you can imagine, with politicians presenting a bill is easy. It's the recovery of your money that is a question mark.

"Yes, we've had some bad experiences with clients not paying up - especially when they hear something negative. But we have figured out ways and means of handling those things..."

Which is something I bet they teach only in the *kurukshetra* of life. Not at IIT!

"Write offs have come down drastically," adds Saurabh.

Besides, they are a little choosy now, about who to work with!

The business has grown slowly but steadily. In the first year there were barely 8-10 clients. In 2006-7 the number tripled, with business coming in from elections in UP, Uttaranchal and Punjab. There was no looking back - the total number of clients served till date is now over 225.

"Last year was quite good," smiles Saurabh. "Loads of elections." Including Lok Sabha.

"Yes, but that means less clients, more work. Each Parliament seat covers 5-8 assembly constituencies, depending on the state!"

A typical project for an assembly hopeful involves speaking to around 5000 people. And takes a month and a half.

As a matter of principle Political Edge will take up work for one client in a constituency. As the brand name suggests, the idea is to give a candidate an 'edge', over the competition.

So how large is the market for this super specialized service?

"Take 543 parliamentary seats and then add the total assembly seats. That's around 4000-5000 potential clients."

What's more, there's no effective way to reach them. Except word of mouth. So what kind of turnover* has the company managed to achieve?

They look at each other, then at me.

"Interesting question."

"OK, forget exact figures. Give me a range," I prod them.

Ah, but it's complicated. Like Michael Jackson, the question is 'black' or 'white'?

"You are able to draw a decent salary for yourselves?" I ask.

"Yeah."

"Similar to what you will be earning outside?"

"No, no."

"But we are hanging on," says Saurabh. "The thing that pushes us is *ki*, we are getting repeat clients every year and we are adding more and more clients. It's an inverted tree, basically. Five years down the line it would be huge."

But the maximum client base is 5000...

"Yes, and of that we don't expect a conversion ratio of more than 25%. So 1200 clients, and since elections happen once in 5 years - 200 clients a year."

But then there are many more elections to target - right upto municipal level. And the idea is to offer value added services such as assessing the 'winnability of candidates' and even providing a 'War Room' service for the last 2-3 weeks of the elections.

---

* The company's revenues are 'under Rs 5 crores'.

> **"Even for an MLA focusing on 200 villages in 30 days of campaign is not possible. We figure out which areas to focus on - it's basically maximising the output for him."**

"What we are doing right now is building a data bank, an expertise. We are building knowledge plans about areas, localities, communities, how do they react and all those things. All this will come handy - in time."

Diving deep into your chosen ocean, you find not just oysters, but pearls...

Political Edge also has plans to start a division catering to the social sector. The logic is the same - NGOs need independent feedback to understand if their various programs are having the desired impact.

"So far we've done about 18 projects for NGOs but not made any money on it. It's something we're exploring."

The employees at Political Edge number around 100 - 80% of whom are field staff. All fresh guys - simple graduates from any field. No past market research experience.

"We are not particular about stream because we want to train them in our method. We don't want them to do the kind of research that is being done in India", says Saurabh.

Adds Gaurav, "We have met people from all leading agencies, the surveyors, the supervisors and... I think many cook up results!"

The point is, a senior guy at HLL may buy an agency's take on rural UP even if the details are somewhat sketchy. But here the MLA is already an expert on his people, his area. The research has to be 'kickass' to be convincing.

So how do they manage the accuracy? Like all questionnaires here too, there are cross-checks. But there's also the simple principle of trust and personal bonding.

Initially the founding team was in the field day in and day out, but now there is a 3 tier system: Surveyor, Team Lead, Project Manager. Project managers report to Saurabh and Gaurav.

"The team that we are talking about stays on our payrolls. And the way they work, its basically more about commitment and hard work. It's a hard job. So one who does it well graduates to team lead and then project manager."

There is churn, but it's at a manageable level. Or maybe it's just the way they choose to see it.

"At any point in time if we have 50% good guys in our team, we can always take one guy each under their wing and double our team in no time", says Saurabh like he was solving a differential equation.

Politicians *ki haar-jeet ki estimation to roz hi hoti hai, apne bare mein kya rai hai*?

"In terms of money I would say in 5 years we want to grow by 5 times."

Adds Gaurav, "We will be interlinked with numerous thinktanks. with political parties and the new leadership which is coming up. We will offer strategic inputs."

The one thing both are clear about is the need to maintain focus; to work only with clients in the political domain. This clarity - or pigheadedness, some might call it - led to a split between the founding partners.

"The original company was 'Info Edge' but last year - in 2008 - we split due to internal differences. Now the parent company is called NDimensions and the brand is 'PoliticalEDGE'."

Although life is good, work does get hectic.

"Odd hours and sudden travel gets stressful at times. Staying single has helped me a bit on this front," grins Gaurav. Saurabh, meanwhile, has tied the knot with childhood friend Pankhuri.

So ultimately, has Political Edge made a difference? Saurabh and Gaurav both certainly think so. The Gandhi *topis* are becoming conscious that just playing politics is 'old school' and not enough. Even the most *khau peeu* type politican must show some 'development', some result.

"Our idea is wherever he is on a scale of 10, he should move towards 10. If he is 2, we will at least make him 2.5."

And someday they may even *join* politics, I think. Whatever they do, they will have an edge. And keep living on the edge.

Doing something they care about.

And that makes all the difference.

ADVICE TO YOUNG ENTREPRENEURS

Saurabh Vyas

I think it's more of a gut feeling that yes, I want to do it now and you have to take the plunge. That's the basic funda.. Why after one year - I don't know. It could have been 2 years, but it was just the decision.. yes let's do it!

Gaurav Rathore

If you are trying to do something new, first of all you have to believe in it. Otherwise, don't do it. Because you will not be able to stick to it.

For any company the first year or two years will be difficult. You might have a brilliant idea, but you will have to stick it out for a year or two years before you can make any real money or do something which has any impact. If you don't believe in the idea, two years is a long time.

Photo courtesy: '*Outlook Business*'

KING OF
POP

Satyajit Singh,
Shakti Sudha Industries

Satyajit Singh was comfortably placed in life, distributing consumer durables. Yet, one fine day he shut down that business, to take on the challenge of commercialising *makhana*. In doing so, he has found a mission if life and brought benefits to thousands of marginalised farmers.

It looks like a thermocol ball.

And feels like one too.

A product with no smell, no taste, no particular reason to be on your dinner plate.

Can you really make a Rs 50 crore business out of it?

Well, Satyajit Singh has done exactly that. And that too in the industrial wasteland of Bihar.

Satyajit is breathing new life into the *makhana* as well as the farmers who harvest it from the shallow ponds of North Bihar. He has organized the trade, networked the farmers, introduced new technologies - and it all started with a chance conversation on a flight.

A conversation that ultimately led him to shut down a *pakka* business as a distributor for BPL and take the dirt path - into *makhana* country.

I sit in Satyajit's office in Patna, surrounded by *makhana*.

Makhana posters, *makhana* polypacks, *makhana* snack food.

I see his machines which grade and separate 16 varieties of *makhana*.

I savour some lightly roasted *makhana* 'pop' - it's delicious!

And I think to myself, something might appear to be bland, or boring. But when you add to it the *tadka* of passion, of enthusiasm, of *'karna hai* at any cost'...

That project can be the most exciting thing in the world; that person is truly blessed.

KING OF
POP

Satyajit Singh,
Shakti Sudha Industries

Satyajit Singh was born in the district town of Jamui but moved to Patna after completing class 10.

"I studied MA (History) and I was the University topper. At that time there was a craze for joining IAS, so I too appeared for the examination."

Satyajit cleared the 'Mains' twice but not the interview. So what was the next best option? He decided to get into business.

It was an unusual decision for the son of an advocate and public prosecutor. The family had land and property but Satyajit was the first to 'go out' and start a business.

"I took up an agency for BPL products in Bihar and quickly understood what is marketing, what is sales and distribution."

The business was flourishing - by 2002, the agency was clocking an annual turnover of Rs 9 crores. Life was good, life was comfortable, but then a strange thing happened.

Satyajit was traveling from Delhi to Patna. The gentleman seated next to him on the flight was one Dr Janardhan.

Dr Janardhan was working with ICAR (Indian Council for Agricultural Research). He was in fact the director of the National

Research Centre for 'makhana'. A plant peculiar to north Bihar, cultivated in shallow ponds.

Dr Janardhan remarked, "For the last 3 years I have been searching for an entrepreneur who will do something in the area of *makhana*." Satyajit was intrigued.

He said, "What is this *makhana* crop all about - can you explain to me?"

Over the next three months, Satyajit traveled to villages in Darbhanga and Madhubani, and saw for himself how *makhana* was grown, and harvested.

"I saw how much pain farmers had to take in cultivation but how little they got in return.

The entire market was dominated by middlemen."

Satyajit told Dr Janardhan, "You want someone to set up an industry? Or do social service?"

Clearly, you could not set up plant and machinery and simply start processing raw material. Much would have to be done to make such a project commercially viable.

But the idea excited Satyajit.

"Overnight, I took a bold decision. I shut down my distribution business and started work on the *makhana* project."

Bana banaya setup, good income, 10 to 6 routine - why leave it all to venture into the unknown, the uncharted? Because. Something inside you has been stirred and shaken.

Satyajit spent two years in the wilderness, getting a feel of the market and the supply chain in agriculture.

"I visited *mandis* across India, understanding how the business works. I also spent a lot of time in the villages where *makhana* is produced."

Makhana - or foxnut - is grown in ponds. It is actually a fruit, similar to pomegranate (*anaar*). When ripe, this fruit bursts and its seeds are scattered at the base of the pond.

These black seeds are collected, roasted and then hammered open. The end product is spongy and white. A very labour intensive process, and mostly done by women.

"It's a very difficult process. *Jisne isey puraane zamaane mein ijaad kiya wo mastermind hoga,*" he exclaims.

Now in any other state, Satyajit could simply have gone to the *mandi* and picked up as many tons of produce as he desired. And set up a processing plant.

But Bihar has no *mandi* system at all*. Satyajit quickly realised that his work would have to start at the very first point in the supply chain - the farmers.

"I decided we should approach the panchayats and ask them to identify the *makhana* farmers in their area."

The idea was to train and network the farmers, improve their livelihood. You build a relationship with the farmers, you build the supply chain. Makes perfect sense, doesn't it?

Bankers were not convinced.

"In 2004, firstly, there was no investment climate in Bihar. No industry, no support from government. No one had ever done a project in *makhana* before. So the question always came up *ki bhai*, how will *you* do it?"

It's a question that brings out the best in an entrepreneur.

After a careful study of all project parameters, Satyajit's heart and head were both saying: you are on to something big. Big enough to warrant a project cost of Rs 70 crores over 5 years.

And he started by putting in Rs 1.5 crores of his own money - surplus from his earlier business - to kickstart the project. He used the capital to set up a small R&D unit.

"For two years we only tested the product, sent it to CFTRI Mysore and did trial marketing all over India."

It was in mid-2005 - in the midst of this trial phase - that Zee TV launched the much hyped *Business Baazigar*. The show promised a platform, as well as venture capital, to the best ideas from entrepreneurs across India.

Satyajit applied, was accepted and even made it to the top 10 finalists. But at that point, doubts set in.

He said, "I have put in my own money and one and a half years of my time into R&D for this project. I want to understand what exactly is venture capital.. How will you make my project happen?"

They said, "We will only help the top 3 finalists and then their projects will become our projects. You will work as a CEO."

"The moment they said this *maine ticket kata liya*. I told them, 'You have only one option: please eliminate me'!"

---

* The APMC Act was abolished by Govt of Bihar in 2006 without any alternate arrangement with the private sector

"Managing the supply chain - getting the crop from the farmer to the factory - was the biggest challenge."

In fact, Satyajit was in a hurry to get back home because finally, the state Industrial Development Corporation had allotted land for his project. The problem was, it was already occupied - by anti-social elements!

"It was the time of President's Rule in Bihar. I approached the Chief Secretary Mr G S Kang with the issue. He ordered the district administration to remove the anti social elements and hand over the plot to us ."

Now, Satyajit started approaching banks with his presentation. Finally, Bank of India agreed to lend support.

By this time Nitish Kumar had come into power; the investment climate suddenly improved. The government appointed Mr S Vijayaraghavan as the Industrial Development Commissioner.

"My Vijayraghavan is a very positive frame of mind person... *is project ko aage badhane mein unka bahut bada haath hai."*

The logic was simple: Bihar needs industrial development. But you need some homegrown success stories, before you can attract outside investment.

Satyajit's project thus became the first to be 'approved' by the State Investment Promotion Board.

R&D completed, land allotted, factory coming up, finance and even government support - great. But the first and foremost task remained - procurement of *makhana.*

"The problem started with 'resource mapping'. We could not trust the government statistics."

The state agriculture department would show 200 hectares in a certain area under *makhana* cultivation; the ground reality would be 35 or 40 hectares. You simply had to go to the grassroots level and work from the bottom-up.

"First thing we did was approach the *panchayats* and ask them to identify for us, the *makhana* farmers in their village."

These farmers are 'registered', given photo ID cards and a bank

"Do kaam side by side hoga nahin, is liye maine distribution line band kar di aur makhane project mein full time lag gaya."

account. This involves documentation, transportation, complications.

"In rural areas the internet is down most of the day, so the bank operates only two hours," adds Satyajit.

So why go through all this trouble?

The first reason: Banks do not provide working capital based on cash transactions.

The second and equally important: To empower marginal farmers, 80% of them *angoothachhaap*.

"I had read about Verghese Kurien and the white revolution he brought about. He gave his entire life to that cause... With *makhana* I saw an opportunity to do something like that. Something that would make a difference."

And how...!

In 2004 farmers were selling *makhana* for Rs 40/ kg to middlemen, with no guarantee of when they would actually get the cash in hand.

Today, the procurement price of *makhana* fixed by Shakti Sudha stands at Rs 130 per kg and as soon as the produce is weighed, the money is transferred to the farmer's account.

"We have registered 7000 *makhana* farmers, so we touch the lives of 35-40,000 people directly." says Satyajit. "But even those farmers who still sell to the middleman benefit from the benchmark price set by us."

And how does Shakti Sudha decide on this price? It depends on the 'cost of production'.

Let's say there was a drought, or a flood last year - Satyajit will factor this in and offer Rs 15 more per kg.

"The cost can easily be absorbed by the end consumer, but for that farmer the extra money can make all the difference," he says.

It helps, of course, that 90% of the world's *makhana* production happens to be in north Bihar!

Another intriguing strategy - increasing the procurement price by Rs 5 every month. Starting from Rs 125 per kg in the month of September going up to Rs 170 by April, when the 'season' ends.

"We did this to motivate the farmer to keep up production, make more effort."

So far so good, but not enough. Satyajit soon realized that farmers were reluctant to travel outside their village to sell their produce. So Shakti Sudha would have to set up local collection centres catering to 250-500 farmers.

Each centre would offer the facility of a raised platform and a common *chulha*. In addition, the panchayat would provide a common godown.

Every centre is manned by 4 employees of Shakti Sudha who are known as '*makhana mitras*'. Tasks are neatly divided; while one person looks after the training, procurement and opening of bank accounts, the other manages the computer, the on-the-spot accounting and despatch of goods to Patna.

There is of course, a centre 'in charge'.

"I am also a frequent visitor; in fact 70% of my time still goes in the supply chain management."

Today Shakti Sudha has 17 centres, with plans to put up another 24 in the next 1 year. The cost of setting up each centre is Rs 10-12 lakhs and it is an investment which banks still refuse to fund.

Satyajit has therefore hit upon the idea of public-private partnership.

"Our biggest concern is how to reduce the cost of identifying and registering the farmers. We are working with agencies like World Bank and RBH in 7 blocks."

Satyajit also wants the Ministry of Agriculture to share with him

"I had read about Verghese Kurien and the white revolution he brought about. He gave his entire life to that cause... With *makhana* I saw an opportunity to do something like that. Something that would make a difference."

some of the funds allocated to ATMA (Agricultural Technology Management Agency).

"ATMA spends Rs 40 crores a year but is yet to create even 100 FIGs (Farmer Interest Groups) in Bihar. I said, 'Give us the project on pilot basis for 5 blocks. I will put up 100 FIGs in each block'!"

And it's no empty boast.

"*Jitney log baahar se aate hain* - World Bank, IFC, ADB - all are sent to see the model of Shakti Sudha which is a success. *Ki kaise humne contradictions ko negotiate karke develop kiya practical taur pe.*"

And Satyajit enjoys sharing his experience, his knowledge, with anyone who wants to learn from him. To see how enterprise can bloom, even in an industrial desert.

"I am not from the *makhana* producing part of Bihar, nor from business community. *Mera door door tak makhane se koi rishta nahin lekin phir bhi main is field main aaya.*"

Aur apna raasta banaya.

Take the Rs 70 crore project outlay - Satyajit certainly did not have the 25% required by the bank as his 'contribution'. But he found a working solution.

He said, "I will take funding from the marketing phase - gestation period is not required. So the project itself will be generating revenue from day 1 and taking care of my 25%."

So for example in in year 1, Shakti Sudha took Rs 6 crores from the bank and also posted revenues of Rs 8 crores. The surplus* took care of the promoter contribution; and thus the cycle continues year on year.

In 2007-08, Shakti Sudha achieved a turnover of Rs 22 crores and the following year this figure shot up to Rs 50 crores.

"This year I believe we will do Rs 100 crores, but it all depends on procurement. I can sell as much *makhana* as I can get to the factory - that is hardly the problem!"

In season, at any given time, you won't see more than 10 tons of *makhana* at the Shakti Sudha factory. Everyday the produce comes in, it is graded, processed and despatched.

If Satyajit's first battle was the supply chain, his second was with the *mandis*. High quality standards and excellent packaging made Shakti Sudha a force to reckon with - in no time.

"90% of the *makhana* in India sells in *boras* or jute bags. We are the

---

* *since most of the surplus is reinvested, actual 'profit' is very modest. In 2008-9, profit was Rs 1.5 crores on a turnover of Rs 50 crores.*

> *"Agar Bihar mein Chankaya aur Chandragupta ki jodi hoti hai to main kehta hoon ki Dr Janardhan mere liye Chanakya hain. He is the one who motivated me to take up this project."*

only ones who provide poly packaging and in different sizes like 5 kgs, 8 kgs, 10 kgs etc."

Another recent coup was an order for 1400 tons of *makhana* from the Vaishnodevi shrine board. They had been searching for a supplier for the last 3 years - in vain.

Conquering the wholesale market might have been good enough for most, but not Satyajit. He could see the next big opportunity - making a commodity into a brand - by reaching out to the end consumer.

This means selling *makhana* under the Shakti Sudha name directly to consumers. And not just plain *makhana*, but a slew of value added products.

"When we studied *makhana* at CFTRI Mysore we found that the protein component and macronutrients are very high. This crop has medicinal value; definitely our ancestors who made it part of *puja* rituals were aware of this value."

With health becoming so important to urban consumers, here was a market waiting to be tapped. With help from the Indian Institute of Packaging in Mumbai and Flex Industries in Noida, Shakti Sudha mastered the nuances of snack food packaging.

And after much experimentation in the 'taste' department, Shakti Sudha has produced a range of 'ready to eat' *makhana* products. This includes roasted snack food ('*makhana* pop'), *kheer* and even an '*atta* mix'.

"Put 500 grams of our mix into 5 kgs of *atta* and you have a great source of protein. I have it everyday, myself!"

Shakti Sudha is targeting 100 towns across 15 states, mainly in northern and western India. And here, the BPL experience is coming in very handy.

"I know how to track my salesmen, how to get the distributor to work for me, how to take advance payment... what should be the reporting format."

As well as how to enter a new market, which newspapers to advertise in, what advertisement will work on TV. This is evident from the simple but effective Shakti Sudha campaign. Created by Oberoi multimedia, but based on Satyajit's idea.

"Our proposition is *makhana* - 'natural healthy and tasty'. *Saare desh ki mummiyan ise hi recommend kar rahi hain... hamein kisi celebrity ki zaroorat nahin hai*!"

The tagline is "*makhana... apna desh, apna khana*."

"Because it is somewhat associated with our religion and culture I have given it that slogan, that this is our 'national product'."

With a modest budget of Rs 5.5 crores, Shakti Sudha will also have to focus on trade promotions. Here Satyajit has a simple idea - with every packet of Shakti Sudha *makhana*, the *kheer* or snack food will be given free.

Despite all this, there is resistance.

"Retailers in urban market want to work on percentage margin whereas we work on per kg margin," he explains.

In fact, Shakti Sudha cuts out the middleman and thus offers much better prices to customers. Large retailers are keen to procure from the company, but it has not quite worked out.

"Reliance Retail asked us for 100 tons but they wanted 90 days credit. I refused."

Since Shakti Sudha pays farmers upfront, the company operates *only* on cash and carry basis - no matter who the buyer.

It is clarity of vision and determination, which has brought Shakti Sudha thus far. And will take it many miles further.

" Our tagline is "*makhana.. apna desh, apna khana*." *Saare desh ki mummiyan ise hi recommend kar rahi hain.. hamein kisi celebrity ki zaroorat nahin hai*!"

> **" I knew that this project would yield
> me nothing in the first two years but in
> time to come it will give me 'everything'.
> It will give me the prestige from IAS."**

"My objective is to work with small and marginal farmers," says Satyajit. "Improving their lives helps me expand the market further."

This could mean negotiating with the government to lease out ponds for 7 years, instead of just 11 months. Or bringing the benefits of numerous horticulture schemes which they are unaware of.

From next year Shakti Sudha will also train *makhana* farmers to grow herbal plants in the same ponds - during the 'off season'.

And in what will be a major change, the company will start using a machine to actually 'pop' the *makhanas*. It is far more efficient - when manually processed 10 seeds yield just 3-4 *makhanas* while the machine extracts 90%.

But what about the 10-12,000 families who will be put out of a job? Satyajit has an alternate livelihood in mind for them.

"In North Bihar there is something called as '*chaur* land' - this is land which is 2-3 feet under water and not used by anyone. There are 15-17,000 hectares like that and we are asking the government to lease out four acre parcels to landless and affected farmers."

Thus more *makhana* will actually be cultivated. And the raw seed will simply be sold to Shakti Sudha who will process it into *makhana*.

What might look like a tasteless white foodstuff to some, is a life's work for Satyajit Singh.

"I was always looking for something which I could devote my life to. *Ek aisa kaam hai jisme mein zindagi ke pachchees tees baras daal sakta hoon...*"

Looking back, it was the right decision.

"I knew that this project would yield me nothing in the first two years but in time to come it will give me 'everything'. It will give me the identity and prestige which I wanted through IAS. The chance to do something good for the people."

In villages across Bihar, there is love and respect for Satyajit - which means the world to him. And there is recognition - from no less than the Chief Minister. Nitish Kumar inaugurated the Shakti Sudha factory in 2006 - making it the first 'success story' for the Bihar State Industrial Promotion Board.

Satyajit is also Chairman of CII in the state, which means he 'sells' Bihar to potential investors at roadshows around the country. Where does he find the time?

"*Time nikaalna padta hai.*"

And there is never enough of it, is there? Certainly not for his wife Sudha and their two schoolgoing kids.

"I must thank my wife for her support, especially in those first two years. When the income flow stops and savings are getting diverted - even her FDs are getting broken - the family feels some tension..."

She did not waver, or interfere.

"*Shakti* is Ma Durga and Sudha is my wife's name - that's how I came up with the name 'Shakti Sudha'.

There is *shakti* within each of us, around us, enough for all of us to be like Satyajit.

To make the impossible possible; to power our dreams.

ADVICE TO YOUNG ENTREPRENEURS

I have one simple advice: There is no shortcut in life, go for details. For any big achievement you need patience and devotion.

If you understand what you are doing and plan it in detail, you will definitely be successful.

But these days I see most people don't want to get into details... they don't want to work at the micro level. They want shortcuts.

If you take the shortcut you cannot achieve major goals or a big vision.

When you start something new, initially resistance will be high. Like in our case, middlemen did not want us to go to villages and train farmers.

But then we won over the resistors and made them our partners. If you study Bihar society closely you will see that when someone does something new, people first laugh at him.

If you persist, they will criticise you.

But when they see you are undeterred - and you are succeeding - *aapke saath aakar khade ho jayenge aur apke success mein apne yogadan ki charcha karenge* .

So focus on your project, your mission - not what people will say.

Lead the way and others will follow!

FAR FROM THE MADDING
CROWD

Sunil Bhu,
Flanders Dairy

He was a city boy who knew he wanted to work on a farm. Right after college, Sunil went to Belgium, where he learnt all about making cheese. That's what he's been doing at Flanders Dairy for the last two decades, and enjoying every moment of it.

"This place smells of milk!" is my first reaction.

Umm, what else will a cheese factory smell like, I kick myself.

As Sunil Bhu carefully brews a cup of designer coffee for me, I admire his farm, his factory, his life.

Sunil is an Average Guy in every sense of the word.

Except that unlike the usual average guy, he knew himself.

Sunil knew he enjoyed animals - working on a farm, milking cows and making cheese. So what if these weren't the things that regular people from middle class families usually do?

When *you* know what you want, no one can really stop you.

Sunil wakes up each day, excited about making his next ball of cheese.

Excited about working with his hands, creating something new.

And I think, life is kind of like milking a cow! You can make delicious stretchy-stringy cheese of it; or simply let it curdle and go sour.

What would you prefer?

FAR FROM THE MADDING
CROWD

Sunil Bhu,
Flanders Dairy

Sunil Bhu is a thoroughbred *Dilliwala,* although his parents are originally from UP.

"My father, for his time, did something different. He was one of the first pilots with Indian Airlines."

Sunil grew up in South Extension and went to St Columba's school where the education was good, but he was not a very bright student.

"My mother used to be happy if I managed to pass and luckily... I did manage that!"

After class 12, Sunil went on to Pusa - the well known Institute of Hotel Management in Delhi. Nobody insisted he take up any particular 'line' but both his sisters had already done hotel management.

"I simply followed in their footsteps."

Besides, Sunil's mother had started a restaurant - his father managed it after retirement.

"It was called Kamalika and it was a popular place in its time - right opposite IIT. I used to hang out there, help out a bit after school. I made some very good friends there," he recalls.

Zindagi ki gaadi badh rahi thi, but there was no great ambition to get into the 'fast lane'

"The only thing was I did not want to work for somebody. I knew that very early."

In fact, Sunil skipped the internship which was a mandatory part of his course; so he does not even have a graduation certificate! But he has no regrets.

"I just wanted to do what I felt like doing."

What he felt like doing was working with animals - living on a farm, milking cows.

"We had this book in school called 'Far from the Madding Crowds' by Thomas Hardy. It was all about the pastoral life. Somehow, that book made an impression on me."

At the same time the idea of doing something related to cheese crept into his head.

Back in 1985, cheese was quite scarce - no one knew much about it in India. But that did not deter Sunil.

"I had a friend from Belgium, so I asked him to find out if there was any farm where I could work - not for money, just the experience."

The friend located such a farm and Sunil landed up in Belgium, with 'nothing clear in his head'. But things did not quite click.

Sunil tried his luck at another farm nearby. .

"Can you come and pull out the weeds?" asked the owner.

"Sure," replied the 21- year-old.

And that's where it all began - in Diksmuide, a tiny town in the Flemish province of West Flanders. Thousands of miles away from life, as we know it.

"And your parents did not have a problem with all this?" I wonder.

"No… I mean they did not really understand why and maybe they did not like it, but no one ever stopped me."

In fact, Sunil's sisters chipped in to help him buy a cheap ticket. He even managed a one year visa - ostensibly to study about microbiotic food.

Things just 'fell in place'.

"As luck would have it, the farmer - Marc - was starting out in cheese making at that time. I traveled with him to Holland and France to see the techniques others were using."

Making cheese is really a family business, a closely guarded secret passed on from one generation to the next. But Marc, being European, managed to open doors quite easily. And Sunil quickly absorbed it all.

"We would come back to the farm and implement various methods, so it was a very good learning experience!"

Life is really about being in the right place, with the right person, at

> **"I wanted to work on a farm - to be with cows, be with animals. And somehow I connected this with cheese, which was quite scarce in our country then!"**

the right time.

The right chemistry.

"Communication could have been a big problem," muses Sunil. "But Marc had an interest in languages. He made that effort to learn English and I also learnt some Flemish - so somehow it worked out!"

After two years in Flanders, Sunil returned to India.

"I was not one of those people who wanted to settle abroad. You are your own boss in your own country, anywhere else you are always number two. So I came back."

What would he do? Well, he did start making cheese but at the time it was not really a business. More just to prove to the family that he had learnt something in the two years spent in Belgium!

"My mother had a little piece of land - this farm - and she gave me one cow."

Talk about 'working' capital!

Initially, the cow was actually kept in the backyard of Sunil's house in South Ex.

"I can't believe it."

"Yeah, my friends used to laugh! "

They said, "People take their dogs out for a walk, you are taking your cow out! "

He said, "So what!"

And Sunil milked that cow and made his one ball of cheese everyday.

"There is a certain process of pressing the cheese - I used to press it under my bed!" he recalls.

But quickly, Sunil realised that conditions in India were very different from Europe. It was far easier to make cheese in Diksmuide than in Dilli!

Indian milk is different, Indian climate is different, Indian tastebuds are different.

Trial and error, *pateele mein experiments chalte rahe.*

"I went back to Belgium for short durations - to learn more - but meanwhile I was helping out with my dad's restaurant. The cheese thing was more like a hobby, something I did on the side."

And that's how it remained for close to eight years. But even as a hobby, his talent was quickly recognised.

A friend knew the owner of Steakhouse, a famous gourmet food store in Delhi

Sunil offered them his cheese.

The store owner tasted it and said exclaimed, "If you can make a hundred balls like this, bring them to me!"

That was the birth of Flanders - a small homemade ball of cheese bearing the logo of Sunil's 'first cow'.

Slowly, Sunil went from one ball of cheese a day to two.

From two balls a day to five.

Each ball sold for ninety odd rupees but it was hard manual labour.

Made, quite literally, with your own hands.

Of course, one cow could only yield milk for two balls of cheese in a day so eventually Sunil increased the workforce.

He bought more cows.

"More cows of course meant shifting here, to the farm. And I got someone to start working with me as well... it just grew little by little over the years."

As did Sunil's love and his passion - for cheese.

And no matter how much he perfected the technique, there was always more to learn. Wherever he happened to go.

In 1989, he was in northern Italy, eating at a little pizzeria.

He asked the owner, "Where does this cheese come from?"

The Italian answered, "A dairy close by."

The next day Sunil decided to go see for himself. It was a huge factory, quite unlike the one in Belgium.

"I explained to the lady at the reception that I am a cheesemaker from India. She asked me to wait."

The boss was not available, so in the meantime Sunil and his friend were treated to lunch at a fabulous restaurant.

"I was thinking to myself, these guys might be expecting some major collaboration! But no, nothing like that - it was simple hospitality."

The owner was a short Italian man who patiently heard Sunil's story.

Then he said, "I started out exactly the way you did! You are welcome to come and be in my factory and learn whatever you feel like learning."

Sunil spent three months at the factory and learnt how mozzarella cheese was made - in a commercial way. The Italian way.

"Italian cheese is more favourable to our conditions and suits the Indian palate better. So I bought some small machines and started off production of mozzarella cheese."

In 1988, Sunil's father passed away. No one in the family was keen to carry on the restaurant, so they downed the shutters. Leaving Sunil to do what he loved best - making cheese.

But it was only in 1994 that cheesemaking reached a scale which you could call an *enterprise*.

At this stage Sunil was handling 500 to 600 litres of milk a day, turning them into 70-80 balls of cheese. There were 20 odd cows on the farm and the the turnover touched Rs 25 lakhs that year.

This is probably the point at which Sunil started seeing himself as a businessman.

"Yes, it did become a business but I am still very passionate about it. It is a business which I love!"

And what exactly does he love?

"I love that it gives you the freedom to excel in what you are doing and you can keep going higher and higher and higher - there is no limit!"

But, isn't every ball of cheese you produce similar to the last one?

And the way you do it certainly does not change...

"True, but you can keep making your systems of working better.

Like?.

"Well, starting from milk collection. There are so many ways to make collection of milk better in our country! India may be number one in production of milk in the world but if you look at the per capita yield, it is very low."

How you feed the cows, how you milk them and how you store the

> **"I am still doing manual labour even today.
> I like it so I put on my boots and work
> everyday from the morning till afternoon -
> I can never tire of it!"**

milk in clean and hygienic conditions - these are all areas Sunil is constantly working on.

And although the story of Flanders began with a man and his love for animals, that story has now been rewritten.

"I used to have my own cows there came a stage when I realised I was spending 75% of the time on the animals and just 25% on making cheese. Whereas it should have been the other way round!"

So three years ago Sunil 'gave away' his 30 cows to another farmer and now he simply buys all the milk that suppliers can bring him.

Recognise your limitations; focus on what you love, what you're good at.

Says Sunil, "I realised at an early stage that I should not be trying to do everything myself. So I did not get into marketing - I got a distributor."

What Sunil focuses on then is making the best cheese he possibly can - mascarpone, gouda, mozzarella - the works.

Today, Flanders churns out between 500 to 600 kgs of top class cheese everyday, 7 days a week.

Sunil is on the farm every morning at seven. And there is non stop action upto 12 noon. By 12.30 the cheese production for the day is completed; by four it is all packed and ready to go.

"I have a small team of eight people working with me, as well as my nephew Gaurav. All of them have been with me since many years and they're equally passionate about what we are doing."

Simple people, not highly educated, trained from scratch.

Exactly the kind every entrepreneur needs...

The process of making cheese involves attention to detail. As well as physics, chemistry - all the stuff Sunil never paid attention to in school!

"Machines break down, you fix them, work with your hands - that's the physics part!"

Learn the hard way.

"The farmers come in twice a day, we collect the milk. Then each and every sample is checked in the laboratory - that's chemistry."

Fat percentage, protein, calcium content - after it's all okayed the milk is kept in cold storage. The next morning it's piped into the vats at the dairy, pasteurized and processed - depending on the kind of cheese being made.

To cut a long story short, you make the 'curd', cut it, drain it and mould it into shape. Every batch is quality checked.

"80% of our business comes from restaurants and hotels - we are now a recognised brand," says Sunil with visible pride.

Flanders' revenues have now crossed Rs 5 crores, but Sunil says turnover is 'not important'.

"The business is self sustaining - we have no loans or liabilities* - and we are getting better and better at what we do. There is a growth factor!"

So there is no ambitious business plan? No burning desire to make Flanders the leading cheese brand of India?

"No plan. Let it flow and it flows itself."

But what if some venture capitalist comes to you and says, "Here's $20 million. Now set up a Flanders factory in six different parts of India?"

"I don't know if I would want to do it!" he says, without hesitation.

Growth is happening - but in the modest and organised way that Sunil prefers.

"Working on a farm is very good but there are certain drawbacks. So I am shifting the unit to an industrial area."

The point however is that the way in which Sunil works would more or less remain the same. Hands-on and personal.

"We work on the same 25-30 percent margin as any industry but don't forget it is hard work, physical work."

Work brings its rewards but at a fundamental level, it must be its own reward.

And beyond work, there is life. *A lifestyle.*

"I go back home in the afternoon, go for a swim in the evening. I have a two-year-old daughter now, I spend time with her. "

---

*Apart from one bank loan of Rs 25,000, Flanders grew from internal accruals.

Marriage and family happened late in life for Sunil - when he felt ready for it. And that feeling came at age 38. Wife Deepali now manages the Flanders 'office' and marketing. She is equally enthusiastic about cheese

It's all worked out rather well for the boy who was not that bright in studies.

But followed his heart, his instinct...

"I have been able to do what I wanted to do which is very important in life."

Because revenues are mere numbers; a dream is infinite.

ADVICE TO YOUNG ENTREPRENEURS

If you get the opportunity to do what you are really meant to do, what is coming from within you - go for it. Start your own legacy!

Be one pointed. Don't waver and don't look too far ahead - just go step by step and it comes to you.

I was not an extra bright student - I realised in the beginning itself that I should not pursue higher goals in academics because I had my limitations.

Be aware of your limitations and find what you are really good at! I could not be the top guy in academics but I can be the top guy in cheese.

Be the top guy in whatever you are doing you don't have to follow an already taken path - you can make your own path.

Lastly, don't start counting the bucks too early. Be passionate and dedicated and money will follow.

ELECTRIC
DREAMS

Chetan Maini,
Reva Electric Car Company

Chetan Maini was crazy about electronics - and cars - as far back as he can remember. It's this passion that led him to pursue the dream of producing an electric car. Today, Reva is not only producing such vehicles but licensing its technology to the likes of General Motors.

The first time I saw a Reva car, I thought it was 'cute'.

But hey, would I really want to *own* it?

That's a question Chetan Maini is familiar with. On paper the electric (or battery driven) vehicle makes great sense. So why exactly do we stick to diesel and petrol?

Well - it's complicated. There's the oil lobby, the auto lobby and the this-is-the-way-things-have-always-been-done lobby. There just aren't enough people in the world who believe in this new technology.

But then Chetan came along.

At 13, he was building go-karts.

At 20, he built a solar powered car.

At 24, he was leading an electric car project.

At 31, he *launched* this car.

And he is still working, perfecting, enhancing his vehicles.

Dreaming of the day that you and I will junk our gas guzzlers and go electric.

At his nifty little factory in Bommasandra - an industrial area just outside Bangalore - I admire a couple of the 'next generation' Revas.

I'm still not sure if I would buy one, but I am sold on the drive, the determination and the can-do spirit of Chetan Maini.

ELECTRIC DREAMS

Chetan Maini,
Reva Electric Car Company

Chetan Maini was born in Bangalore, and he was crazy about all kinds of electronics, as far back as he can remember.

"I remember making my first radio in fourth standard, by sixth standard I was building remote control planes. Then I moved into assembling remote control cars!"

Luckily, Chetan's father recognised his passion and encouraged it - monetarily, and otherwise.

"Dad had friends who were experts in certain areas. He'd call them over for a drink in the evening and make sure they spent an hour helping me out."

What's more, Chetan had his own 'hobby room' - a converted terrace where he spent most of his day. Working with milling machines and lathes, on some project or the other.

"In fact we were three brothers... and my hobby room was bigger than the room we slept in," recalls Chetan.

One summer Chetan spent the whole three months of his vacation building a go-kart. He picked up an old engine and components from the junkyard and did the job on a shoestring budget of Rs 1500.

A fairly large sum back then - I wonder if Chetan was the proverbial rich 'spoilt brat'

"We were comfortably well off but my parents never flaunted it. If I needed five rupees for lunch my mama would give me exactly five rupees."

Money does not grow on trees; it is hard work tending the plant.

Chetan's father certainly knew that! Sudarshan Maini was an engineer who quit his job with Mico Bosch to start his own engineering company - way back in 1973.

A bold move for a man with a young family to support.

"At a very early age I saw how much pride he had in his work; he always wanted to do something that is different."

And that certainly rubbed off on Chetan.

Like most of his classmates at Bishop Cotton, he started preparing for IIT JEE. But in a couple of months Chetan realised IIT was not the place for him.

"I wanted something more hands-on, something to do with automobiles," he declared.

"Why don't you apply to schools in the US," said his dad.

The University of Michigan was Chetan's first preference - because of its proximity to the auto hub of Detroit. And fortunately, he was accepted.

"I studied mechanical engineering but I spent fifty percent of my time on extracurricular projects. In my first year itself I worked on a 'supermileage' car which would give 400 kilometres to a litre!"

In his second year, Chetan became very passionate about the 'solar car' project - an inter-university competition where teams built a car from scratch. The University of Michigan team was one of 35 teams chosen to participate.

It was a completely hands on project - from welding body panels to wrestling with machine parts.

"I was working with General Motors as an intern. I would be at GM from 7 am till 4 pm, drive two hours to the Michigan International Speedway where we tested the car... and spend 4-5 hours on the track!"

The months spent building, testing and perfecting resulted in the University of Michigan team standing first among the 35 universities which raced their cars.

At the end of the race a rival team member remarked to Chetan, "We spent only $40,000 while you guys spent a million dollars, so of course you came first!"

Chetan replied, "Sure, but we put our heads together and raised the million dollars. You could have done that as well!"

It was an important lesson in teamwork - from getting the B-school

> # "My brother flew the planes that I took months to build and made sure he crashed them. And then again I spent months rebuilding them."

guys to help in raising sponsorship, to understanding weather and solar patterns. The University of Michigan pooled in many hands, many heads and many hearts, to make it happen.

Next stop: World Solar Championships in Australia. Racing across the outback from Darwin to Adelaide - a total of 3200 kms - competing against the likes of Mazda and Honda!

"On day one we actually finished ahead of Honda* and everyone was shocked. How could twenty year olds beat large OEMs?"

For Chetan, it was an awakening.

"Anything is possible," I realised.

Back at college, Chetan spent his final year working on a formula race car.

"To me these projects *were* my education. I enjoyed my classes and got decent grades. But the night before an exam you would often find me reading about things which interested me. And had nothing to do with the syllabus!"

At this point, Chetan got excited about electric cars.

"We were four friends who understood each other very well. We would meet around once a month and put together business plan ideas in this area."

One of the four friends was Dave Bell, whose father Dr Lon Bell was a PhD from Caltech. Dr Bell had founded a company called Technar - which he'd just sold to TRW - and was looking for something interesting to do.

He said, "Well this sounds really good! Why don't you come and join me?"

Thus in 1991, Chetan joined Dr Bell's startup.

"In the first summer we were just seven of us in the company. We built the platform of an electric car and evaluated many different technologies."

---

* *University of Michigan finished third at the end of the championship*

It was a huge learning experience but Chetan felt he needed to study further. So he took a year and a half off for a Master's at Stanford. Apart from attending a great program which integrated mechanical and electrical engineering, Chetan got involved in building a hybrid-electric car.

After graduating, he returned to work with Lon Bell at Amerigon. The company continued to work on electrical vehicle technologies but also moved into other high-end automotive technologies.

There was much to do there but Chetan was feeling the urge to return home.

"I was visiting India once a year and started getting a feel for how things were changing here. The economy was opening up, pollution was getting crazy. Things that I used to do as a kid - like cycle to school - had become impossible!"

Surely there would be a market for an electric car in India? While most companies - including Amerigon - were focussed on high end cars for US and Europe, Chetan was convinced that the future lay elsewhere.

In cost-effective city mobility solutions for India, China and South East Asia.

"Dr Bell allowed me to travel around Europe and US to evaluate the market and understand what was working, what was not."

Chetan realised that the *way* in which technology was developed led to a very high cost structure.

"I remembered my solar car days. Back then we did not know how to do things, so we explored so many different ideas and processes."

The explorer finds many new routes, when he does not have a map. And that is what Chetan and his team decided to do - explore cheaper and better ways of building a car.

"For example, you build a car and put its wheels. Why can't we do it the other way round and have a running chassis? That is the kind of brainstorming we were doing as the project started to take form."

In December 1994, Sudarshan Maini happened to be visiting the US. He met Dr Bell, liked the man, liked the idea, and proposed a joint venture for the Indian market.

At a party, Maini Sr met Frank Wisner, the ambassador to India at that time and mentioned the project.

"Does it have a name?" asked Frank.

"Not yet," said Sudarshan.

"Well, why don't you name it Reva!" suggested the ambassador who had just been introduced to Reva Maini - Chetan's mother.

What's more, in Sanskrit, '*reva*' means a new beginning, which is exactly what the project was all about.

Incidentally, the Maini group run by Chetan's father was already making simplified electric cars like trolleys for factories, fork-lifts and golf carts. As well as manufacturing precision automotive components for companies like General Motors and Bosch.

So what was the big deal about manufacturing a Reva car then?

Well, there are hundreds of companies making auto components; but just a handful who sell cars. It's like the second extra from the left, dreaming of becoming a Shahrukh Khan...

Of course, it did not happen overnight.

Chetan ran the team on the Reva project in the US, working closely with the team in India. But it was a fluid sort of arrangement.

"I would come four times a year back to India and I had several engineers from India come down there. There was an MOU but we didn't have a formal agreement till 1999."

For five long years the two companies worked together to get the tech specs right - the business side would come later.

"In fact both parties would put in investments and work but I wasn't representing my family at that time. I was working for Amerigon, drawing a salary, but leading an entire team much older than me!"

At the time Chetan was barely 24. In fact, he had offers from large companies at 2x the salary but turned them all down.

"If I had worked for any other company it would have taken me fifteen years to get this kind of experience," says Chetan.

So what was the team doing for five long years?

"We made initial prototypes - then we had to test them on Indian road conditions and also make sure the final product would be cost effective."

The first prototype took a year to build. In 1996, the first 'car' was shipped to India and by the following year it had been thoroughly tested. In fact, Reva even secured ARAI* certification in 1997.

Things were looking good - both for the India and the US sides of the project.

* *Automotive Research Association of India (ARAI)*

> **"We we were given a lot of independence. I cannot recall a single time my parents asked me to study - they just trusted us a lot."**

The state of California had declared that by 1998, 2% of the cars on its roads would have to be electric. So many companies were keenly investing in electric vehicles and technologies.

Then, in late 1997, the regulation disappeared. And so did interest in electric cars.

"It was probably because of lobbying by oil companies and auto giants. Whatever the reason, we found the business of electric cars going down the drain..."

Both the Maini group and Amerigon had put in a lot of time, effort and money into Reva. Now it all seemed pointless. But Chetan was not one to give up easily.

"I came to India, sat down with the family and they saw my passion on this..."

The Mainis asked, "What do you need to make it work?"

Chetan said, "I have a plan - these are the facilities we need, this is the kind of money."

And the family agreed to support this crazy dream - with facilities, land & buildings and surplus from the existing business.

Chetan then went back to Dr Bell and said, "I have commitments from my family, I have some funding. Let me move to India and start making cars!"

In April 1999 Chetan moved back to Bangalore.

"It was a turning point because I think till then I was very technology focussed - now I was looking at Reva as a business."

Something few could envision.

"With oil at $20 a barrel it was not a hot proposition for VC funds. So I went to institutions like ICICI and TDB and raised debt financing of around Rs 15 crores for the project."

Chetan was constantly asked, especially by bankers, 'Who else does it in the West... are they successful'?"

"I definitely think electric vehicles are a hot proposition... but only very forward thinking people who see something five years before are able to understand my vision."

The answer is no such example, sir, but that does not mean *main kar ke nahin dikha sakta*!

In five years of R&D, the Reva project created ten patents in energy management, new ways to manufacture parts and make the end product more affordable, more 'India proof'.

"Even for the first car we made, I shipped steel from India. Because I knew when we start manufacturing, that's what we'll be using!"

A crucial issue was the 'charger' - the heart of the electric vehicle.

"We procured chargers from ten different manufacturers - all of them failed within one month. They simply could not handle Indian brownouts and blackouts!"

Reva then had to develop a charger to 'military specifications'. One which stood rock solid even if there were ten powercuts in a night, or poor earthing.

Other designed-for-India features included dent-proof, rust-proof body panels and automatic gearshift - making it easier to drive.

To do all this, Chetan first had to assemble a team. Which was easier said than done...

"I interviewed close to 400 people in Bombay, Delhi, Pune over two weeks!" he recalls

What kind of people was he looking to hire?

"I needed R&D, I needed vendor development, I needed marketing, I needed an entire organization!" he replies.

R&D was the tough bit because there were no people who'd worked on an electric car. In fact, in 1999 it was difficult to find engineers in India with R&D experience on any kind of car.

So Chetan did the next best thing. He hired young people for passion, and equipped them with skills.

"I would say that for the first two years, 95% of my time was spent in R&D. I practically lived with these guys."

Every night when Chetan got home his wife would say, "There goes another shirt"!

Stained with lubricant and *mitti...*

"I talked to every supplier, shared with them my vision... because they have to be convinced about why to invest with you!"

On the positive side, *yeh kaam kisi ne kiya hi nahin tha*, so no one had an idea how difficult it was! And Chetan never *made* it look hard.

"If you say we are building a car from scratch it's a daunting task. But if you break up the project into small steps - it is much easier."

One small step for the team, one giant leap for team spirit!

Chetan would challenge his young team to do in 15 days what was estimated to take a month.

"When I would ask why do you need a month, no one had an answer. They would go back and finish in maybe 18 days what a regular company would complete in 3 months."

Over 2 years, Reva built 40 cars. These cars were tested for a million kms before Chetan felt he was ready to launch - in 2001. Just then, a bolt from the blue.

"One month before we launched, taxes were doubled for electric cars... What's more, taxes for regular cars actually came down."

The subsidy of Rs 1.05 lakhs which had been provided to electric cars was also withdrawn. Just bad luck, or greater forces at work?

Sometimes the best defence is offense, and Chetan certainly tried to build support for his cause.

"I got IIT involved, I got IISc, and bunch of other companies and suppliers. 35 of us got together and tried to create awareness by setting up a body called the Electric Vehicle Association of India."

But no one really had the time or energy to think about how India would benefit 10 years from now, by adopting electric vehicle technology. The organisation fizzled out, but Reva kept its promise and launched the first electric car in India - in July 2001.

The company sold 150 odd cars in its first year of operation, all in Bangalore. And who were these buyers?

"We had customers who were seventy years old and our youngest one was nineteen. We had army officers, we had doctors, we had some IT people and a lot of women drivers. 50% of our customers, in fact, are women."

Reva did not spend a single rupee in advertising but made great use of PR. When you have an interesting product, you don't have to beat your own drum - you let others beat it for you.

Trust builds up slowly, especially for a never-been-seen-before product, from a never-been-heard-of company.

"When people walk into a showroom to buy a regular car, all they're doing is negotiating price and figuring out the colour. When someone walked into a Reva showroom, we had to sell them the *concept.*"

There were other concerns. Who was this Maini group and what if they folded up tomorrow? Chetan addressed the issue head-on.

"In those days every auto company offered one year warranty. We were the only company that offered a three year warranty."

The fact that Reva focussed only on Bangalore helped. The company was able to fix customer issues immediately. Once a month Chetan invited customers for tea and got their informal feedback and suggestions.

"We incorporated many new features in Reva on the express request of customers."

"So would you say the first year was the toughest?" I ask him

"Mmm... I think that were different challenges, at each stage," he says.

The first 5 years it was getting the technology right, then the focus shifted to raising money and putting together a team. Actually, every day was a new challenge...

"When I went to certify the Reva, they refused saying there is no law to certify an electric car, so we can't do it. I spent 6 months with ARAI and the government framing laws for electric cars!"

But yes, post launch things started to move. The core technology was working, money was less of an issue and suddenly, overseas markets started opening. Quite by chance!

An entrepreneurship group called 'Leaders Quest' goes around the world every year and looks at different things. In 2002, they came to visit Infosys and a bunch of companies in India.

"I was part of the 'Young Entrepreneur' organisation and through that they wanted to come and see Reva."

Well, they came and simply loved what they saw. Three of them approached Chetan and said, "We would like to see this car in London."

Three months later they returned, with a concrete proposal. A radical one.

"Let's do a different model, let's do everything online and create a different way of marketing cars in UK," they said.

Reva shipped 16 cars to UK in December 2002, where they were tested for a year, under British conditions.

"First thing, we had no clue what happens in winter. We had to develop special heating technology for the batteries. Then there were a lot of regulatory issues in Europe we weren't quite aware of."

In January 2004, the Reva electric car went on sale. For once, the timing was perfect. Londoners were now required to pay a congestion charge of five pounds for bringing their vehicles into the city.

Reva is the only car which does not attract congestion charge. In fact, Reva owners get free parking and free charging in many areas. That itself created huge buzz for the car!

Then, there was the seeing-is-believing approach.

"We launched the car by organising test drives at 16 locations in London city. And we hired environmental science students who were very passionate about clean technology to explain the benefits."

Reva also turned the conventional delivery model on its head.

"You order online and we deliver your car at home or at work, which is unheard of in UK. We also created a home servicing model for electric cars using on-board computers to diagnose problems - another first."

Reva retails for 7000 pounds; the company has so far sold over 1000 cars in the UK. Of course, the brand is known as 'G Wiz' in that country! And that's not the only point of difference. In India, Reva was a vehicle for the cost-conscious middle class buyer. In the UK, it became something of a fashion statement.

"I talked to every supplier, shared with them my vision... because they have to be convinced about why to invest with you!"

> **"I led by example - people learnt to be hands-on because of what they saw. If there was a problem I went straight to the car and slid underneath it"**

"Nine out of ten customers in the UK owned a high-end BMW, Porsche or a Mercedes Benz. They were top investment bankers, lawyers, celebrities - people who were very influential."

The company had to deliver a much higher level of service, and of perfection.

"You know in India, you might ship a car with a speck of dirt on the brake pedal - that's unacceptable in the UK. The level of detailing we had to go into was a huge cultural shift."

And it was very good, it grew the organisation. Both Chetan and his technicians spent weeks in the UK, understanding the market and its dynamics.

"The overseas experience helped us grow five years faster. We *needed* to be challenged by customers to increase our quality levels and become a global company."

What's more, margins were much higher in exports. And that certainly helped!

Of course, funding from the parent company - the Maini group - run by Chetan's father and two brothers continued.

"I think we grew Reva at the cost of other businesses which could have been far more profitable. But we were all committed to this project, and kept it going."

Maini group also set up divisions to support Reva, like a plastics division, a chassis division and a charger division. Over time, these divisions attracted other clients like Leyland and Volvo - making them independent business units.

All this support was valuable, but the company needed more money to grow rapidly. In December 2006 Chetan raised his first round of VC funding - $20 million from Draper Fisher Jurvetson, Global Environment Fund and Fursa.

Much of this money has gone into creating next generation technologies.

"How do we make cars go faster?"

"How do we make them go longer?"

"And how do we make them charge quickly?"

These were some of the questions the tech team grappled with.

"We set a target of launching one new model and one new variant every year*. And we are also putting up a new plant which can produce upto 30,000 vehicles a year," says Chetan.

Seems like a tall order for a company which sells barely 3000 units a year today. But Chetan has a roadmap in place.

"Today, we are test marketing in ten countries. That means we have between 4 and 20 cars there, we have a distributor in place, we've figured out regulatory hurdles..."

Commercial sale in these countries will start, very soon.

Similarly, in India, Reva has test marketed the car in Delhi, where CM Sheila Dixit has been very 'positive'. In fact, at a global level, Chetan sees 'change' is in the air. Starting from President Obama talking about a million electric cars on the road by 2015, to several EU nations which have announced a 5000 euro subsidy for such vehicles.

"Fundamentally, there is more awareness on climate change and more interest in renewable energy."

So, does Chetan see a day when Reva will be selling 10% of the cars in India ?

"I don't know," he replies. "I would want 10% of cars in India to be electric - they don't all have to be Revas."

But they could certainly be *powered* by Reva. By technology licensed from the only company in the world with 85 million kms of experience on electric cars.

"What we have to offer will probably help another automaker save three to five years, so there are going to be lot of opportunities, several business models emerging in this space."

I think Chetan is right. This is not just a car company but a knowledge company. 33% of Reva's employees are in R&D and they're all passionate about this baby. Reva could well be the 'Intel Inside' of the electric car industry.

In September 2009, General Motors became the first auto major to tie up with Reva to produce an electric version of the Chevy 'Spark'. More will surely follow...!

*Currently Reva is available as REVAi (with lead-acid batteries) and REVA L-ion (with lithium-ion batteries). Two new models - NXR and NXG - will be launched shortly.

Despite its many small successes, Reva is still in startup mode and yet to break even. So work-life balance has definitely been elusive.

"I would not have been able to do this without my the support of my wife Kim. I do work Saturdays, I do carry work home... But Sundays are only for her and for the kids."

Chetan squeezes in yoga thrice a week, as well as a bit of cycling. He used to enjoy driving the Reva car, before Bangalore traffic got to him. He still travels in a Reva, of course, but an 'extended' version where he can sit on the backseat.

"I also have a custom Reva which is a convertible - a fun car for evening use!"

As you might expect, 99% of Chetan's journeys are electric. But ultimately, it's not just about Reva...

"My dream would be when I go to a traffic light, everything around me is quiet. There are electric bikes, electric three-wheelers, electric buses and electric cars."

And there's the quiet satisfaction of being more than a market leader.

The satisfaction of leading a movement.

<u>ADVICE TO YOUNG ENTREPRENEURS</u>

You need to have a very strong belief in your idea to make it happen. Any idea that you take up - irrespective of what the world believes is - you have to see it through.

The second thing is when I found myself facing a problem, I would sleep over it. When I took a look at it in the morning... I tried to see opportunity. I found that worked very well; it made me positive and I was able to push that within the group and the company.

In hindsight, what may seem like a setback was actually just the push you needed - to try something new, to stretch your limits.

PAPER TIGER

Mahima Mehra,
Haathi Chaap

She wanted to work in recycling, but not with an NGO. So, she ended up starting a business in handmade paper. Along the way she discovered many interesting things, including an unexpected use for elephant dung.

Mahima Mehra hates to 'sell'.

"I am here in Mumbai for the very first time, taking around samples of Haathi Chaap products. It's difficult for me - I've never been the marketing type!"

In fact, Mahima is not really the kind of person you expect to see running a business. But don't be fooled by her mild mannerisms - this is one tough lady.

As a strong headed young woman of 24 she ventured into the badlands of UP in search of small producers of handmade paper. Her passion for recycling eventually led her to develop paper from the dung of elephants - sold under the quirky brand name 'Haathi Chaap'.

This unusual enterprise is getting her a fair bit of attention, which she finds amusing.

"I look at all the stuff we make and sometimes wonder, "*Logon ko kyun pasand aa raha hai?*'

Elephant poo or not, it's par for the course. Another day spent working in an industry she enjoys, with people she likes to work with, at a pace she sets.

Mahima has taken the *kora kaagaz* of life and written out her own answers.

More power to elephant potty, and to people who can take the poop out of convention!

PAPER TIGER

Mahima Mehra,
Haathi Chaap

Mahima Mehra was born and brought up in Jaipur.

"Traditionally we are business people. My parents were in the jewellery line but I was never interested in that. I always wanted to do something in recycling!"

After completing her graduation in psychology from Lady Shriram College in Delhi, Mahima decided to pursue her passion. She joined an organisation called Jan Seva Ashram, hoping to work in vermi-composting. Instead, she was assigned to the handmade paper division.

"Living in Jaipur, I had been exposed to handmade paper. Often we would take our bicycles and ride out to a small town called Sanganer which is famous for this craft."

At Jan Seva, Mahima enjoyed working with paper, especially the aspect of 'recycling' which is at the core of handmade paper. What she did not enjoy was working in an NGO.

"I thought there was too much attention being paid to form-filling, diluting the essence of working for a cause."

The only other option was working in an academic organisation, doing research. But Mahima preferred to be in the field, working with her hands.

"I wanted to do something with recycling but I also wanted a certain lifestyle, certain comforts in life... Actually, I never thought I would start a business, I don't really have the temperament for it! This just kind of happened."

After 7 months at Jan Seva Ashram, Mahima quit and simply started working with paper. The year was 1995. The capital investment was Rs 12,500 - borrowed from her family..

"What did I use it for? To buy myself a table, a chair and some paper," she laughs. "Really that was all I needed!"

In the initial few months Mahima did only jobwork. She bought handmade paper from the market, and created folders by hand. She would then go around her own neighbourhood and areas close by, looking for buyers.

"I'm not really a marketing person. Nor am I an expert in craft - in fact I am quite clumsy! It was all very hit and miss, I simply learnt on the job!"

This continued for about a year and a half, which is when Mahima met her mentor, Bernd Merzenich, at the Indo-German Export Promotion Council. Impressed by the quality of work, he introduced her to a couple of his friends who wanted to work with handmade paper from India. They booked an order for stationery worth Rs 7 lakhs.

"The wonderful thing was, they gave me half the money in advance! And they went on to become my distributors for Germany, and very good friends."

Mahima decided it was time to start making her *own* paper and headed to the tiny town of Kaalpi in Uttar Pradesh. Why Kaalpi? Because unlike Sanganer - the other hub for handmade production in India - Kaalpi had smaller producers.

"Apart from the recycling aspect, I had also decided to work with small, family-owned units. What's the point of helping those who've won export awards earn a few bucks more?"

And so it was that Mahima - then merely 24 - took the train to Kanpur. Followed by a three hour road journey, sitting on top of a tempo. Her first impression: *bilkul beehad bazaar*. A town in the middle of nowhere.

But the really difficult bit was not getting there; it was a *woman* getting there and wanting to do business.

"Kaalpi is the kind of place where women basically stay indoors. The men there would not even look up and speak to me!"

And when Mahima showed them paper samples, most would simply reply, "*Nahin ban sakta hai...*"

> **"I had a strange set of social skills - I could either talk to people in villages or in foreign countries. My regular middle class social skills were rather sad!"**

Finally, Mahima located one small unit in Kaalpi run by three brothers who were interested in taking up her work. And with the kind of spark she was looking for.

"For me the most important aspect when I look for a small producer is a sense of creativity... sense of adventure *ki haan hum yeh bhi kar sakte hain*. Rather than just wanting to earn money out of doing the same thing again and again... Udai had that quality."

But of course, it meant frequent trips from Delhi to Kaalpi, in the first year. Getting through on phone actually took longer than simply getting onto the overnight train - which is what Mahima got used to doing.

Around this time, Bernd Merzenich returned to Germany and started working for a fair trade company.

"Let's design some packaging for organic food!" he suggested.

And that's how 'Papeterie' - which is what Mahima had named her little company - suddenly became a much bigger business. From a modest Rs 15 lakh turnover in the first two years, by year four revenues had jumped to Rs 40 lakhs.

"We created packaging for Darjeeling tea, meant for export markets. This in fact became the 'bread and butter' for the company."

Working with Udai, using age-old techniques, Papeterie produced paper which was so high in quality that when it was tested in Germany, they concluded, "This is good enough to eat!"

But what actually makes handmade paper so attractive; what is the 'eco' element to it? Well, first of all handmade paper is completely wood-free.

The raw material commonly used is cotton rag - what we know as t-shirt cotton or hosiery. This cotton is pulped and thrashed into tiny pieces in a large machine known as the Hollander Beater; after which it is washed in a roller drum. This process continues for several hours.

Now all you need is a wooden vat filled with water, in which you put a mould - or a giant *chhalni*. Pour the right amount of finely shredded pulp into it and voila - a layer is formed!

On drying this layer turns into a sheet; coat it with starch, smoothen between rollers and there, you have 'paper'.

"The advantage in places like Kaalpi is that even today, there are people who use the purest form of paper making."

The eco aspect is also reflected in Mahima's attempt to make handmade paper a part of everyday life, and not just something to use as a *shaadi ka lifafa*.

"I've been using handmade paper in my Laserjet and Deskjet printer for years! Of course we need to add a special coating to make that possible."

Exports, packaging, production and the joy of working with paper - all this kept Mahima busy enough for six years. Then, she met Vijayendra, a small producer based in Sanganer. And life took a new and interesting turn!

At the time Vijayendra was in bad shape - he had a small paper-making unit, but no orders. In fact, he used to work in a *bhatti* - or brick kiln - to make ends meet.

Vijayendra came to Mahima with some samples of decorative paper.

She said, "We don't work with this kind of *kaagaz*. Can you make something else for me?"

The discussion went back and forth. A few months later Mahima was in Jaipur and going up to Aamer fort to celebrate *navratras*. Vijayendra was with her.

"We both looked down and saw mounds of elephant dung and joked, 'This has great fibre. We should make paper out of it'!"

The moment passed and Mahima returned to Delhi. But the idea remained in her head.

"You think there is scope?" she asked Vijayendra.

"Haan... *bahut* scope *hai*," he replied.

It was a bizarre thought but she decided to do a bit of research on the internet. And surprisingly enough, paper *was* being made from elephant dung in countries like Sri Lanka, Thailand and Malaysia. Although it seemed to be more of a hobby than a business.

This got Mahima thinking - what's the harm in trying it out? She told Vijayendra to start experimenting.

"We took 6-8 months to figure out the process. Initially the paper was too brittle because we used only dung! Then we started mixing

> **"Kaalpi is an interesting place, part of the famous Chambal valley. The first time I went there they asked me, '*Aapko Phoolan Devi ke husband se milwa kar laayein*'?"**

cotton fibre and the texture improved."

In 2003, Mahima sent some samples to her German clients and they agreed to stock a range of products. But a year and a half later they said, "It is not working."

Mahima was not surprised.

"I was constantly telling them that this is not a serious product; it has a very high humour quotient. If you use sober motifs of elephants and grey colour it's not going to sell!"

So life went back to regular, elephant-free paper until 3 years ago, Mahima suddenly decided, let's do something - here in India.

At the time Papeterie was doing steady business of around Rs 70 lakhs per annum.

"The turnover had been pretty much the same for several years - but that never bothered me. When someone asked me, it got me thinking for precisely 25 seconds and then I said, 'Naah. That's not my priority'!"

So selling 'elephant poo paper' under the quirky name Haathi Chaap was really more about challenge. The desire to see how far can we take a crazy idea...

Well, Haathi Chaap did take off - in more ways than one. Over the last 3 years Papeterie's annual revenues have crossed Rs 1 crore. The Indian market was finally ready for something *different*.

"When I started out handmade paper meant an Anokhi bag, or a wedding card. Now people are looking for well designed products, novelty products."

Papeterie sells Haathi Chaap paper in sheet form, and in the form of stationery and children's games. These include *pithu*, snakes and ladders and ludo. In fact, children's products sell the fastest. Products are retailed through eco stores or niche stores which stock humorous and funky stuff.

"There are two kinds of growth; one is that you sell more and two is PR and publicity. Suddenly the work I do has become much more visible!"

---

* Haathichaap sales are expected to touch Rs 15 lakhs in 2009-10. For list of outlets stocking Haathi Chaap visit www.elephantpoopaper.com

Haathi Chaap constitutes only 10% of Papeterie's business but it's the part that gets talked about and written about! Meanwhile getting into retail has certainly increased the volume of work on hand.

The core team at Papeterie is just five people, and it's the kind of place where everybody does everything. Paper is sourced from 3-4 producers; products are manufactured at a nearby workshop on jobwork basis. Mahima and her team manage the design of products, booking of orders, despatch of goods and overall co-ordination.

"The complexity has increased because generally a shop will order about Rs 3000-5000 worth of goods. Whereas in exports we deal with just one large client."

This has meant slightly longer working hours for Mahima - which she is trying to sort out. But where does she see all this going? Will the business grow or just remain steady?

"There are physical limitations right now - the unit Vijayendra operates is very small. I've often been advised to expand but I can't steal the idea from him. So we will grow together."

Mahima's plan is to buy land on the Delhi-Jaipur highway and get Vijayendra to put up a bigger unit. The idea is to produce more paper as well as promote the whole concept of 'paper tourism'. Get school kids to come and stay over the weekend, actually make paper with their own hands.

"I want to expose more people to Haathi Chaap - not just the logo - but the experience!"

Mahima's other dream is to transfer the technology - open small pilot projects in villages next to wildlife sanctuaries.

"If elephant dung can provide a source of income, there would be more respect for wildlife!"

The first such project Mahima tried to implement did not pan out - they decided to open a spa instead. But she is now working with an organisation in Udaipur, making paper from camel dung. Currently

> **"You can't just say elephant paper is eco-friendly, or it's a novelty. You have to sit down and design products from it which people want to buy."**

Papeterie buys dung from them and transports it to Jaipur, where it is converted into paper.

Mahima is currently helping raise funds to set up a unit in Udaipur.

"These are the kind of projects one wants to be able to do in terms of expanding rather than just selling more!" she says.

Luckily for Mahima, she works with people who share her values. Her client in Germany is actually one of the faster growing fair trade organisations in Europe. Fair trade means complete honesty and transparency.

"I sent them my price list and told them exactly how much money I was making; they sent me their price list and how much money they were making."

Margins are comfortable - the standard range is 40% (before overheads) but the Germans in fact always encouraged a slightly higher profit to take care of contingencies. Mahima in fact likes to earmark a small portion of monies earned towards 'development'

8% of Haathi Chaap's profits go towards funding an elephant ambulance in Jaipur. And working with small producers remains a priority, although it's tougher to find genuine ones. And dealing with them is not easy.

"When you work with small producers you get very involved in their personal problems. My first supplier in Kaalpi - Udai - took a family dispute so seriously, that one day he simply said, *"Ab main kaam nahin karoonga."*

A couple of the other small producers Mahima started working with are now several times the size of *her* company. But they still work with her, out of loyalty.

"You know, I could have gone about this business in a very cold-blooded commercial way, and I would have been 4-5 times the size I am now. But it wasn't a very charming or attractive idea."

Ultimately, paper making was an enterprise born out of passion. Passion for recycling. Passion for a simple life, well lived.

"All I ever wanted was enough money to pay my rent and to have a regular middle class lifestyle. With enough leisure time for myself."

Her family - which was initially skeptical - has accepted her unconventional choice of career.

"Women don't work in Jaipur even today. At best, they may have a tailoring unit, they may be teaching, they may be doctors-engineers but they don't do male-dominated things like manufacturing!"

In fact, six months after she began Papeterie, Mahima was also wrestling with personal issues.

"I got divorced at that time and so I put my heart and soul into this business. I had to pick up the pieces, hurry up and really do stuff because I wanted to be financially independent."

And independent she remains.

"I am self sufficient in what I do - I've never felt the need for a partner in business."

Mahima may believe in recycling paper, but her ideas on life and on business are all her own. And those are the most precious natural resources of all...

ADVICE TO YOUNG ENTREPRENEURS

If you have an interesting idea just follow through with it! I have seen a lot of youngsters with an idea who don't pursue it, because they are scared. There's no reason to be scared, India is a great market for entrepreneurs. If it's an interesting idea - just a wee bit different from what's already in the market - it will work.

You must be very adaptable if you want to work in a business at a social or rural level. It often happens that you have a target and you find your supplier has taken off 2 months - for a *shaadi*. It's very frustrating so you have to be patient!

I was never scared, I never once thought, "This will not work". Considering I am not at all business minded. If I could do it - anyone can.

GENTLEMEN PREFER
LETTUCE

Samar Gupta,
Trikaya Agriculture

Samar was a city boy with no burning ambition in life. But when life threw up a challenge, he decided to face it head on. Over the last decade Trikaya Agriculture has matured from a hobby into a flourishing business. Ever expanding the boundaries of 'what can be grown' in India.

You meet people like Samar Gupta at Bombay Gymkhana. They claim to be in 'manufacturing' or 'consulting' - and have business cards to prove it - but no one knows exactly what they do.

The truth is most of them don't do anything, because they don't need to. Samar could have been one of them.

Son of Ravi Gupta, the iconic founder of Trikaya Advertising, he was comfortably placed to lead a life of ease. Not particularly ambitious, at 32, Samar was happy 'helping out' dad in his hobby business of agriculture.

The 'Wake up Sam' moment came when Ravi Gupta passed away at the age of 59. Leaving behind a small company which was losing Rs 2 lakhs a month, and was probably a crazy idea to begin with.

Well, challenge brings out the best in us and so it was to be. Samar put on his hat, picked up the hoe and cracked the whip. With grit and determination, head and heart, he made a roaring success of the business.

In doing so he became a lover of plants, a patron of fruits, a son of the soil.

Samar's story tells me that whether you are born with a wooden, silver or platinum spoon, life is about finding 'meaning'. Something to do on this earth which fires your spirit, moves your soul.

So get down, get dirty, get going... find it!

GENTLEMEN PREFER
LETTUCE

Samar Gupta,
Trikaya Agriculture

Samar Gupta is a third generation Bombayite.

"My grandfather came here from Haryana, I grew up at Napean Sea Road. But from class five onwards I went to boarding school - Mayo College in Ajmer."

Samar was never 'academically inclined'; he loved reading but was definitely not the kind of guy who would mug the night before the exams. And neither was there any pressure from the family to do so.

"My dad - Ravi Gupta - was an advertising man. And he was super liberal in every sense of the word."

Ravi Gupta was, in fact, a legend in the ad world. He worked in the client servicing department of a very successful agency of the '70s known as MCM. Unfortunately, the agency went bust and he found himself at a loose end.

At the age of 35, he set up his own agency - Trikaya.

"I was about 12 years old at that time and I remember for the first two years he struggled a lot. Since he could not get any advertising clients, he would run around and get print jobs, do calendars - that kind of stuff."

And then Trikaya bagged the prestigious Thums Up campaign, from which there was no looking back.

The agency became a 'creative hotshop' - an example for others to follow.

Meanwhile Samar was following no particular path or ambition. He enrolled in St Xavier's college, to study liberal arts. After two years he transferred to Tufts University, near Boston.

"It was an amazing experience. I took courses in economics along with Greek tragedy, typing and comparative religion! But at the end of it - I came back home, came back to India."

The year was 1986. Now the easy option was - join Trikaya Advertising. Learn the ropes, put in your time and one day - take over from the boss. Your dad.

But that was not to be.

"I trained with Trikaya for a few months, but I didn't have the aptitude for this sort of work. I am too outspoken, hate reporting to someone, don't work well within structures!"

So, he did the next best thing. Became the boss at the family-owned printing press - a small business started by his mother to make greeting cards.

"What was really important for me with the printing press was that I was not answerable to people."

An opportunity to benchmark yourself - against yourself.

Samar loved it, and slogged his butt off. The same client would call three times a day, ask him to come across 'immediately' and take details of the next job.

"I would hop into a train and go to Kalina - sometimes twice a day. When you are young you have a lot of energy!" he grins.

Lekin usey karne ke liye motivation chahiye. And the thrill of turning around a loss-making company was motivation enough. In less than two years, the press was making nearly a lakh and a half a month - which was a lot of money, back in 1988.

Samar said to his dad, "I don't see why I should generate profit and take a salary of Rs 5000 a month. I want the business for myself."

Dad replied, "Son, it's a family business."

Samar walked out of the company in a huff.

"I sat around, sulking. Partying too hard. Though we'd fought I continued to live in the same house. My dad was a patient man - he took a lot of crap from me!"

Ultimately Ravi Gupta introduced Samar to a close friend - the brilliant and eccentric Pheroze Engineer. The man had just started a company called 'Ceasefire' and offered the hot-headed young man a job. As his third employee.

"It was fascinating because Pheroze had such a fine mind. Working with him, at least once a day I would say to myself, 'What an

> ## "If I had any other partner I would have fought with them. Now whatever mistakes I made were entirely my fault... and I made a lot of them!"

insight... I would never have thought of that'!"

In the three years Samar spent at Ceasefire, he learnt a lot. The company grew from three employees to one thousand. As Pheroze Engineer's assistant - or *chamcha* as he calls it - Samar was completely hands-on, building the business.

"I handled all the advertising for Ceasefire, bought the hoardings, ensured things happened on schedule. Because Pheroze was a bit of a maverick it was a decent fit, but at end of three years we fought and I left."

The year was 1992, and once again Samar was at a loose end. Partying too hard, with no particular plan in mind about what to do next.

That's when Ravi Gupta said, "Son, I need your help."

By this time Trikaya - the advertising agency was a huge success. Where Ravi Gupta needed help was his agriculture venture. Well, it was not so much a venture as a labour of love.

"Dad had bought six acres of land in a hilly, jungle area, fourteen kilometers from Lonavala. Every Friday at five o'clock he would hop on to the Deccan Queen... Spend two nights there, and take the Sunday evening train back to Bombay."

The idea was to get away from the city, get close to nature. And no, it was not an opulent farmhouse but a *farm*. A *zopadpatti* like structure, without even a bathroom.

"You had to crap in the jungle - that kind of thing. My dad was absolutely into that life and I got the hang of it too! My brother and sister rarely came - they preferred city life."

As Trikaya's fortunes improved, the property was upgraded. A *pakka* structure came up, but it was still very much a farm. A place where you grow things.

"My dad could not go there and just... put his feet up in the air and kill time. He always wanted to be doing something, so we grew vegetables."

But, with a a difference. If the world is growing tomatoes, *kakdi* and *baingan*, why do the same thing? Why not take up a challenge?

"My dad used to travel abroad once a year. so he would bring back seeds - lettuce, Chinese cabbage, broccoli. And that's what we planted."

People said, "You can't grow lettuce in India - it's too hot, it's just not possible!"

And that's what made it all the more exciting. The entire operation was trial and error, learning and unlearning. For every five times a crop was sown, one would survive and get harvested.

"The first five years, we ate it ourselves... gave it to friends. It was not really a business. But in 1987, after five years of dabbling in it, my dad decided to get more serious."

The Lonavala plot was irrigated by well water; when the well ran dry the crop failed. So Ravi Gupta leased another plot of land, in Talegaon, next to the Mulshi river.

Excellent, so now you actually had a truckload of exotic vegetables to sell. But was there a market? A very tiny one - mainly five star hotels, air kitchens, the odd *subziwallah* at Peddar Road. To service them, Ravi Gupta believed things would change.

"Trikaya Agriculture was incorporated in 1991, but it was rough. When I stepped into the business, it was losing two lakh rupees a month."

Liberalisation was just kicking in, the share market was booming. Ravi Gupta was taking money out of one successful business - the advertising agency - and pumping it into a basket case. Agriculture.

Samar said, "Why don't you just invest in the market, build your retirement fund!"

But Ravi Gupta would have none of it.

"This is where I definitely give him credit. He had the vision to start the business - and stick with it back then."

Sensing the pain point, Samar agreed to step in and handle the marketing side.

"I went and met all the five star hotels and very passionately told them, "We can give you broccoli, we can give you iceberg lettuce. All the stuff you are importing, we can give you at 1/4th the price."

The chefs were delighted, until a few weeks later Samar returned with a sorry face. Four out of five crops were still failing, so how could he guarantee supply?

"You can do it once, you can do it twice, but the third time you cut a really sorry figure. I had a big showdown with my dad."

What was the point of marketing two tons of Chinese cabbage when ultimately, you produced only 20 kgs? Why bother to hardsell to clients?

"I was really rude to my father, I told him he was just flying a kite."

Ravi Gupta was hurt, but in his characteristic quiet way he said, "Come with me. I will show you what we are doing on the farm."

It was summer, extremely hot. There was a manager on the farm by the name of Kishore who promised that in seven days, a couple of truckloads of Chinese cabbage would be harvested.

"Come, let's go see it," said Ravi Gupta.

There was no *pakka* road; after trekking half a km in the mid-day heat, father and son arrived at the plot. To find a patch of land which had not been ploughed. Where seeds had not even been sown.

Kishore had been lying through his teeth.

"We looked at each other and said, 'This is what we are up against'!"

Kishore was fired on the spot. Packets of imported seeds were found, spilling out of an abandoned drum. It was not a pretty picture.

"You see, my father was used to working with professionals. In Bombay, if you told a manager to do something, it got done. You did not personally check on them, or micro-manage!"

Despite these horrors, Ravi Gupta did not give up. He continued to handle the production in his gentle, love-thy-neighbour style. And gave Samar a free hand - in marketing. As well as a 50% stake in the company, to keep him motivated.

And yet, in 1997, Trikaya Agriculture was making losses; it was heavily subsidised.

"I remember one month there was no money to pay salaries and my dad simply called the Trikaya accountant and wrote out a cheque for one lakh rupees."

And this is the way it might have continued, *dheeme dheeme, aaraam se*, had Fate not intervened.

In late 1996, Ravi Gupta was diagnosed with stomach cancer. He passed away in May 1997, at the age of 59.

"He would not even discuss the possibility of dying... let alone a formal handover or division of assets. It was just so sudden...," he trails off.

> ## "When I took loans from the market at 32% interest, I was told, "*Yeh Dawood bhai ka paisa hai.*" Just to let me know I had to give it back."

The family got lucky. Grey Advertising from New York already owned a 55% stake in Trikaya Advertising. They were keen to buy out the rest. Narottam Sekhsaria was MD of Gujarat Ambuja Cement - an important client of Trikaya and a close friend of Ravi Gupta.

He negotiated the deal, and it was a sweet one.

"My mom did a brilliantly generous thing, rarely done in most *bania* families. She kept 2/5th of my father's estate and divided the rest equally among the three of us."

Hmm, lucky you! *Aagey kaam karne ki zaroorat nahin*!

But, it wasn't quite like that. Although there was a sizeable 'cash' element to the settlement, access to it was limited for the first three years. And, Samar got substantially less. Instead, Sekhsaria transferred all the shares of Trikaya Agriculture to him.

He said, "Samar, you may not see it now but one day you will thank me for this."

And, he does.

"Best deal I ever made," he exclaims.

To be sure, the company was losing money; everyone had given it up as a lost cause. But Samar could sense the potential, the light at the end of the tunnel.

"Had the shares been divided between my brother, my sister and me, I would have been answerable to them. I would probably not been able to do things exactly as I wanted - make mistakes, but ultimately find my way!"

And what were those things?

In 1997, Trikaya Agriculture had revenues of Rs 25 lakhs, and was making losses month on month. The very first thing Samar had to do was simple: stop bleeding.

"Dad was a bit of a dreamer. He said, 'I am sick of the Indian market, I want to export.' So we were exporting snow peas to Australia."

It was not a viable proposition. Over two years, the company lost Rs 25 lakhs trying to make it happen.

"The moment my father passed away I shut it. Actually, I flew to Perth and met the buyer. He was lying to us, claiming to receive spoiled goods."

There are crooks in any kind of business, and more in some trades than others.

"Vegetables?" remarks Samar, "You have to look really hard to find an honest man here."

Samar decided, *eent ka jawaab paththar se.* No more treating people softly, giving them benefit of doubt, believing in their inherent goodness.

"My dad insisted we must build 'relationships' with vendors. He would sell cheap in summer - when we were the only people who could supply lettuce. The idea was that the vendors would then buy from us in winter as well."

The reality was that in winter, there were many suppliers and vendors simply bought from whoever sold the cheapest.

"I introduced a 'morning' price, a price which fluctuates from day to day. Take it, or leave it!"

People whispered, "Ravi Gupta was a great man... this fellow will destroy everything."

Samar took it in his stride. This was no popularity contest; it was a battle for survival. And it had to be fought on many fronts.

"A farm is not like running a factory - there are tremendous variables. Too much sun, too little sun, too much rain, too little rain... If the manager wants to fool around, he can have a new excuse for the next hundred weeks!"

You need people you can trust, people who *deliver*. Samar quickly fired half of the employees on the farm. They had been slacking, taking advantage of their soft-hearted *bade sahab*.

> **"I tend to be aggressive and in your face which I think is required in the vegetable business. It's full of sharks!"**

Now, of course, there was no Ravi Gupta. No *annadaata*, no life support for the company... In fact, Samar borrowed money at 32% interest, to tide over the initial months. Simply to pay the staff and keep the tractors ploughing.

"The pressure of actually running a business and keeping your cashflows positive sank in. It was a huge dose of reality for me."

The 'tough love' act with vendors, with employees - saved the day. Everybody realised Samar meant business, and business it was that got done.

"I got lucky, I was in the right place at the right time," he shrugs.

Demand for exotic vegetables was growing in leaps and bounds. Samar leased a stall at Crawford market and it did brisk sales. The star attractions were broccoli and iceberg lettuce.

"Iceberg, in particular, was - and is! - very difficult to grow in Indian conditions," says Samar, with obvious pride. It's an expertise which gave Trikaya a definite edge.

What was the secret? Well, attention to detail - lots of little things. Importing the right seeds, using 'seedling trays', frequent weeding, drip irrigation and very importantly - cold storage.

"Funnily enough," says Samar, "The cold store was set up for the client in Perth. Well, that did not work out but it helped us become a major supplier of lettuce to McDonald's when they entered India!"

Life works in mysterious ways... And solving those mysteries - or at least puzzling over them - is what keeps the entrepreneur busy, day to day.

And once he took over, the first couple of years, it was really about *being* there. Putting in a ten hour day on the farm - or in the office - then spending four hours doing 'research'. Learning new techniques, finding new plants to grow. Fertilising the mind with the abundant resources available - on the internet.

One thing Samar realised was: farming ain't rocket science. You don't need to set up fancy greenhouses with Israeli collaboration. In fact all the companies which put up those capital intensive projects have since gone defunct.

"Technology can be simple - take these seedling trays," he says, holding up something like the plastic contraption we use to make ice cubes in the refrigerator. "You take care of the plant when it's a baby - in the first month - automatically it has a much better chance of survival."

"I have a little angel on my shoulder taking care of me."

The trays contain coconut dust - not soil - so the seedlings are not exposed to pathogens. The trays are kept in simple greenhouses for one month. Then, workers remove the plugs* and plant them in the field. Ready to take on the sun, the wind, the world.

It's an expensive business, with each tray costing Rs 250. At Trikaya there are 5000 such trays - an investment of over Rs 15 lakhs.

"It's always tempting to cut corners, buy cheap quality trays. But if you take shortcuts, you will fail. We learnt that lesson early on!"

Another lesson - never put all your eggs in one basket. Scatter your seeds, hedge your risk. And you can do that in many ways.

Take the mix of crops. Trikaya agriculture was the first to introduce a host of exotic vegetables - baby corn, cherry tomato, yellow squash.

"We created the market, we made decent money. Then, the pyjama-clad farmer next door caught on, prices fell and it became unviable for us!"

That's why Trikaya agriculture grows not 5, not 10, but 80 different kinds of vegetables. Including some, which have little or no demand today.

"See this," he points to a beauty with dark green leaves and a succulent red stem. "This is Swiss chard. I don't have many customers for it, but we're promoting it!"

Fennel, parsley, chives, pandanus leaf... Think of a five-star-menu-vegetable, and it's here. Greens, reds, yellows and the heady fragrance of herbs in the air. But what if the *dhotiwallahs* figure out how to grow these too....

Well, lettuce remains Trikaya's trump card.

"Our niche is in items which are delicate, which cannot just be stuffed into a *bori*. We store vegetables at 2 to 4 degrees centigrade soon after harvesting, and transport them in refrigerated vans. The average farmer cannot afford to do all this!"

And neither can he invest in a plant with a German vacuum-packing

---

* A plug is a self-contained unit which ensures seedlings can be transplanted without tearing the roots.

machine, which is what Samar did to bag Subway. Today, his biggest buyer of lettuce, and one who has made Trikaya its sole supplier of this sandwich-essential.

In a sparse and super-hygienic facility, cap-glove-coat-and-boot-clad workers tear apart and then sort lettuce leaves. Insect free, fresh and crisp leaves are then vacuum-packed, giving the delicate vegetable a shelf life of 7 days.

"Supplying lettuce to Subway and McDonald's is big business. You know McDonald's alone picks up 30 tons a month! But, we continue to supply 5 kgs a day to folks like Oberoi."

And to 160 other such institutional clients.

Their chefs also buy sweet marjoram and leek and radicchio. Introducing the adventurous Indian to the sight, smell and taste of new veggies. Which Trikaya hopes will one day find their way to the dinner table...

"We're growing by 25% a year. And that's because India has changed, people are experimenting with food, trying out new things!"

Ten years ago, there were 4 stalls in Crawford market selling exotic vegetables, now there are 40.

"But," points out Samar, "They are all pure traders, while we grow *and* we sell. So there's no middleman - out of every Rs 100 the customer spends, Rs 80 goes to Trikaya."

And remember, that's tax-free income. A privilege only the agriculture sector enjoys.

"Of course, I don't think such exemptions were meant to benefit people like me," he shrugs. "But that's how it is..."

And as an 'outsider', Samar has learnt - the hard way - that it's best to keep a low profile.

"A couple of years ago, we had a slight *tapori* problem at one of our farms.. The locals came and said 'You have to employ only our people.' And they threatened violence."

Samar promptly shifted his 'head office' from Induri 7 kms away to Babhidhal - nicknamed as 'Babydoll'. This land is leased, not owned by Trikaya. Which means the owner - a '*dada*' in the area - keeps the peace.

Sow not your seeds in a single farm; Samar has been expanding, across geographies.

In 1997, Trikaya agriculture was a single farm near Talegaon, of 55 acres. Today it has 225 acres under cultivation across 7 farms. The majority in and around Pune, but also 12 acres in Ooty and 22 acres in Konkan.

"In Konkan we grow ultra-tropical crops and in Ooty, fruits and vegetables which thrive in colder climate."

But how does one manage all this? Ensure seeds are sown every week, transplanted at the right time, growing healthily and ready to harvest...

Well, it's a combination of soldiers and systems.

The 'field marshal' is Hari Manje Gowda - whom Samar has known since they were both 13.

"When he came from the village, he knew only Kannada. Within a year he was speaking Hindi, Marathi, English and handling all kinds of admin work at the agency!"

But the desk job wasn't quite suiting him. So, back in 1989, he was sent off to the farm.

"Hari took over from Kishore - the crooked guy who hadn't even been planting the seeds. Basically, he was thrown into the deep end and he simply shone."

Optimistic, hard working and blindly loyal, Hari is the Man Friday who holds the fort at the farm. Ably supported by two young agricultural college graduates. Satyavan Pawar, who's seen eight summers at Trikaya and Ravi Wagh, who's been around for fourteen.

"Between the three of them, they handle all seven farms beautifully. There is no need for me to micro-manage!" laughs Samar.

Of course, he is involved in the planning, the strategy.

"I referee the monthly meetings where the sales and production teams sit down together and decide how much to grow of which crop."

Trikaya Agriculture is now a Rs 6.5 crore operation*, employing 35 people in Mumbai - in the marketing office - and 240 workers on the farm.

"Vegetable farming is very labour intensive and it does not come cheap. The minimum wage for agricultural workers is now Rs 120 per person, per day!"

While many employers simply wink and undercut, Trikaya pays in full. Because it's the right thing to do and because, money is hardly the force which drives Samar.

---

* Lettuce and broccoli bring in 40% of Trikaya's revenues.

> **"The first time my dad took broccoli to Crawford market, the wholesale vendors laughed, saying, *'Yeh to sada hua gobhi hai.'* They wouldn't even buy it for the price of cauliflower!"**

"At the age of 17, I decided I want to be single, I don't want to have children. I'm just not a very domestic person, a person who wants that kind of responsibility."

So there's no incentive to save, to 'leave something behind'.

"It was never about buying my own flat quickly, or salting away money so my kid can study in the US. Anything I earned was pumped back into the business. I keep buying more land every year!"

The most important thing for Samar - to learn a lot, do work that's interesting. And at Trikaya there's been plenty of opportunity for both.

"People say, *'Arre tarkaari bech raha hai!'* But it's a good business. You don't deal with sophisticated people, most of the time you don't speak English but I don't have any hang-ups!"

And neither is he hugely ambitious.

"Mr Sekhsaria asked me recently, 'Samar can you take Trikaya from Rs 7 crores to Rs 35 crores?...' And I don't have an answer..."

The question is not just 'can I do it' but 'do I really *want* to do it'?

In 2007 Samar did set up a processing and canning unit, to manufacture gourmet foods such as pickled onions, paprika and jalapenos. And, he's quietly been building brand 'Trikaya' by labeling the produce he sells to retail customers.

Scaling up to the next level will take a whole lot more: money, manpower, messy expansion. And there is no dearth of investors.

One such gentleman told Samar, "I am willing to put in Rs 30 crores, the risk is mine. What are you afraid of?"

Samar replied, "That's exactly what I'm afraid of... This is my life. My legacy. I have a responsibility towards the people who work for me...!"

It may look like an easy business, a lucrative business. Nothing ever is. You plant 12 types of beans and one might click...But you keep at it.

"We have a special plot - an R&D plot - where we constantly try out new plants, new varieties. And my latest passion is growing fruits."

I get a taste of *seetaphal* - a giant, almost seedless variety which will hit stores sometime soon. And that's just the tip of the custard.

"I went to Hawaii to learn how to grow 'palm heart'. This summer I'll be in Ecuador, staying with this amazing guy who's a fruit farmer... learning all I can from him!"

There is delight in his eyes as he speaks.

The seed of possibilities, yet to come.

Mehnat ka phal, ever so sweet.

ADVICE TO YOUNG ENTREPRENEURS

If you are from the city and want to get into farming, first thing, don't be in a hurry. You won't be making a quick buck. The first two years, you'll be learning, you'll encounter problems - completely unexpected ones.

Find your niche and find what excites you. Growing Alphonso mangos on a hundred acre farm may be a good business but there are so many people doing it. It's not a challenge - and that's what keeps me going. Challenges, doing new things, different things.

And remember, as you sow, shall you reap. It's true in farming, and pretty much everything in life...

Sow good 'seeds' and you will reap rich dividends.

ZUBAAN

Creative people need a platform to express themselves. When that talent is unique, the platform must be created. And in doing so, the artist too becomes an 'entrepreneur'.

THE
STORYTELLER

**Abhijit Bansod,
Studio ABD**

As a young NID graduate, Abhijit Bansod wondered why *desi* designers were always inspired by the West. He went on to pioneer the uniquely Indian 'Heritage' and 'Raga' collections at Titan, and now runs his own product design company.

When Abhijit Bansod emails me his office address I am intrigued.

"Lakeview farm, off Whitefield-Old Airport Road."

I brave two hours of cacophonic morning traffic in Bangalore to arrive at an oasis of peace. I am greeted by natural light, oxygen-rich air, and one very grounded designer.

"Show me your watch? It's a Raga!" he exclaims with delight.

How ironic - the designer meeting his design creation on the wrist of a just-introduced stranger.

I tell him how much I love this watch, with its slip-on bracelet style.

He nods, like he's heard it a million times before, but still can't get enough.

And why not!

It was the vision of Abhijit Bansod which transformed Titan into a design-centric company telling genuine Indian stories. Not through advertising, but in the DNA of the product itself.

Abhijit's story illustrates how one passionate individual can influence an entire system.

That you have to be patient and bide your time - to reap rich dividends.

And creative people and business managers can complement and supplement each other.

To create a new economic raga.

THE
STORYTELLER

Abhijit Bansod,
Studio ABD

Abhijit Bansod was born and brought up in Nagpur. It was a carefree childhood, with no burning desire to be a 'topper'.

"My rank was 50+ in a class of 80. That gave me a lot of freedom to do what I really wanted to do..."

Close to Abhijit's home was a lake, and barracks from colonial times.

"My brother and I spent most of the summer holidays jumping in the lake, swimming and doing anything and everything outside the house."

Both parents worked in government offices. Mom with the Employment Exchange, dad in the Commissioner's office.

"So luckily our home was *khaali* in the afternoons..." he grins.

Children without 'something to do' and someone to watch over them would scare the hell out of modern parents. But Abhijit is grateful.

"It gave us so much hands-on experience in dealing with people, in dealing with situations, improvisation." Let a kid think for himself; he will find his own solutions!

Still, the problem of 'what to do in life' remained.

"I used to really like doing many things with materials. But I had no idea that I would ever be an artist or designer. I actually failed in 'elementary' - the basic drawing examination - and my mom said, 'I don't think you are meant for this'!"

Besides, 'designing' was not a career option kids from Nagpur were aware of in the mid-eighties. It was engineering, medicine or IAS.

So after class 10, Abhijit actually became 'really serious' in life and secured decent marks. Enough to make it to the Government Engineering College in Karad. But more than mechanical engineering, Abhijit found himself drawn to design and all things creative.

"I used to make posters. My friends would design the software for games while I developed the interface."

It was but natural then for Abhijit to apply for a design program. He was accepted at both IDC (Industrial Design Centre, IIT Bombay) and NID (National Institute of Design, Ahmedabad).

IDC was paying a stipend but after visiting NID Abhijit just *knew* he had to be there. He took an education loan and the day after his last engineering exam, he was at the campus in Paldi. Taking his first class in projects.

NID was a once in a lifetime experience. It was about learning and unlearning, yet retaining the essence of who he was through it all.

"I am a stupidly optimistic kind of person. I always see lots of possibilities and make something from what I have, rather than miss what I don't have!"

And that included skills such as presentation and sketching, which Abhijit was learning for the first time - at age 23.

So NID was a bit of a struggle. What's more, Abhijit felt like a cultural misfit. Everything was so *Western*. There was no connect with the user - the *aam aadmi* of India.

What's more, marketing was seen as an enemy of design.

Seniors would say, "In companies you have to fight with marketing to get ahead."

The product was seen as one thing, and the 'brand' as something else altogether. Which simply baffled Abhijit.

Meanwhile, with his very *desi* bent of mind, Abhijit did a couple of projects at NID using natural materials and crafts.

"I specialised in product design. I really wanted to do things inspired from India. But my intention was not to use craft as a *craft* but to combine it with international sophistication."

Create something emotional, evocative, with an identity quite its own.

> **"Ideas take time to get accepted -
> I don't give up! The other tool I have is
> to visualise. It doesn't cost anything, it's
> just the effort of sketching and putting
> down what I can see in my head."**

NID exposed Abhijit to a variety of disciplines - textiles, graphic design, animation, video, ceramics. You learn so much by merely looking - but Abhijit went a step further and loved to collaborate.

"I used to take help from textile design for colours, graphic design to build things around the product... I think it helped me to understand how each one really brings in a different way of thinking and you can still co-exist."

And in fact create magic.

Abhijit had the *keeda* in him of doing 'something different'. For his diploma project, he approached Bajaj, with the idea of doing a 'people's car' in an autorickshaw base.

The company showed no interest at all.

"That did not happen," he grins. "But maybe it was a good thing for me. The auto industry is too slow, it takes 8-9 years to develop a product!"

Instead, Abhijit found himself at Titan, working on wall clocks. Here again he had the idea of combining the old with the new. To bring traditional craft to a precision industry.

The craft he chose was 'Etikopaka' - the famous wooden toys with lacquer colours made in a small Andhra village by the same name.

Abhijit went and lived among the artisans, and observed them carefully.

"I learnt how they developed amazing colours from vegetables. How their model is completely sustainable and how can I replicate what they do - but at a different scale and in a different industry."

The idea was not to create one loftily inspired piece of art but *democratise* good looks. Because beauty can be affordable, and mass-produced. But how do you industrialise a lovingly hand crafted object? That was the challenge!

After each visit to Etikopaka, Abhijit would come back with a prototype and then sit in the factory with the engineers. Chiselling out the finer requirements of production.

The hard work paid off when this diploma project with its uniquely Indian inspiration won second prize at an international design competition. And it wasn't a mere showpiece - over 4,000 of these clocks were sold. The company was thrilled and offered Abhijit a permanent position.

The year was 1998 and Titan already had five product designers. But they were not really *designing* anything.

"Gents watches were inspired from the Swiss markets and ladies watches were miniature versions of gents watches. So it was very boring!"

Design was a support function; the company was led by marketing.

Of course, as a young designer you were only dimly aware of all this. The first task at hand was to understand the A to Z of making a watch.

"A watch is very small, very precise, it's very personal because you wear it on the body. There were certain norms in the industry at that time which we had to follow. Within that yes, we were innovating, but nothing very radical."

Abhijit spent five years on the job, absorbing and understanding everything around him.

"Then I reached a stage where I could contribute. I could say, "This is the way it should be, and they would listen to me."

Abhijit got his big break in 2002 when he produced the 'Heritage' collection. A range of fine, high-end watches drawing inspiration from Indian architecture through the ages.

"There is so much influence of history. Starting from the pure Hindu base (*mandala*), to the Buddhist influence during Ashoka's time. Then you come to Rajputana-Islamic mix and of course the colonial period."

"I don't give so much importance to skills- they can be acquired! What you need is the right attitude."

The watches were born, not out of a marketing need but pure gut feel. The vision of a young designer.

But soon enough, the marketing team realised the power of storytelling. When you had something unique and interesting to say, you did not need an ad budget running into crores! You could make an impact with just Rs 20-25 lakhs.

To illustrate, the 'Heritage' collection was launched in conjunction with Music Today. Musicians like Taufiq Qureshi were invited to jam at the launch, and dedicate a composition to each watch.

Both the event and the watches received wide critical acclaim. Subsequently, the collection also did brisk sales*.

The 'Heritage' collection was a turning point not just for Abhijit, but for Titan as a company. Design began *leading* the marketing effort. It inspired new ways of reaching out to the consumer, of getting him to the store.

This turnaround led to the introduction of 'Raga', Titan's range of watches for the Indian woman.

"We decided not to be a me-too brand. We will celebrate the Indian jewellery through 'raga' forms - no one in the world will have those kind of watches."

Thus was born a one of a kind range. Bangle and bracelet forms took over from leather straps. Dials reflected the Indian sensibility, matching the vibrant colours and design of traditional clothes. Yet, with subtlety and a sense of class.

"Then we did a collection called Black inspired by 'digital life'. We upgraded the Casio kind of watch from gimmicky kid stuff to a thing of beauty and sophistication."

Of course, it was not a 'purely creative' process. The design team would sit with marketing and understand the target segment - what kind of person the collection should appeal to. Then comes the

> "I had studied Japanese design philosophy, Scandinavian design philosophy, Italian design philosophy and I used to wonder... Is there an Indian design philosophy?"

---

* Till date the Heritage collection has generated revenues of over Rs 20 crores .

"I think 'Heritage' also worked because we were ready for it. All eyes were on India - Bollywood, curry, Arundhati Roy. The things we used to label *desi* were suddenly very cool."

design brief, based on which you arrive at the 'story' which needs to be told to take the product to the next level. The level of experience.

At every step of the way there is a lot of communication, exchange of ideas. At the end of it, the design team presents its 'story'.

"Generally designers are asked to present many options. But here if they wanted four, we would present five designs. That is the confidence I gave my team - we have followed a process and we are sure of what we are doing."

Once the designs were selected, marketing got into the act and asked the advertising agency to start thinking about communication. By the time watches were in production, the promotional material and strategy would be ready.

"Not that last minute you give a creative sounding name to the collection - maybe while doing the shoot. That used to happen, it still happens in many industries, even today!"

Over the next 5 years the design team created collection after collection. Each with its own distinct identity.

Fastrack was transformed from a fuddy duddy range into an iconic youth brand. Within Fastrack there were fun collections like 'masala' using East-meets-West style of an MTV.

"We took a pure Indian element like the Maharastrian *chaddi* and made a style statement, but not in an obvious or loud way."

At the other end of the spectrum the team produced Nebula - a range of luxury watches.

"Using gold and diamond alone will not sell the watch. You need to give each piece some meaning, an emotional connect," explains Abhijit.

But detailing matters as well. For the Nebula collection the team worked with calligrapher Achyut Palav.

"We just thought it would be so amazing to bring these two things together."

"Though at home you are so Indian, outside you put on a Western façade. So if it is a 'corporate collection' you will put Roman numbers on the dial!"

Design inspiration comes from immersion. For the Heritage collection, that meant visiting palaces and absorbing the influences. Then picking one key element - like the *jharokha* from Hawa Mahal to communicate the essence of Rajputana.

"When we worked on the 'Chocolate collection' for Raga we went to chocolate factories, chocolate shops, chocolate spas. You need to absorb the experience before you can express it through design!"

And once you do, you need all the support possible at the factory level.

"It is a huge investment in terms of tooling. We need the right specifications, and you have to keep pushing manufacturing to deliver exactly what you want. Things they've never done before!"

In any other place the designer might be told "Sorry, not possible."

Here the impossible *had* to be made possible; the company's future depended on it.

"So, it's like being an intrapreneur?" I ask.

"Yes!" he agrees. "Your work does not end at the drawing board. You work to take it from dream to reality."

And in what is a very rare honour, Titan even gave Abhijit his name on the back of every Heritage watch.

"The faith they had in me was amazing… It's a culture of freedom and complete trust."

In fact from the very beginning, Titan allowed designers to keep doing something 'on the side'.

"I didn't freelance for other companies, but I did my own work. I developed a line of home accessories - and it was all about telling stories. Really fun stuff."

Abhijit held exhibitions in Bangalore, Chennai and Delhi but it was never a serious *business*. It could have been, had he quit and focused his energies there instead of sticking with Titan. But he has no regrets.

"Corporates have the power to globally reach the masses, which I could never have."

Yet after close to 10 years with the company he felt the urge to move on and explore the world.

"I had worked with everything from plastic to platinum in watches. I felt the time had come to pursue other dreams."

About two years ago he spoke to the management - they requested him to wait for a year. He was asked to develop the new team and of course complete work on Heritage collection II - something very dear to his heart.

Abhijit officially left Titan in October 2008, leaving behind a team of eight designers. He now runs 'Abhijit Bansod Designs' - or Studio ABD - a company specialising in product design and the 'Indian story'.

In less than a year, ABD has produced one iconic product: a table lamp for BPL.

"The design brief was to do something so that kids can study when the electricity goes during exam time. The lamp would provide 6 hours battery backup - that's all I was told"

From that point how do you bring out the 'story'? Through everything, starting from the form.

"First of all, I had to push them to do smaller batteries, because you can't have a large inverter sitting on your table!"

Then came the story of 'Halo'. The lamp became the friend who comes to help you - so much so that it seems to be saying hello as it glows in the dark.

"Because it was for kids I have given it soft corners and a jelly-like, animated form. It almost feels like the lamp is talking to you, bending its neck! Also, we used LED, which is a new kind of lighting - unlike bulbs it does not produce any heat. In fact Shankar Netralaya has certified the quality of light."

"I had no idea I would ever be a designer. In fact, I failed in 'elementary' - the basic drawing examination - and my mom said, 'I don't think you are meant for this' !"

It's a marriage of technology and imagination - and amazingly, took just seven months to actually reach the market. Even more amazing was the fact that it was manufactured at BPL's own factory in Kerala.

"I got power from the MD to get what I wanted done. I had his complete trust and authority."

The factory was told, "Whatever Abhijit says is right. Now find a way to get it done!"

The result is stunning. The 'Halo' lamp* has got amazing reviews worldwide and a growing fan following.

"Some 200 blogs have written about the product - Koreans, Japanese, Spanish - and it is just power of design. There may be many products in LED lamps but this is that one iconic product."

Like the iPod?

"Exactly."

So there is a kid from Bangalore, studying at the Doon School. He has taken 10 lamps back with him in various colours - for his friends.

"It is wonderful to see that we are creating this community which is so bonded to something. That is why Apple is Apple and others are just products."

The question is, how do you replicate over and over again this process - whether for a small enterprise or a big industry. The four member team at ABD constantly ponders over that.

"Product design is a very short cycle as compared to the large cycle of learning, absorbing, seeing things together, new materials, experimenting. We try and visit many fairs - material fairs, interior fairs, craft fairs, watch fairs, everything possible."

Studio ABD works with the best of exhibition designers, copywriters, and so on - for specific projects. And advances in CAD/ CAM technology certainly make it easier as well.

"The client can see a rendering which is 100% like the actual product and take a call. We make a dummy product which can be

> "Give us a chance to create an iconic product. But don't ask us to only change your outer shell, it has to come from *within*."

* This lamp is sold by BPL under the brandname StudyLite.

> **"If you start seeing design as the core of what you do, the way you do business will change. In India, Titan has done it, so has Tata Motors."**

tested with consumers, shown to dealers and so on."

With a hi-tech prototype machine available, it takes just 3 days to create a working model of the design from the dummy reference!

Among other notable work, ABD designed the IPL trophy. And also has a range of very interesting products, some of which are scattered around the office. Others he shows me on his PC screen.

Terracota computer speakers.

A vase inspired by devotees who pierce their tongues.

An incense stick-holder which keeps the ashes from falling everywhere.

"There is a belief that this ash should be disposed off only in a certain manner, so these rituals become systems and systems become products."

Speaking of systems, Abhijit has created a new design process inspired by the cycle of *karma*.

"Today designers are not responsible for their creation from birth to death. So again the idea was to really bring in the Indian way of life, where we reused almost everything.

Using RFID technology it may actually be possible - someday - to track a product from the time it is created, to the end of its life.

At a more practical level, ABD has growth and revenue targets. Well, sort of.

So far business has come in mainly on word of mouth and on the basis of Abhijit's credentials.

He realizes it will need someone who can focus on business development.

"I believe I will find that person and spend my time on the creative process. We do not want to be a design service provider, we want to be known for design consultancy which creates and helps companies innovate and connect people through storytelling."

"You have to figure out what to do from your heart and your stomach."

This could mean projects for companies, or even licensing of ABD designs to anyone who wants to take them to scale, commercially.

"Let someone manage everything and make a lot of money; we would want just a part of it."

Of course, Abhijit would like to build his own brand - and is looking for funding. But he is also quite content doing what he does right now. From the beautiful little haven he has created at Lakeview farm (can one even call it an 'office'?!)

Abhijit grins like he knows exactly what I mean.

"Our studio was in this small one BHK place earlier and I used to tell my wife, "Amrita, imagine if we get a place here -at Lakeview Farm." I realised 'dil se maango to mil jaata hai'."

The windows are open - a gentle breeze is blowing in.

"I get good sleep at night and lots of oxygen."

And I am sure - sweeter, more spectacular dreams.

<u>ADVICE TO YOUNG ENTREPRENEURS</u>

We have to really be proud of where we come from and I think the genuineness will reflect in what you do. Your work should reflect an Indian design vocabulary.

It could be opulent, it could be minimal, but it must *celebrate* who and what we are.

Instead of another vaccum cleaner which looks like a spaceship why not a hi-tech *jhaadu* suitable for Indian homes.

Many designers are very good at their craft, but if you want to make an impact and reach out to many people, you have to learn how to manage the business of design. This could mean partnering with an entrepreneur who can sell your vision and market your products, because designers aren't very good at that!

TRUTH SHALL
PREVAIL

Paresh Mokashi,
'Harishchandrachi Factory'

Paresh Mokashi wanted to be an actor, but found his niche as a playwright and director on the Marathi stage. A chance reading of Dadasaheb Phalke's biography led him to on a new adventure - a widely acclaimed feature film which was India's official entry at the Oscars in 2009.

Paresh Mokashi has a face which speaks as loudly as his words. His eyebrows vault, eyes dance and mouth frequently breaks into an expansive grin.

The man has reason to be pleased with himself. His first ever feature film *Harishchandrachi Factory* - made in Marathi, with no big stars, no songs, no dance - was India's official entry to the Oscars for the year 2009.

But, it took twenty years for Paresh to become an 'overnight success'.

Drawn to theatre and acting as a college student, Paresh struggled for many years before finally making his mark as a writer and director on the Marathi stage. *Lekin is bande mein kuch keeda tha, kuch alag tha.* Every play he did stood out as 'crazy' and different.

Paresh is an eccentric genius, and therefore, it is hardly surprising that he set out to make a film about another eccentric genius. The father of Indian film making, Dadasaheb Phalke.

Phalke was an entrepreneur, a man who took risks to realise his dream. He raised capital to finance his great adventure of making India's first feature film. Never once doubting his *paagalpan,* or thinking *ki yeh* nahin *ho sakta hai.*

Which is exactly how Paresh made *Harishchandrachi Factory* 96 years later.

Whatever the year, whatever the era, you can live your life like it's a movie.

Write your own script, and direct it with confidence.

One day you'll give your grandchildren a speech on life well lived...

And it will feel like an Oscar.

TRUTH SHALL
PREVAIL

Paresh Mokashi,
'Harishchandrachi Factory'

Paresh Mokashi was born in Pune, son of a journalist.

"I did my schooling in Dr B N Purandare Bahuvidh Vidyalaya, Lonavala. After SSC, I went back to Pune for my higher education."

Paresh joined Modern College in Pune and enrolled for a BA in geography.

But he spent most of his time dabbling in Marathi theatre.

"I used to act when I was in school - everybody does that. But when I came to Pune it was a big world, a different world. I was exposed to lots of things and one of them was professional theatre."

Paresh joined the 'Theatre Academy'* - a well respected theatre group known for staging plays like *Ghashiram Kotwal, Mahanirvan, Mahapur, Begum Barwe* and *Teen Paishyacha Tamasha* (adapted from Bertolt Brecht's 'Three Penny Opera').

"I started doing small roles in their new productions as well as helping backstage with props and costumes."

In 1990, Theatre Academy started collaborating with GRIPS Theatre, Berlin - a famous German theatre group which focuses on children. GRIPS does not believe in the typical fantasy, magic or *raakshas* type stories. Their productions are inspired by realistic themes, such as single parenthood. But seen from the point of view of children.

"These plays were highly entertaining as well as educating - for both parents and kids. I became the lead actor of that movement - of the plays we adapted from GRIPS and staged in Marathi."

* *Jabbar Patel, Mohan Agashe and Satish Alekar were some of the names associated with Theatre Academy*

At the time, Paresh was completing his last year in college. After graduating, he joined Theatre Academy 'full time'. But it was not a commercial kind of set up. Theatre Academy didn't pay its actors - everybody was in it out of sheer passion for theatre. But then came the question of *rozi-roti*.

Perhaps theatre can remain a hobby, *bete*, while you go get yourself a real job?

"For the sake of my family, I gave the UPSC exam, even did a computer course. But my heart was not in it. At the same time I was not working hard enough to establish myself as an actor... So my family must have gone through hell at that time!"

In the mid 90s, Paresh shifted to Mumbai. Luckily, his family owned a flat in Dadar which he could use as a base.

"During those days I got friendly with Sanjana Kapoor, who runs Prithvi Theatre. I became part of the core group which worked on the annual theatre festival. Apart from that my struggle to get acting roles continued - without much success!"

The trouble was Paresh was no good at auditions. Only producers or directors who had seen him on stage offered him work.

"I did a couple of Marathi films as well as some television episodes. But it was not very satisfying. I realised that I will not go far because I am not the kind of person who is successful in self promotion. A very essential quality for any actor!"

So it was a tricky phase, a phase when there were many questions, and few answers. Yes, he was finally earning enough to survive. But what of the future? Would he remain a mere spectator on the stage of his own life?

And then, in 1999, destiny opened a new door. Prithvi was organising an international theatre festival and looking to stage some contemporary Indian plays. Sanjana Kapoor somehow got to know that Paresh had written a couple of plays - just for fun - during his Theatre Academy days.

Back then he had been busy with acting and nothing ever came of the scripts.

Writer-director Ramu Ramanathan ordered, "Read them to me!"

Both *Sangeet Debunchya Muli* and *Watanachi Usal* were complete black comedies. Ramu loved them and declared, "Paresh, this is great stuff, it has to be part of the festival. You choose which one to stage and direct it as well!"

"Entire credit goes to my family for supporting me for a very long time. I started earning - surviving on my own - only in my late twenties!"

Paresh chose to produce *Sangeet Debunchya Muli*, a satire where two girls are performing *kirtan* and discussing various problems.

"They came to the conclusion that at the root of every problem on this earth there is this divide between male and female. If we destroy this division everything will be fine. So how to do it? Let's transform all males into females!"

As crazy as the idea was, the production was a hit. Paresh Mokashi, the actor took a bow; Paresh Mokashi, writer-director was born.

In spite of being an experimental play of just 60 minutes, *Sangeet Debunchya Muli* did over 100 shows all over Maharashtra. And Paresh's next play was an even bigger hit.

Mukkampost Bombilwadi was set in 1942 - a time when the freedom movement was sweeping India, while world war raged across the globe.

"I joined the two events and Mr Hitler accidentally lands up in a coastal village in Konkan. At the same time some people are trying to blow up the only police station in Bombilwadi!"

The idea for this black comedy came to Paresh from the daily reports of bomb blasts in Kashmir and Punjab at the time. The thought struck him, what will happen if one of the bombs does not explode?

"It was a funny situation but I did not want to set it up in the contemporary times. Because that was not a new thing on Marathi stage, in fact it's the standard formula we use in one act play competitions."

So Paresh went back in history and chose to set his play in 1942. *Mukkampost Bombilwadi* itself went on to create history by staging over 500 shows, many of them house-full. It was a big shock to everybody, that this kind of play could do a lot of business.

The critics said, "*Hamein to pasand tha* but we never thought that even layman audience will love it!"

In fact Paresh himself was not convinced the play would be commercially viable. He casually read the script to a few friends, not thinking it would ever get produced. But people started talking about it, in theatre circles.

One day two young boys - Santosh Kanekar and Abhijit Satap - came to Paresh.

"We want to produce *Mukkampost Bombilwadi,*" they said.

Paresh warned them, "I don't know if it will work with the audience. We may have to stop after 4-5 shows - are you ready to take the risk?"

"We love the play, we have to do it!" they replied.

"Abhijit and Santosh were still in college but they were so committed, so enthusiastic. They were not doing it for money alone but passion for theatre."

Of course they also put up Rs 2 lakhs to make it happen - a large sum of money back in 2001. But the gamble paid off, with a 500 show run. A full house earned the producer Rs 25-30,000 per show. The producers made handsome profits, the cast and crew got their per-show royalties.

Paresh went on to script another laugh riot - *Lagna Kallol.* Supported by the same producers, the play did over 200 shows.

Having made a name in the comedy genre, in 2005, Paresh tried something completely different. *Samudra* was a 'science fiction mystery', based on the ancient tale of *samudra manthan.* Kind of like a 'Da Vinci Code' set in contemporary India.

"People were surprised with the subject but you see my other grand passion is doing objective research on our ancient books - such as Ramayan, Mahabharat, Ved, Upanishad. In fact I sometimes say that is my main career and everything else is extra-curricular!"

Paresh got interested in this activity after the Ayodhya issue flared up in 1992.

"When I was watching all that madness - of Ayodhya, of bomb blasts - I asked myself why people blindly follow one stream of thought or another. I decided to take on the objective research of our scriptures, and reach my own conclusions."

First is *granthadikshitsatya* or book-based truth. Go back to books first, see what is written in them. But go to the original texts - or refer to the literal translation. And no, it's not mere armchair research.

"I am planning a big archaeological tour - that is another way to look at it. Then there is the question of 'historicity' of the books. What part is imagination and what part is history. And the science mentioned in the books - how much is miracle, how much is actual science."

It is an eccentric pastime, you might say, but this is one of the many mental munchies bubbling in the mind of Paresh Mokashi. A man who thinks differently, writes differently, lives differently.

Which is probably why, when he read the biography of the eccentric genius Dadasaheb Phalke, there was an instant connect.

"When I read Bapu Vatave's book on Phalke, I was struck by the subject so strongly that I started seeing things in front of my eyes. In 4 hours I finished that book of 200 pages and decided right then and there to make my first ever feature film on this subject!"

It was that quick and final a decision. And writing the script did not take long either. Paresh researched his subject further, at the Film Institute, the National Film Archives and a couple of other books and experts. And not only Phalke, but the whole process of film making, which was very primitive back then.

"The final script was ready within two months time - it was that intense an activity. And then, I started looking for money which is when the adventure began!" he grins.

But, he says, it was a very typical adventure. Every first time film maker has to go through this experience.

"People don't trust you. They don't know if you are capable, or if you will mess up! It is a big investment, so I can't blame them. Besides, I was a very stubborn chap!"

Paresh was clear about one thing: he would make this film exactly the way he was 'seeing' it. In Marathi, with no big stars, no song and dance sequences, very simple treatment.

That scared the hell out of producers.

"Paresh, do it in Hindi - that's where the money is!" they said.

"*Chal ek gaana daal de - sirf* title track," said others.

But Paresh refused to budge. "I will wait for someone who will let me do it my way," he said. After waiting for three years, he decided to produce the film on his own. To do this, he mortgaged the house owned by his family in Dadar.

"What can I say... Plenty of people have done it before me and I am definitely not going to be the last! If you are passionate and dedicated enough about a particular thing you will do all these 'mad' things!"

Yes, it adds some glamour to Paresh as a director, but what he really wants to do is quickly change the subject and talk about the film itself.

Harishchandrachi Factory is the most expensive film ever made in Marathi, with a budget of Rs 4 crores.

"We needed a big budget because it is a period film. Not only did we have to erect sets but also look into details like what kind of film equipment was used back then."

The film was mainly shot in Pune, Mumbai, Karjat and London (the city where Phalke went to learn film technique). *Harishchandrachi Factory* went on the floors in April 2008, and was completed in December of that year. And it was first screened at film festivals around the country.

From day one, *Harishchandrachi Factory* received rave reviews. Then, it started winning awards at every festival. "Best Film", "Best Director, "Best Story." Interestingly, despite being a biographical subject, the film was not 'heavy'. In fact, in typical Paresh style, it has a strong element of comedy.

"There is a bit of resistance, few people don't like it. But at Signs 2009 in Kerala, Mani Kaul - a typical serious film maker - was on the jury. He gave us the 'Best Film' award. So people are seeing my point!"

Which is that *hasya rasa* does not have to be slapstick, or *atishyokti* - where you blow something out of proportion. The 'comedy' in *Harishchandrachi Factory* is something like *Life is Beautiful.*

"*Life is Beautiful* can be called a comedy but at the same time it talked about how people dealt with life in a concentration camp - which is a serious subject! See, there are some very spirited people who don't take 'balance sheet' of the situation..."

They simply win over their circumstances with their attitude towards life. And Dadasaheb Phalke was exactly that kind of person. Now all of us know that Phalke was the first Indian to make a feature film - *Raja Harishchandra* - but how exactly did he do it?

"*Arre baap re,*" says Paresh, "It's a terrific tale!"

Imagine a boy born in Trimbakeshwar, a pilgrim town near Nasik in 1870. He shifts to Mumbai to study at JJ School of Art.

"An urban rich fellow joining JJ in 1890 was normal but a boy from the village, that too born in a Sanskrit pandit family - that was unusual!"

> # "I don't do trial and error writing.
> I wait till the story and the characters
> reach a certain level of development in
> my head, and then start!"

Phalke went on to study in Kala Bhawan, Baroda and then set up a still photo studio in Godhra. When that did not work out he learnt magic tricks from a German magician who was touring India and started performing under the name of Professor Kelpha (a re-arrangement of P-H-A-L-K-E!)

"He was that kind of eccentric and strange person. And only this kind of person would dare to do something different, without caring about financial status, family background, where is my next meal coming from...the typical emotional ups and downs."

In fact, Phalke walked out of a lucrative printing business after a quarrel with his business partner. And that's when he stumbled upon a tent theatre showing a silent film called '*The Life of Christ*'. He was awestruck.

" Why can't we Indians make films like this, showing our Indian gods on screen", he asked himself.

At the age of 41, Dadasaheb Phalke decided to go to London and learn film making. He cobbled together the money to make the first Indian movie '*Raja Harishchandra*'.

"It was an incredible adventure for Phalke as well as his wife and two kids. That's what the movie *Harishchandrachi Factory* has tried to capture - the spirit of adventure."

"There is something universal about the theme that touches almost anyone who sees the film. That this amazing story was reaching people almost a hundred years after the original *Raja Harishchandra* was made would have been reward enough for Paresh.

But then, came a most resounding recognition. *Harishchandrachi Factory* was selected as India's official entry to the Oscars for the year 2009.

It happened like this. The Film Federation of India decided to change its selection process and invite not just big name producers and directors, but any film made in any language, to vie for the honours.

"The regional film federations were asked to nominate the top three films in their language - that's how *Harishchandrachi Factory* was shortlisted. And finally it was selected by the jury!"

The film instantly grew in stature and many distribution houses approached Paresh for rights to release the film. After negotiating with 4-5 different parties Paresh decided to tie up with UTV and Paprika Media.

But he hasn't taken the easy way out by simply selling the film to someone; he remains a partner, with a share in the profits.

"See, it is all my money, so there is no pressure to release the film as quickly as possible to recover as much money as you can. I could wait for things to 'ripen'..."

Harishchandrachi Factory released nationwide on January 29th, 2010. Although the film did not make it to the final shortlist at the Oscars, audience response has been positive. It's the kind of film that grows, by word of mouth.

This marks 'The End' of another dramatic chapter - who knows, what next! But looking back, Paresh Mokashi can see how it all adds up. Every experience, every influence, every bit of struggle.

"Including my years without employment," he grins.

"I am not from any film school, nor have I ever even assisted anyone. The first time I was on a film set as a director was for my own film. But in my Pune days I was exposed to good cinema, to world cinema. All those... *sanskar jisko kehte hain...* were there."

Paresh knew how to make a good film, and how to make a bad film. And when he got his Big Idea, he took his chances.

"I am not such an ambitious person. I let things happen...but yes, whatever I do I give it my best!"

And none of it would have been possible without the support of family and friends. Such as 'Indian Magic Eye' - run by his pals from Theatre Academy days - who were the executive producers of *Harishchandrachi Factory*.

"They took care of everything...!"

Proudest of all, are the parents and brother who stood by him at every stage. Who let him vegetate and 'gestate and luxuriate in the *chakravyuh* of his creative juices. For almost two decades.

"Of course it is all because of them... if they had not given permission, I could not have mortgaged my property. I could not have made this film."

Like Dadasaheb Phalke, it's been one grand adventure for Paresh Mokashi. And something tells me there is more to follow.

Because life is beautiful and bountiful and full of breathtaking possibility.

When to thine own self thou stay true.

ADVICE TO YOUNG ENTREPRENEURS

Don't listen to anybody's message - that is my message.

Don't look for anyone's advice. Just do things the way you want... This is also an advice but not an *advice* advice. That's all I have to say... I did not listen to anybody so how can I tell them to listen to me!

AVATAR

Krishna Reddy,
Prince Dance Group

In a small town in Orissa, Krishna Reddy assembled a group of daily wage labourers and formed 'Prince Dance Group'. This troupe won the hotly competed 'India's Got Talent' show, enthralling the audience with its unique brand of mythology-inspired choreography.

The first time I saw Prince Dance Group on *'India's Got Talent'*, I was blown away.

Who are these silver-painted, surreal dancers? Where have they come from, and who has taught them to move like this?

The answer to these questions was a revelation. 'Prince' is a group put together by 26 year old Krishna Reddy. A boy from the sleepy little town of Behrampur in Orissa, with no formal training. Just a passion for dance.

Like Eklavya learning archery, Krishna picked up dance by observation. Honed it through practice. Then, took it to the next level with the power of imagination.

After struggling for seven years - performing at small shows, earning a pittance - Krishna had the burning desire to 'prove himself'. To stand out in the crowd; to create an impact.

To do this, Krishna thought like an entrepreneur; he came up with a Big Idea.

Got his team to execute it flawlessly and captured the 'market'.

The minds and hearts of the voting public.

Krishna's story says to me that talent is where it all starts.

But desire to excel, to push yourself beyond the limits, to do that which has never been done before is what lights you up inside. Makes a prince out of a commoner..

May we see many Krishnas, in many avatars.

AVATAR

Krishna Reddy,
Prince Dance Group

Krishna Reddy was born in Behrampur.

"My family is originally from Andhra Pradesh, then my father was transferred to Orissa. He is in 'electrical line'."

A worker, with the state electricity board.

Krishna was the youngest in a large family - four brothers and two sisters. He did not care much for school or for studies. But he was passionate about one thing - dance. Not that he had any formal training, but *dekh dekh kar seekh liya*.

"One of my older brothers is also into dancing, I used to watch him and copy the steps. In those days Prabhu Deva was very popular - he was my hero!"

Krishna got a chance to shake a leg at the annual Ganapati puja. And at small competitions in and around Behrampur. When his brother started a dance group, Krishna became part of it and discovered a bigger platform. A world beyond his small city.

"We used to go to Bhubaneshwar, Puri and Hyderabad to perform. Sometimes we won small cups and shields - it was very exciting! I also got to perform solo on stage - under the name 'Prince'."

After completing class 12, the Krishna 'Twinkle Toes' Reddy decided, "Enough of studies!" He decided to form his own dance group - 'Prince Dance Group'. But how does one begin? Where does one get members?

Krishna simply went house to house, looking for students to teach. In no time, 8 kids signed up, paying a fee of Rs 100 per month. In less than 2 years, that number doubled to almost 20.

"*Kharcha chal jaata tha*," he recalls. But, Krishna was not happy. Yes, he was paid by these doting, middle-class parents but they saw dance as one more means to achievement.

"If I took one student on stage for a show, the other parents would pester, 'What about my child?' Their rivalry and jealousy disturbed me."

In 2004, Krishna decided to stop the classes; give up teaching middle class kids. Instead, he started going village to village. He travelled by bus, 30-40 kms from Behrampur, looking for youngsters with a passion for dance.

But once again, the ride was not smooth.

"I had a group of 7-8 boys in Tata colony. *Sab acchha chal raha thha par phir log pareshaan karne lage.* They said, "You cannot practice here." So small-small problems like that I had to keep dealing with."

In 2005, Krishna finally struck a rapport with a completely different set of people. He began teaching a group of *mazdoors* - or daily wage labourers. *Magar kyun?*

"I always liked to meet such people. From childhood I used to see they work so hard, *subah se shaam tak kaam karte hain. Magar phir bhi mast rehte hain. Agar main unki khushi ke liye kuch kar sakta hoon to mujhe bhi achcha lagega.*"

Krishna approached a group of *mazdoors* in Ambopur village and asked them, "Dance *seekhoge?*"

They readily agreed.

Thus every night, after dark, when the boys were done with their day's labour, they gathered at the Kali mandir. In a small room adjacent to the temple, they surrendered to the power of dance.

"We used to practice till about 2 or 3 in the morning. *Kuch bhi, apne style ka, jo bhi mujhe aata tha, main unko seekhaata tha.*"

And these young boys were actually excellent students.

"*Woh meri baat maante the...* They knew nothing about dance so they never argued with me!"

But why would a dozen boys spend hours every night, tapping their feet... Only to wake up next morning to work with their hands, at construction sites?

Because Krishna Reddy gave them the hope of a better future. A future he imagined for himself each time he saw the contestants on the popular television dance show 'Boogie Woogie'.

"I used to watch 'Boogie Woogie' and learn from the dancers, think about what I would have to do to compete and win against them!"

Krishna told his boys, "*Dance se tum bhi kuch ban sakoge... Magar uske liye mehnat to karni padegi*"

*"Mujhe laga itne din se hum dance mein hain
lekin kuch bhi haasil nahin hua... jo bhi ho
mujhe yeh competition jeetkar dikhana hai."*

And they believed him. Just like his family, which left him alone to practice his dancing with the CD player or TV on full volume.

"My brothers were all working. Maybe since I was the youngest there was no pressure on me to go and get a job..."

Only his mother would sometimes remark, "What will you get out of this dance mania? *Kuch kaam-dhandha seekh le - baad mein kaam aayega!*"

But Krishna was convinced, *ki ek na ek din dance mein hi main kuch karke dikhaoonga.* And he carried on, honing his craft. Along with the boys from Ambopur, Krishna continued to train some of the talented youngsters he had identified in other villages.

"I used to pay their bus fare or they would come by cycle. We used to perform at small shows once in 3-4 months. There we won Rs 500, Rs 1000 - and it used to be a big thing!"

In 2006, Krishna decided to try his luck at 'Boogie Woogie' and travelled to Kolkata with his 16 member troupe for the auditions. To finance the trip he pawned his motorbike. Competing against 1500 participants, Prince Dance Group was selected for the next round, to be held in Mumbai.

Once again Krishna scraped together money to make the journey. This time, he took along a female dancer (and her mother) because he'd been told it would improve his chances of winning.

From Behrampur, the group first went to Hyderabad. Then, they boarded the train for Mumbai.

Krishna asked a policeman, "*Dadar kab aayega?*"

The man replied, "Six o'clock in the morning - don't worry, go to sleep."

But Krishna could not fall asleep and when the train made a halt at around four am, he peeked outside the window. The train was already at Dadar!

In the mad scramble that followed, half the group managed to get off the train, while half remained on board.

"*Main daud daud kar sab ko neeche utaar raha tha*... they were throwing the luggage off the train and jumping off one by one. Finally I got off the train thinking we'd all made it."

But when they took a headcount they realised two were missing. The train was picking up speed when one boy who was still on board came to the door.

"Stay where you are!" pleaded the group on the platform

He jumped off anyway, and got badly hurt.

One boy was still on the moving train. Krishna asked his group to stay put exactly where they were and got into the next train headed in the same direction. At CST he found there were a dozen trains on the platform. Somehow he located the boy and returned to Dadar.

But now the rest of the group was missing! Bystanders said the police had taken them away.

"This was just a month after serial bomb blasts of July 2006. There was high alert at all stations."

The railway police asked, "Where you have come from? Show us an ID proof."

Krishna had no documents, nothing to satisfy the authorities at least. He had been trying the numbers of the 'Boogie Woogie' organisers - no response. Finally, he called a friend in Behrampur and said, "We are in trouble - do you know anyone in Mumbai who can help us?"

The friend arranged for someone to come down and vouch for the group. Finally, they were allowed to leave. But there were more troubles to come.

"Somehow we managed to reach the 'Boogie Woogie' office. But we had no place to stay..."

The hotel booked by the organisers was too expensive - Rs 500 per person, per day. Krishna decided to try and find a cheaper place.

"I went to a *basti* for the first time. I saw people sleeping on the footpath, eating on the footpath - I got scared. Even our village is better than this, I thought, at least everyone has a house to call their own!"

He was taken to a 'mess' - a cramped little room where 150 people slept back to back. No, it would not do! Till 10 pm Krishna continued looking, walking from here to there on foot. Finally he put up his hands and said, "*Main haar gaya hoon.*"

He decided it was best to take the next train back home. But when Krishna called the organisers they said, "Because of you, 'Boogie Woogie' will lose face. Do you want that to happen?"

With a heavy heart, he agreed to take the five hundred rupee rooms - Rs 8000 a day for the entire group. For a stay of eight days.

"We used to eat only once in a day, in order to save money," he recalls.

With only fire in their bellies, Krishna's group danced their way into the finals. But once again, there was a problem. A bag containing all their costumes and the CD they had practiced on had been left behind on the train.

On the morning of the competition, Krishna procured another piece of music and composed a routine. He decided to use silver paint in lieu of costume - and in this makeshift manner they went on stage.

"We were in a bad state by this time... I had no money left to settle the remaining hotel bill. No money for food. *Magar us din bhagwaan ne meri sun li...*"

Although Prince dance group did not win the competition, judge Javed Jaffrey was so impressed by their performance that he gave them a consolation prize of Rs 75,000. In cash.

Moreover, the exposure on 'Boogie Woogie' brought its own reward. Prince Dance Group began getting more enquiries for shows. They began performing at marriages, at colleges, and cultural programs. And the money got better too.

"We used to get around Rs 10-12,000 per show, although mostly we had to spend on our own for travel and food so we did not make much profit."

Despite the small success he had tasted, Krishna still did not have the confidence to negotiate a price, demand extra for conveyance. Or give a fitting reply to people who said, "*Abhi tum star nahin bane ho...* why should we pay you more!"

Because money was tight, Prince Group lost many talented dancers.

"I could not pay my boys on a monthly basis so many would go to Hyderabad or Mumbai for work and then I would have to find new boys to train for dance."

But like any startup, Krishna dealt with the attrition and carried on. Prince Group became a regular at 'Boogie Woogie', performing every year between 2006 and 2009. Twice, they managed to reach the runners-up position. Always, they captured many hearts.

In fact Ravi Behl, one of the judges of the show, offered Krishna support by arranging a room for the troupe. *"Kisi ko mat bataana, sirf tumhare liye karte hain,"* he added.

Despite some recognition, and support, Prince dance group could only scrape by. Travel, food expenses and daily wages of Rs 80-100 ate up any small earnings that came their way. Then there was the cost of all those glittery costumes...

Par gaadi chal rahi thi, dheeme dheeme, when one fine morning Krishna heard about a competition that would change the course of his life. A show called 'India's Got Talent' on the recently launched channel 'Colors'. With prize money of Rs 50 lakhs.

Krishna knew this was his big chance. *Kuch karke dikhaana hai.. magar kya?* Ordinary *jhatkas* and *matkas* would not do. There would be many people with many talents - he had to do something which would stand out!

"I sat up all night thinking... If I have to get selected, if I have to win, I have to do something related to our culture, our country... *apne desh par, apni sanskruti par kuch karna hai."*

Krishna visualised a completely new kind of dance; never seen before by anyone. A dance which was not about individuals performing steps, but the whole coming together to become greater than its parts.

Thus was born the 'Krishna' act where the fluid movements of silver painted bodies*, and a blue-hued Krishna playing his flute produced a veritable visual feast*.

When the group performed the act during the elimination round, it received a standing ovation. Judge Shekhar Kapur called it a 'world beating act' . He went on to add, "Your act proves that to be an artist you don't need resources, you don't need professional training. *Dil chahiye, kala chahiye!"*

After the selection, each act was given a month to prepare for the next round. That's when Krishna choreographed the famous 'Flag Act' set to the tune of *Saare Jahan Se Achcha*.

In this sequence, dancers painted orange, white and green created stunning formations. Also showcased were two physically challenged members of the troupe - Padmanabha Sahu (24) and Telu Tarini (13). Both the audience and the judges had tears in their eyes, at the end of the performance.

Expectations from Prince Group were high in the grand finale. And once again, they did not disappoint.

---

*The silver paint is powder-based while the blue paint is distemper. It takes 1-1.5 hours to put on and 2-3 hours to take off.

The *Dashavtar* act depicting the ten avatars of Vishnu was described as 'zen like', even transcendental.

But would it bring in enough SMS votes from the public, to win the contest?

Luckily, Prince Group had caught the eye of Orissa Chief Minister Naveen Patnaik. He called Krishna before the contest and said, "Krishna - you focus on your performance, the entire state of Orissa will vote for you!"

Patnaik personally campaigned for Prince Group, the Oriya media lent its full support and ultimately the boys from the brick kilns got the maximum votes.

Prince Group won the 'India's Got Talent' contest, against all odds.

And what of the prize? Krishna gave the Maruti Ritz car to the village of Ambopur, to be used by the community as an emergency vehicle,

"They have supported me, looked after me, fed me, believed in me... I thought if this car can be of some service to them, why not!"

Of the Rs 50 lakhs cash prize, Rs 20 lakhs went in taxes. Krishna gave Rs 1 lakh to each of his 20 group members; the rest of the money is being used to renovate the Kali *mandir* where he once practiced.

"*Yeh sab bhagwaan ka aashirwaad hai,*" says Krishna. "Earlier I did not even believe in God, *magar dheere dheere mujhe yeh ehsaas hua. Main pehle kahaan tha, aur aaj kahaan hoon...*"

Krishna - as well as his dance troupe - are stars in Orissa.

"We have got respect, and recognition. What more can I ask for?"

More shows, more platforms to perform - and all that is happening. Sony Music has signed a two year contract with Prince Group. They promote their client, negotiate fees and contracts and take care of all the hassles like travel and living arrangements.

"They get a commission, we get a monthly fee. I am happy. Now we can focus only on our dance."

What's more, the Orissa government has announced a cash prize of Rs one crore and four acres of land for the group to build a dance academy.

"*Mere liye sabse khushi ki baat hai ki meri wajah se bees-pacchis logon ki zindagi ban saki hai.* There are still many hundreds of youth in our villages who have talent, who have potential, but not enough

---

* *Videos of all three performances can be seen on YouTube.com. Search for 'Prince Dance Group'.*

opportunities. *Agar main unko bhi raasta dikha sakoon to aur bhi acchhi baat hai...*"

If you can imagine it, you can make it happen.

That's Krishna Reddy - labourer of love, prince of hearts.

ADVICE TO YOUNG ENTREPRENEURS

Only your own hard work will take you ahead, do not depend on anybody else to show you the way.

Money is not a hurdle, *mehnat karne waale ko, dil se kaam karne waale ko sab kuch milta hai.*

CALL OF THE
WILD

Kalyan Varma,
Wildlife Photographer

At 22, Kalyan Varma had a 'dream job' with Yahoo. But one fine day he quit and pursue his passion - wildlife photography. Today, he is a living example of an 'idiot' who's living his dream *and* making a living, out of something he truly loves.

When my brother was little, he wanted to be a BEST bus conductor; when I was little, I dreamt of becoming an astronaut.

When Kalyan Varma was little, he said to himself, "I wish I could live in the jungle watching animals all day!"

Today, my brother is a brand manager with a multinational corporation.

I am a writer who looks up at the stars and thinks, maybe - some day.

But guess what, Kalyan Varma actually spends his days watching animals in the jungle. And, taking their pictures.

Kalyan Varma represents the big dreams of the little people.

Dreams that generally fall by the wayside, as we grow up and get 'real'.

But the reality is, we can make our lives what we want them to be.

We can clear a path through the jungle of expectations and limitations and be the Tarzan swinging from the vine of our true potential.

Aiiiiiiiiieeeeeeeeeeeeeeeeee! But what about practicality?

As I sit in the iconic Koshy's eating the blandest of vegetarian continental lunches, I think to myself: "Most of us live like this cauliflower, smothered in rich white sauce..."

And then we look for some tabasco, to spice it up.

But if you create your own special recipe for 'success', like Kalyan did.

It will fill not just your stomach but your heart, your mind, your soul.

CALL OF THE
WILD

Kalyan Varma,
Wildlife Photographer

Kalyan Varma was born in Vishakhapatnam.

"My father had a public sector job, so we used to travel a lot. I got to see different places, meet different people."

Kalyan studied at Kendriya Vidyalaya - a government school - which, he says, was a good thing. But moving every three years meant making new friends at each new K.V. Not so good!

From Vizag to Gulbarga, then Vijayawada and finally one year in Canada; Kalyan finally settled down in Bangalore - after class 10.

"I did my college here, and worked here, so now I more or less consider Bangalore to be my 'native place'," he says.

Kalyan was an average student - he had his ups and downs. Like any kid growing up, he had 'dreams'.

"As a kid you always want to be an astronaut, you want to be a pilot. I wanted to sing - which I tried but I failed. And I wanted to be in the forest. Watching *National Geographic* - Jane Goodall especially - I always said, 'Hey I want to be in the jungle watching animals all day'."

All day - ha! The closest Kalyan got to wildlife at that age was a day trip to a sanctuary, when the family went to Ooty on LTC.

"*TV tak theek hai, bete, aage padhai karo, kuch bano!*" was what a concerned dad would have said.

But luckily, around the same time, Kalyan also fell in love - with computers. It was the early 90s; there were so many exciting developments in that field. Hackers, in particular, fascinated the young man.

"I started computer programming very early, and that was a very nice thing to do, while I was still in school. And I really enjoyed it. So somehow the way the industry was growing and your parents also push you, I guess, computers was the easy thing, the thing to do."

Besides who could make a career out of wildlife?

Kalyan joined PES College of Engineering (PESIT), in Bangalore. A good college, but not the best. What's more he did not even get a seat in computer science!

"I was okay with academics, so I didn't get the top engineering college, or even the C.S. branch. But I wanted to be in Bangalore so I took up mechanical engineering at PESIT. I also liked robotics a lot so I thought maybe I could mix both - somehow."

Not getting the branch - or college - of your choice is devastating for most students but Kalyan took that lemon and made lemonade out of it.

"College was great fun, it was also the time when Linux and open source became hot, the internet was spreading. I was bunking classes but not just to hang around in the canteen. I also spent hours in the computer lab playing with all these things."

From his second year of college, Kalyan began working part time, doing some Linux consulting and networking.

"It was good fun because I was a mechanical student, but I was kind of taking care of the computer science lab. So it was very weird in fact!"

You get a degree, you get domain expertise - but often it is only skin deep. But when you have passion and seek out knowledge, it radiates from every part of your being. And that is how Kalyan Varma, mechanical engineer, got placed with Yahoo.

"They offered me a job in my third year of college. I always liked security and I was put in the security department of Yahoo - so that was great for me. Back then Yahoo India was a 'startup' and a great company to work for."

It also paid extremely well.

"I had the highest salary in that batch from Bangalore... about five and a half lakh rupees, for a fresher."

The year was 2001.

"I wasn't doing justice to my security career and I was not doing justice to wildlife. I had to make a choice."

Working at Yahoo was a 'ball'.

"Every guy tries to screw around down with Yahoo - break into the system. So we were on our toes 24 hours!"

Being a dotcom company, there was no 'boss' as such, a 22 year old could actually be 'in charge' of security.

"I made my own projects, my own challenges. So I really loved my work, dabbled in cryptography and things like that. I can take pride in all this because in Yahoo even small things you do have a huge impact."

Each time you log into Yahoo - even today - a little piece of code written by Kalyan is probably still at work there.

"Things like domain keys - which is a standard for email security - I was part of the design team. Even Gmail uses the same protocol now."

You can feel the pride in his voice.

"So a lot of people think that I got disillusioned by the cubicle job and quit but I loved my job actually, absolutely loved it. I won the Superstar Yahoo Award in 2003 I think - which is like the best in the Yahoo worldwide."

Wonderful, but then, why did he quit? Well, more than one reason.

By late 2004 Yahoo had grown - a great deal. From one small room where Kalyan was the fifth employee, the company now had 1000 people on its rolls and was no longer a startup. It was, a corporation.

"Hierarchy started coming in, people wanted to manage things. Yahoo India was heading into a traditional Indian software company setup and I was just not at all comfortable with that. I just didn't like it."

Meaning, turn up in office at 9 o'clock, follow dress codes.

"I was a shorts guy, come in at 6 in the morning. Some days work for 22 hours, some days for 3 hours. I always used to finish my work but now they wanted some kind of..."

Discipline?

"Unnecessary discipline. I like discipline, I'm for discipline when it increases efficiency but discipline for the heck of discipline is wrong."

Kalyan was disillusioned with the job but the final straw came when they asked him to either shift to the US, or move to a different department.

Neither choice was appealing.

Kalyan quit Yahoo India in late 2004. He was 24 years old.

At this point Kalyan had offers from other companies - including the likes of Google. But he was very clear about what he did not want to do. More of the same, more of the easy, more of the 'what I already know'.

"After college I started working within one week... this was one time when I had no responsibilities, no nothing so I thought, 'Let me just do something completely different in my life'."

And that something was, wildlife photography!

Now even while he was at Yahoo, Kalyan had started dabbling with the subject.

"I'd bought a good digital SLR camera. In those days it cost over a lakh, but I could afford it you know."

Like many yuppie software engineers, one of his favourite pastimes was driving out of the city on weekends. Kalyan's trip was to visit wildlife sanctuaries like Bandipur and Nagarhole. And take pictures.

"Wildlife photography was like a marriage of two 'first loves'. I really liked photography and I really liked wildlife... but I had no formal training, in either."

Learning by tinkering, observing and actually doing is a recurring theme in Kalyan's life.

"I don't have formal education in computer science. With photography it is all self taught. With wildlife, I am not a biologist - again it is self taught."

So in late 2004, Kalyan took a radical decision.

"I like wildlife. I like photography. So let me spend some time in the forest."

One can always get back to a job after three or four months, what the hell!

Kalyan contacted an eco-tourism resort and said, "Hey, I want to stay in your resort for three months."

They said, "Well, you'll have to pay."

I said, "I'm not going to pay - what can we do?"

They said, "OK, why don't you work for us. You speak good English, you know wildlife, so you can take our visitors out for a safari, give them a tour..."

The deal was: no salary, only food and accommodation.

I said, "Great - that's perfect for me."

And that was how Kalyan simply packed his bags and moved into 'Jungle Lodges and Resorts' in BR Hills, a wildlife sanctuary near Mysore. A move which was to change his life, forever.

Since he was not taking any salary, Kalyan did not have any major responsibilities as an employee of the company.

"Morning I would go in the jeep safari, evening I would go in the jeep safari. In the daytime I would just take my vehicle and drive around in the forest. It was just the best time of my life."

24 hours in the jungle meant, you got to see and actually be with wildlife. And the people who know them best.

"I would take tribal guys and just follow a tiger for 2-3 days. Follow leopard kills, follow elephants. Learn about birds, play with monkeys. I spent so much time them that they recognise me, treat me... accept me as part of their troupe now."

Wow.

And there were some super-close, super-dangerous encounters with animals.

"The first time I saw a tiger, I just couldn't pick up my camera; I was shivering so much. And this happened another 3-4 times!"

Another time, Kalyan was setting a 'camera trap' i.e. a camera which is tied to a tree. This camera detects heat and hence photos of any animal passing by automatically.

"So there I was, tying the camera to the tree and I didn't realise, just a little above me, at the fork of the branch, there was a leopard. I heard something and looked up and saw it smiling at me from a distance of two feet. It was the scariest moment of my life, I think. I almost peed in my pants that day!"

Kalyan ran for his life and lived to tell the tale! And there were the 'fear factor' moments but it only got him more addicted.

At the end of three months, Kalyan just could not go back. He was loving it so much that he ended up staying in the jungle for a whole year!

> **"One thing that has driven me quite a bit in my life is self learning... I really like that - starting from scratch. Understanding, talking to people, getting into a new field."**

But, reality bites. Kalyan had enough savings to support himself for a year but this couldn't go on forever. And yet, he could not come back and take up a regular, strait-jacketed job (for which he had offers).

"I decided to become an IT security consultant. Because I thought I would be able to spend 50% of my time in the city, and 50% in the forest."

Sounds like the best of both worlds. But turned out, to be the worst!

"I worked like that for the whole of 2006. And that was one of the difficult periods of my life. I could not do justice to either consulting or wildlife."

Kalyan would be in the middle of the jungle and suddenly he would get a call from a client saying, "There's an audit tomorrow morning... you need to be here."

And then while he was in the city, busy with the audit someone would call from there and say, "The tiger just made a kill, why aren't you here to photograph it?"

Kalyan struggled for six to eight months, trying to balance the call of the concrete jungle; of being practical and earning a living. With the call of the wild.

"I was not exactly depressed but I was not very motivated. I would skip work and I lost some clients - that was the cost of being in the jungle." In late 2006, Kalyan got a call from the BBC.

"What helped me was that I was very active in social media, very early. Since 1999-2000."

Kalyan had been blogging since the year 2000. As well as sharing his pictures online.

"I wasn't doing photography for money. So all my output was on my blog. And in the jungle I was 'live blogging' via GPRS. I would write, "Hey, there's a tiger calling outside my window." And then I would actually take a photograph and upload it within 5-10 minutes."

> **"I agree that there is lot of luck involved in wildlife photography but I say, 'The more you work, the better your luck is'."**

The blog* got many fans and followers, both from India and abroad. Some of his work was even featured on the popular website Boing Boing.

Among the many photographs Kalyan was continuously posting, there were several frogs. The BBC wanted to do a film on frogs and they when they googled the term, guess whose name showed up!

That particular film on frogs did not quite work out (permission issues!) but it was a 'foot in the door' for Kalyan. A few months later - in early 2007 - the BBC was doing a film on monsoon and the Western Ghats with Sandesh Kandur, who happened to be a friend.

They said, "Hey, you know the place, we have seen your photographs, we know what you have been doing, so why don't you work with us?"

That was like a Sign. The direction Kalyan had been looking for. He shut down his consulting business and decided to plunge into wildlife, and photography, full time.

"They weren't paying me much but I knew that I've got a break. And I'm ready to sweat it out for few years. I think that's one problem with people also, they want to move up too fast…"

The truth is you have to serve your time.

You have to prove yourself.

You have to be patient, and built to last.

"I started as a production assistant, just started carrying tripods," he laughs. "But it was great because when the UK filmmakers came, whenever they weren't filming, I would borrow the camera. Shoot a little of this and that. And they really liked my work."

After a while, instead of coming down from the UK every time, they just asked Kalyan to shoot the footage!

"I think you build that confidence, you build that relationship over time…"

The operative word being time.

* www.kalyanvarma.net/journal.

Technical skills matter, but maybe about 50%. The rest is how 'sticky' you get with your client. Do they like you, do they trust you, do they believe you will deliver?

In a creative field it does not matter how well qualified you are. Or aren't. You have to start at the bottom and work your way up,

"Yes, but a lot of people are not ready to do that, they just directly want to jump to the top. Like *National Geographic*, they employ 40 photographers and they are 4 million photographers in the world who want to be a *National Geographic* photographer."

So how do they choose one in a million?

"I know *National Geographic* folks now and they say, 'We can't look at technical merits any more. We like to contact photographers who have already done something outside'."

Somebody who's noteworthy on a consistent basis. Not a mere flash in the pan.

"People think I've taken this cool photo, *National Geographic* is going to buy it. No it's not that way, you have to work your way up, earn your credits. Just like a journalist is known for a certain kind of writing - over a period of time."

Of course that time need not be thirty years in this day and age. In three years, Kalyan has come far.

"BBC trusts me enough to put me at par with their foreign crew. They pay me UK rate now, which is 300 pounds (Rs 24,000) a day. Initially they were paying me 20 pounds a day. Then they were paying me 50 pounds a day. But you kind of build that trust, you build that faith. They know I can deliver."

And to deliver one good picture, photographers actually have to shoot one hundred. But of course, there's no standard rule or formula.

"Some of my best pictures were taken in just 2-3 shots because, you know, something just happens and you were there, ready to take that shot. But at other times, you wait, keep trying and eventually you get what you want."

It's the same story with video. For one hour of high quality footage, BBC shoots about 100 hours of raw footage.

Excellence is a function of dogged, invisible effort. No matter where you go.

And it might seem like when you close one chapter of your life and start writing another, that what you did before was a 'waste'. But the truth is, man is a sum of his experiences and the whole is greater than the parts.

"Another thing that helped me make this switch - into wildlife photography - is my technology background. I offered to do many things - like build a web portal for them, set up a live blog for your production."

Baaye haath ka khel for a Yahoo 'superstar' but a great value add for the BBC. Especially since it came free of cost.

"No one in BBC knew how to do all this. They would've had to hire an expensive company in the UK to set it all up. So they were thrilled."

Going the extra distance means taking the initiative, strutting your stuff without asking 'what's in it for me'. Knowing that you will get your due, in the long run.

On many programs, BBC would already have a primary cameraman but invite Kalyan to come and shoot some stills, for their website.

Some of the series Kalyan has worked on include *'Mountains of the Monsoon'*. The other is *'Crocodile Blues'*.

"I've worked on the web presence for various BBC productions and some of their wildlife conservation projects. We've set up a fund raising kind of thing online and a follow up to the series that aired on television."

Kalyan is currently working on a BBC series called *'Chasing the Monsoon'*. He's also made some inroads into National Geographic, with a shoot on King Cobra.

But still, one wonders, can you make a career out of wildlife photography, here in India? Kalyan gets that question a lot, I'm sure.

"In India most wildlife photographers are rich people, the kind who own some big industry. So it's kind of like trophy hunting. You show off to your friends by taking a cool picture of a tiger."

Just a handful of photographers in India make a living through wildlife pictures. By selling to large foreign publications.

On the flip side, it's an opportunity in disguise.

"Since you are the first one in the market you can create the market itself. And that's the approach I have taken in photography."

Traditionally, a wild life photographer goes to Africa to photograph the lions and the cheetahs.

"Fundamentally everything is easy there. It's like a big football field, you just drive up to the lions and the lions are sleeping there and you can photograph them and come back."

So on a 10 day trip you can come back with breathtaking pictures.

"In India, it will be a great thing if you have a glimpse of a tiger in 10 days. So though India has as much - if not more wildlife than Africa - very little had been properly documented."

For example, in the Western Ghats there are five species of primates, of which only three have been properly photographed and filmed.

"*National Geographic* photographers are not going to attempt it, because they have to speak with the locals, spend lot of time, understand the place. But for us - we stay in India, it's in our backyards. I think it's a great challenge, a great opportunity!."

The point is, if you work hard and you are resourceful - you will find a way to make it work. And make money off your work, in more ways than one.

For example, Kalyan has found a way to sell his pictures in the local market. Which is really amazing in a country where we don't have a culture of 'paying'. More so in this age of digital cameras and Flickr, where everyone thinks *isme kaun si badi baat hai* !

"People are not going to buy photographs in India. And even magazines pay you 200 bucks, 500 bucks for a photo - which is peanuts."

But, if you take a photograph and make it into a product, people buy. So Kalyan does not sell prints, instead he uses them to make a calendar and that sells like hotcakes.

"Everybody needs a calendar and instead of putting up something boring from State Bank of India, they actually get a nice looking thing with wildlife pictures. I also sell prints on t-shirts."

Apart from products (which Kalyan designs himself), another source of revenue is workshops. For people who want to learn wildlife photography

"I'm writing software now because it's cool to do it, not because a client is going to pay me $20 an hour. That childish excitement is back in me once again."

"You see all this beautiful wildlife and you come back the next year and realise that it's not there anymore. You can't help but feel like doing something about it!"

"BBC work is not more than 3 months in a year. For those 3 months, I am with them full time - and get paid well. But the remaining 8-9 months I have these other things to keep me busy."

And keep the money coming in. Right now, the products and workshops bring in 50% of Kalyan's annual income.

The workshops are marketed purely through his website - anyone who's interested signs up. The frequency is roughly once a month and some involve field trips - like a rainforest expedition, or tiger photography.

But many are simply held on weekends, in Bangalore. Because that's all the time people have to spare. And Kalyan does not take classes the 'textbook' way. It's about practicals, not theory - the way he taught himself.

"People love it. Others schools are very traditional, starting from the basics and all that. No one has that kind of attention span now. They buy a digital SLR, they're technically clued in, but just want to know how to take better pictures."

Besides, photography schools don't teach the nuances of digital photography. How do you process the pictures, upload them, publicise your work online.

"I take an open source philosophy towards my photography. You go to my website, all my pictures are under Creative Commons license - free on public domain."

It's kind of shocking - because artists and creative people are paranoid about the ownership of their work. Because giving rights to use your creation is the traditional way to make money from it.

But again, times are changing, and Kalyan has a different view on the subject.

"People come back. They love my photographs so much..and some of them say, we'll pay you for your work. Others buy my products."

There's a lesson in this for every creative person out there. You can't stop people from downloading your music or movie - or book - off the internet. But if you can make them your fans, your followers and your friends, you will find some way to make money from them, regardless.

"I take a slightly philosophical approach to this. The reason I take photographs is so that I can share my experiences. I was there, you know. I'm taking these pictures so that other people can 'be there' as well."

"If I restrict those photographs what is the point of it, really. And I think we're in an age where gone are the days when I can say I'm this hotshot photographer, and I have this huge studio and everyone's going to buy from me. It's gone."

Incidentally, Kalyan says that recession has not hit him "at all." He makes more money than thirty-year-old professional photographers in Bangalore.

"The old school is stuck up while I'm so open. I freely give my pictures, my licenses. I say, "Take it - if you like it you pay me. I have 20 times more clients than a guy who says, "Unless you buy it I'm not going to give you."

Out of those twenty freeloaders, two or three actually pay up. So Kalyan ends up making more than the traditional photographer.

"I'm happy to say that today I earn as much as I would earn if I was in IT today. Which is unheard of in photography."

But then Kalyan is more than a photographer. He's a one man photographic enterprise - looking for new markets, new business models to monetise and popularise his work.

The idea is 'give more and get more' - and being on the Linux 'open source' platform from an early age, helped shape that.

"I like to share my work, keep it free. I think if you're good, things will get back to you. And for me, 'being good' is more important for me than making money, Because if you are good, you will make money. It just automatically comes."

OK! But nothing comes 'automatically' and surely it never comes with a seal of approval from the world at large. That first year when he ran off into the jungle, surely people must have thought he was mad?

"Oh, friends thought I had gone insane. Parents were extremely upset. I had the typical Indian setting - a house, a car, a great job.."

And just when mummy was thinking what to write in *bachche ka* matrimonial, there, he throws it all away! How did he handle the pressure?

"I just said that these are not my priorities in life. I am from Andhra so people talk about this thing - dowry, it's called 'valuation'. My valuation just fell to the ground."

It took two years for Kalyan's parents to accept his decision, and now they take pride in his work. But for those two years it was about a guy who did not care what people said, what people thought...

So what lies ahead?

"I'm doing so many things... I'm part photographer, I'm part film maker. I also work with a lot of wildlife NGOs - I help them put together species databases, conservation messages. At times, I even do field work with the forest department."

Basically, it's about being passionate not just about photography, but everything to do with wildlife.

"I just want to get my hands dirty and be a part of it."

Kalyan dreams of doing a cover story for *National Geographic* - and that will happen, God willing, very soon. Meanwhile, he's been chosen as a 'BBC Earth Explorer'. Which means he is paid to explore - around the world - and do stories for the BBC!

As for what he will be doing five years from now, ten years from now. Well, two ways to look at it.

"If I can continue to do what I'm doing today ten years from now, I'll be really, really happy. I'm not looking for a promotion!"

Kalyan keeps his own schedule. Travels when he wants to. Does what he loves. Of course, there's a slim chance he just might chuck it all and try to do something altogether different.

"I think if you love something you can make it happen. Tomorrow if I want to be an astronaut, I'll start an astronomy club, I'll go work for HAL, or better still Virgin Galactic. I'll say, 'Hey can I be a mechanic, I'll work for free for the next 5 years!' I'll somehow get my foot in that door."

Find the door to your destiny, and put your best foot forward!

It will open, trust me.

ADVICE TO YOUNG ENTREPRENEURS

Go all out! Unlike what people think there are great opportunities in India to be a wildlife scientist, to be a wildlife photographer. As I said it's what you make of it.

Second, you need to have passion - more than any qualification. Many people come to me and say, "I've done a diploma in film, tell me how can I work with BBC or *National Geographic*? I want to do wildlife films..."

So I ask them, "How many forests have you been to?"

They say, "None."

Ask them to tell the names of 10 birds in India and they can't name even one! You won't believe it, but almost all the people I know who work with BBC or *National Geographic* - none of them are trained film makers or trained biologists. They come from different walks of life but they are all passionate about films and about wildlife.

You have to find what you love - and make it happen. I worked 3 years without pay, to get my foot in the door. Buying a bigger house or car were not my personal milestones.

Yes, you need equipment for wildlife photography but you can start with a Rs 50,000 budget, a basic camera, a cheap zoom lens. It's like computers; you don't need a Mac book or 4 GB RAM to be a good programmer. You can work even on a mobile phone or an old, dusty PC. Some of my best pictures are with the old, cheap lenses. People still love those pictures.

And finally, you must 'think different'. That applies to every field, whether it's music or art or literature. If your style is completely different either you fail miserably or you take it to a completely different level because people love it. But that's the only way to succeed. To stand out.

START UP RESOURCE

If you would like to contact any of the entrepreneurs featured in this book for help/advice, here are their email ids. Do try and be specific in your queries and a little patient in getting a response!

1. **Prem Ganapathy, Dosa Plaza:** *g.dosaplaza@gmail.com*

2. **Kunwer Sachdev, Su-kam:** *kunwersachdev@gmail.com*

3. **Ganesh Ram, Veta:** *ganeshram@vetaglobal.com*

4. **Sunita Ramnathkar, Fem:** *sunitaramnathkar@hotmail.com*

5. **M Mahadevan, Oriental Cuisine:** *madico55@gmail.com*

6. **Hanmant Gaikwad, BVG India:** *gaikwad.hr@gmail.com*

7. **Ranjiv Ramchandani, Tantra :** *tantratshirts@gmail.com*

8. **Suresh Kamath, Laser Soft:** *kamath@lasersoft.co.in*

9. **Raghu Khanna, Cashurdrive:** *raghu@cashurdrive.com*

10. **R Sriram, Crossword:** *sriram@nextpracticeretail.com*

11. **Saurabh Vyas & Gaurav Rathore, PoliticalEDGE:**
    saurabh.vyas@gmail.com & gaurav.rathore@gmail.com

12. **Satyajit Singh, Shakti Sudha:** *info@shaktisudha.com*

13. **Sunil Bhu, Flanders Dairy:** *sunil@flandersdairy.com*

14. **Chetan Maini, Reva:** *cmaini@reva-ev.com*

15. **Mahima Mehra, Haathi Chaap:** *pooper@elephantpoopaper.com*

16. **Samar Gupta, Trikaya Agriculture***: samar@trikaya.net*

17. **Abhijit Bansod, Studio ABD:** *abhijitbansod@studioabd.in*

18. **Paresh Mokashi, 'Harishchandrachi Factory':** *pareshmokashi@hotmail.com*

19. **Krishna Reddy, Prince Dance Group:** *pabitraforever@gmail.com*

20. **Kalyan Varma, Wildlife Photographer:** *mail@kalyanvarma.net*

STREET SMART- 01

Prem Ganapathy, Dosa Plaza

Inauguration of the first 'Dosa Plaza'
eatery outside Vashi station, 1998

Prem Ganapathy with a friend,
at his open air eatery

With the 'Dosa Plaza' team at one of the
many outlets in a food court today

THE INVENTOR - 02

Kunwer Sachdev, Su-kam

Kunwer, tinkering around

The khadi kurta clad student

The man, the machine,
owner of a Rs 500 crore company

TO SIR, WITH LOVE - 03

Ganesh Ram, Veta

An early picture –
Ganesh Ram (centre),
Rajagopalan (right)

Portrait of a
young businessman

Ganesh Ram – many many reasons
to smile!

WHAT WOMEN WANT - 04

Sunita Ramnathkar, Fem Care Pharma

Sunita, addressing owners of beauty parlours in Nagpur

Sunil and Sunita, with the entire range of Fem products

THE HUMAN TOUCH - 06

Hanmant Gaikwad, BVG (Bharat Vikas Group)

Inauguration of the first BVG office

The office was inside a tabela

Hanmant Gaikwad with friend and partner Umesh Mane — together they have come a long way

SHINE ON CRAZY DIAMOND - 07

Ranjiv Ramchandani, Tantra t-shirts

Ranjiv, in his cartoonist avatar

Ranjiv and partner Vimal Mariwala with some of their funky tees

JUGAAD

LOOK MA, NO HANDS! - 09

Raghu Khanna, Cashurdrive

Raghu, backpacking across Europe

Thank you mom and dad!

Next to a car wrapped-up with an advertisement, by CashurDrive

KITABI KEEDA - 10

R Sriram, Crossword

Sriram and Anita, at the first Crossword in Mahalaxmi.

Life is a beach: Sriram with daughter Kavya, leading a flexitime life

KING OF POP - 12

Satyajit Singh, Shakti Sudha Industries

Satyajit Singh, registering a makhana farmer

Oustide the factory in Patna

Apne desh ka khana — white, fluffy, nutritious makhana

FAR FROM THE MADDING CROWD - 13

Sunil Bhu, Flanders Dairy

Sunil making cheese with his mentor Marc Dournez in Belgium

Gauri - Sunil's first cow

Sunil, in his cheese factory as it is today

ELECTRIC DREAMS - 14

Chetan Maini, Reva Electric Car Company

Chetan as a University of Michigan student, with the 'Sunrunner' car

There are cars, and there are cars, but there is only one 'Reva'

PAPER TIGER - 15

Mahima Mehra, Founder, Haathi Chaap

Mahima in Kaalpi village, with artisan Udai, and a German buyer

Enjoying the rustic life

Making paper by hand even today – a delicate, manual process!

A rare privilege: the designer gets his name on his creation!

Abhijit, wearing a self-designed Heritage watch

The designer with the funky table lamp he designed for BPL – 'StudyLite'

Paresh Mokashi, 'Harishchandrachi Factory'

Directing actors in the play 'Samudra'

A scene from the laugh riot 'Mukkampost Bombilwadi'

Paresh, directing actors in his first ever feature film, 'Harishchandrachi Factory'

AVATAR - 19

Krishna Reddy, Prince Dance Group

Prince Dance Group in a practice session

Krishna Reddy, in the 'Krishna' act for Colors channel

Prince Group performing the 'Flag act' in the semi-finals of 'India's Got Talent'

ZUBAAN

CALL OF THE WILD - 20

Kalyan Varma, Wildlife Photographer

Kalyan Varma in his cubicle worker days

Born to be wild!

Kalyan – loving it in the jungle.
Living each day as it should be!